African American Slavery and Disability

D1481542

Disability is often mentioned in discussions of slave health, mistreatment, and abuse, but constructs of how "able" and "disabled" bodies influenced the institution of slavery have gone largely overlooked. This volume uncovers a history of disability in African American slavery from the primary record, analyzing how concepts of race, disability, and power converged in the United States in the first half of the nineteenth century.

Slaves with physical and mental impairments often faced unique limitations and conditions in their diagnosis, treatment, and evaluation as property. Slaves with disabilities proved a significant challenge to white authority figures, who were torn between the desire to categorize them as different or defective and the practical need to incorporate their "disorderly" bodies into daily life. Being physically "unfit" could sometimes allow slaves to escape the limitations of bondage and oppression, and establish a measure of self-control. Furthermore, ideas about and reactions to disability appearing as social construction, legal definition, medical phenomenon, metaphor, or masquerade highlighted deep struggles over bodies in bondage in antebellum America.

Dea Boster received her PhD in history at the University of Michigan and is an instructor for the Humanities Department at Columbus State Community College.

Studies in African American History and Culture

General Editor, Graham Hodges

For a full list of titles in this series, please visit www.routledge.com

African American Slavery and Disability

Bodies, Property, and Power in
the Antebellum South, 1800–1860

Dea H. Boster

Routledge
Taylor & Francis Group

NEW YORK AND LONDON

First published 2013
by Routledge
711 Third Avenue, New York, NY 10017

Simultaneously published in the UK
by Routledge
2 Park Square, Milton Park, Abingdon, Oxfordshire OX14 4RN

First issued in paperback 2014

Routledge is an imprint of the Taylor and Francis Group, an informa business

Library of Congress Cataloging in Publication Data

Boster, Dea H.
African American slavery and disability : bodies, property and power in
    the antebellum South, 1800-1860 / by Dea H. Boster.
        p. cm. — (Studies in African American history and culture)
    Includes bibliographical references and index.
    1. Slaves—Health and hygiene—Southern States—History—19th century.
    2. Slaves—Wounds and injuries—Southern States—History—19th century.
    3. Disabilities—Social aspects—Southern States—History—19th century.
    4. Human body—Social aspects—Southern States—History—19th century.
    5. Health and race—Southern States—History—19th century.   6. Slavery—
    Southern States—History—19th century.   I. Title.
    E449.B73 2012
    362.1089'96073075—dc23
    2012029116

ISBN 978-0-415-53724-7 (hbk)
ISBN 978-1-138-92070-5 (pbk)
ISBN 978-0-203-11059-1 (ebk)

Typeset in Sabon
by Apex CoVantage, LLC

For Max

Contents

Figures

Acknowledgments

I have been fortunate to receive the help and support of many wonderful individuals and institutions for this project. For their invaluable assistance with my research, I wish to thank Elizabeth Dunn and her colleagues at Duke University's Rare Book, Manuscript, and Special Collections Library; Jane Aldrich, Mary Jo Fairchild, Jana Meyer, and their colleagues at the South Carolina Historical Society; Kay Carter and the staff of the Waring Historical Library; and the archivists at the Virginia Historical Society, the Library of Virginia, the Georgia Historical Society, and the Southern History Collection at the University of North Carolina. I am also very grateful for the support of the Department of History at the University of Michigan, and the Humanities Department at Columbus State Community College. Stacy Noto, Denise File and the editorial staff at Routledge were terrific throughout the publication process, and I thank them for their constructive feedback and assistance.

Many others have contributed to this project by reading drafts, making fruitful suggestions, or offering helpful encouragement. The guidance and unwavering support of my PhD dissertation committee at the University of Michigan—Martin S. Pernick, Joel D. Howell, Martha Jones, and Tobin Siebers—were truly inspiring. I also wish to thank Rima Apple, Jenifer Barclay, Rabia Belt, Daina Ramey Berry, Daniel Blackie, Jeffrey Brune, Susan Burch, John Burnham, Cornelia Hughes Dayton, Jim Downs, Jonathan Edwards, Douglas Egerton, April Haynes, Jerrold Hirsch, Marilyn Howard, Mary Kelley, Wendy Kline, Catherine Kudlick, Jennifer Nardone, Kim Nielsen, Steven Noll, George M. Paulson, Stephanie Patterson, Michael Rembis, Amy Renton, John Sauer, Walter Schalick, Robert Stevenson, Robert Taylor, Judy Weiner, and Daniel Wilson.

Finally, I wish to acknowledge my family for their support throughout this long process, especially my husband, Johannes Wuerdig, whose enthusiasm and love helped to carry me through to the end. Thank you, all.

1 Introduction

"Here Are the Marks Yet"

Early in 1858, Tom Wilson arrived in Liverpool after stowing away from New Orleans in the hold of the cotton cargo ship *Metropolis*. After several weeks in England, Wilson's "own plain, unvarnished tale, taken down as the narrative fell from his lips," was printed in the *Liverpool Albion*. Wilson, then aged 45, had been a cotton worker in Mississippi with a wife and three children before he was sold to New Orleans, away from his family. At his new plantation, Wilson was subject to repeated floggings with a leather strap, as well as having his right bicep cut to decrease his strength and ability to resist punishment. After less than two years in New Orleans, Wilson attempted his first escape from the plantation by running into the alligator-infested Baddenrush swamp, where he was caught by a pack of bloodhounds. The dogs attacked Wilson, enabling Burke, Wilson's overseer, to ride up and shoot Wilson in the hip. As Wilson described this occurrence to his interviewer, he noted "here are the marks yet," and pulled up his trouser, showing "formidable seams" of scars on his calf and knee from the dogs' teeth; Wilson also noted that the fourteen pieces of buckshot in his hip "can be seen and examined at any time."[1]

This "unvarnished" interview of "a poor fugitive slave"[2] was part of a significant trend in antebellum abolitionist propaganda on both sides of the Atlantic. In the 1840s and 1850s, many antislavery audiences were fascinated with the experiences of disabled slave bodies, and detailed accounts of slaves who sustained terrible, debilitating injuries during their bondage were abundant in abolitionist speeches and publications. Antislavery activists were certainly aware that visual images had the power to stir the emotions of their audience, hiring former slaves and fugitives to present their own accounts of slavery and display their bodies on abolitionist lecture circuits throughout the North.[3] On many occasions, the ex-slaves would remain largely silent, appearing before the audience only to agree with the main presenters about the facts of their cases or to present their injuries. It was not uncommon for featured slaves to pull up their skirts or trousers to display scars on their legs, or to expose disfiguring whip marks on their backs. This exhibition of African American bodies was, in many ways, similar to the presentation of slaves at Southern markets and auctions. On the Northern abolitionist lecture circuit, the disfigured and disabled bodies of African American slaves were spectacular texts, and antislavery activists invited their audiences to "read" those bodies in a way not dissimilar to the way slaves' bodies were read at slave markets in the South.[4] Even though the readers of the *Albion* could not actually see Wilson, through his interview and the descriptions of his disabling injuries, they encountered his body as a part of his story and were invited to read his visible disfigurement as a major part of his tale of bondage.

Like the scars on Tom Wilson's leg, evidence of slave disability abounds in primary documents but remains invisible to those who choose not to see it. As historian Douglas Baynton has pointed out, "disability is everywhere in history, once you begin looking for it, but conspicuously absent in the histories we write."[5] Historians have mentioned disability in discussions of slave health or the effects of brutal treatment at the hands of masters, and a few have described famous slaves with disabilities—including Underground Railroad worker Harriet Tubman, abolitionist and women's rights activist Sojourner Truth, insurrectionist Denmark Vesey, Barnum's "Celebrated African Twins" Millie-Christine McCoy, and musical prodigy "Blind Tom" Bethune—but few have examined constructions of disability in antebellum slave society. Marks of slave disability in the historical record are certainly there to be found; the meanings of those marks, however, are far more complex than they appear on the surface. Analyzing disability and slavery involves finding intersections and layers of meaning in two social constructs that were more fluid and contested than many contemporaries would have admitted. Many scholars since the mid-twentieth century have identified constructions and deconstructions of the troublesome category "enslaved" (including race, gender, education, and social status); the popular image of blackness as backward, primitive, and savage; and the intertwined categories of black and white in antebellum American society. However, until recently, historians have been less likely to adopt disability as its own category of analysis or even as a cultural construct.[6] We cannot take for granted simplistic definitions of disability as an individual's deviation from an imagined functional norm or physical ideal any more than we could assume slavery and race were simply inherent individual traits. Instead, it is more useful to approach a study of disability in African American bondspeople from the perspective that disability, like race and slavery, is defined by interactions between bodies and their physical, social, cultural, and aesthetic environments. This relational view of disability rejects the notion that those who are disabled have always been defined in contrast to a central, unproblematic, able-bodied norm and seeks ways to examine how both disability and able-bodiedness were culturally constructed, performed, racialized, commodified, and negotiated. In this sense, the contrast between able-bodied and disabled, slave and master, or black and white cannot be expressed as a simple, fixed binary; as scholars like Daniel Wickberg and Kenneth Greenberg have observed, we must instead seek out the language (both verbal and visual), contexts, and interactions that created and recreated those categories in history.[7]

In this book I analyze the complicated relationship between African American bondage and disability in the antebellum United States. Concepts of race and disability were mutually constituted in nineteenth-century discourses, and race as well as social status was often a signifying marker in definitions of normal and abnormal bodies. Slaves with physical and mental impairments often faced unique limitations and conditions in their diagnosis, treatment, and evaluation as property. Expectations for slave able-bodiedness, or soundness, often were linked with ideas about manageability and influenced how masters applied labels of disability to their human chattel as well as what measures they used to control their bondspeople. Slaves with disabilities could be a significant challenge to white authorities, who were often torn between the desire to categorize them as different or defective and the practical need to incorporate their disorderly bodies into daily life, labor schemes, and the strictures of the slave market. However, ideas about and responses to slave disability went deeper than economic and disciplinary concerns. Slaveholders and other white authorities (including overseers, traders, and physicians) assessed and valued enslaved bodies in idiosyncratic ways, often relying on emotional or aesthetic reactions to disabling characteristics. In essence, slaves with disabilities threatened the delicate illusion of control and stability that white authority figures had constructed but also forced them to confront their own deeply-held assumptions about race, deviance, and defect. Such complex reactions to disability were not limited to white and/or slaveholding observers. Although the majority of voices in the surviving primary record belonged to free, mostly white witnesses, slaves (and their bodies) actively participated in disability meaning-making projects. Furthermore, slaves with disabilities felt pain, loss, and despair but also experienced hope and recognized opportunities to use their defective bodies and minds to negotiate the terms of their bondage; in some cases, being physically unfit allowed slaves to establish a measure of self-control. In these respects, ideas about and reactions to disability—appearing as social construction, legal definition, medical phenomenon, or metaphor—highlighted deep struggles over bodies in bondage in antebellum America.

The project of this book is to reclaim a history of disability in African American slavery from the primary record and to analyze how concepts of race, disability, and power confluenced in the United States in the first half of the nineteenth century. Interpreting disability as a social construct rather than as an individual physical or psychological condition allows us to examine how social, political, cultural environmental, and aesthetic dialogues and relationships created boundaries between normal and defective bodies and minds in the nineteenth century. The culture of the emerging American republic often viewed disability as weakness and dependence, with negative associations to immorality, dishonor, and the grotesque; although there is evidence that slaves themselves did not conceptualize their bodies in bondage the same way whites did, it is apparent that many African Americans shared negative assumptions about individuals with disabilities. Race and disability were mutually intertwined concepts in discourse on bodies, normality, and the creation of "Others" in American culture, and African American bodies in bondage often bore a dual stigma of blackness and physical or mental inferiority. Disability was also used as a metaphor on both sides of the slavery debate in the North and South—proslavery advocates claimed that African Americans were inherently disabled from participating in a free society and required enslavement to thrive, whereas abolitionists argued that bondage itself was crippling to African Americans—and featured prominently in many different issues of slaveholding society. A variety of primary sources—including plantation records, masters' correspondence, estate records, auction advertisements, judicial opinions, medical literature, and narratives written by slaves themselves—illuminate a complicated interaction of factors that contributed to how the slaveholding class assessed disability in human chattel and reacted to disabled bondspeople as bodies, property, and challenges to power. The contradictory classification of slaves with disabilities as "useless" on plantations, although many of them performed necessary and occasionally difficult duties, illuminated tensions between production, profit, and control in masters' assessment and treatment of disabled bondspeople. Similarly, the codified language of slave soundness at market, which encompassed descriptions, physical signs, comparisons, and slave performances on the auction block as well as monetary price, reflected complex expectations and assumptions that slaveholders had for their bondspeople. Southern professionals, such as doctors and judges, played an important role in discourse on slave disability and the regulation of slavery itself, but they ultimately had to contend with the motives and desires of slaveholders, which could limit their authority. Slaves themselves, however, were not mere bystanders in discourse about unsoundness; they were active participants in the construction of meaning around disability and recognized that prevalent assumptions about disability could be advantageous in bondage. In all of these situations, concepts of disability and unsound bondspeople were significant elements of the uneasy power balance of American slavery and mastery. Each chapter begins with a brief glimpse into an individual experience with disability that highlights layered meanings of normal and abnormal enslaved bodies. These accounts, like Tom Wilson's scars, may be read to illuminate complex, intertwined constructions of disability and slavery in the antebellum United States.

Issues of slave disability, particularly assumptions about the inherent mental inferiority of African Americans, were prevalent in early-twentieth-century studies influenced by Ulrich Bonnell Phillips. In his 1918 monograph *American Negro Slavery*, Phillips promoted an image of slaves as childlike, superstitious, and needing proper discipline to control themselves; according to this view of the Old South's "plantation régime," most masters assumed a benevolent teacher role, and most slaves were content with their kindly treatment.[8] The Phillips school, a significant departure from earlier studies by scholars like James Ford Rhodes and W.E.B. Du Bois, dominated views of slavery until the 1940s and 1950s, when new objectivity scholars like Herbert Aptheker, Richard Hofstadter, and Kenneth M. Stampp challenged the conclusion that slavery had been a largely kind and cooperative institution. In 1959, Stanley Elkins presented his controversial thesis that the closed system of power in United States slavery caused significant psychological degradation, resulting in the infantilization of plantation slaves. Relying on much of the same plantation data that Phillips had utilized, Elkins argued that the trauma of capture, shock, and existence under a system of absolute control created the "Sambo" stereotype that, in his view, characterized the degraded mental state of slaves.[9] Elkins's totalizing view of the victimized Sambo figure, as well as his comparison of concentration camp inmates during the Holocaust to African American slaves, inspired a number of important critiques; for example, Eugene Genovese claimed that the Sambo stereotype was far more subversive and complex than Elkins theorized, and scholars like Earl E. Thorpe and Sterling Stuckey argued that the Sambo figure was a myth created by slaveholders to justify slavery, not a reality created by the institution.[10] As a result of the backlash against both the Phillips school of slavery history and the Elkins thesis, scholars more recently have emphasized slave agency and resistance over trauma and have largely avoided any in-depth discussion of slave disability.

Since the 1970s, there have been many important studies of slave communities and cultures that briefly mention disability in relation to the cruelty of the institution, slaves' agency in protecting themselves and their families from abuse, or the use of malingering strategies as a method of negotiation. Ira Berlin's argument that slaves are not "outside history" and should be considered as central historical actors in their own right provided an avenue for examining slave perspectives on labor, health, punishment, and other issues related to disability.[11] Other studies of nineteenth-century society and culture hint at the importance of slave disability in more specific settings, such as the family, courtrooms, slave markets, popular culture, and the abolitionist movement.[12] However, although issues of disability are present in the literature on slavery, most authors mention them only in passing and have largely overlooked how constructs of "able" and "disabled" bodies influenced the institution of slavery. Furthermore, the experiences of slaves with physical or mental disabilities have received little scholarly attention. As Stephanie Camp and Edward Baptist have noted, "slavery studies that emphasized resistance and the capabilities (rather than the troubles) of slave communities were erasing everything that made the plantation evil," including physical suffering that resulted from exploitation.[13] In *The Slave Community*, John Blassingame—a vocal critic of Stanley Elkins—briefly examines the impact of brutality on the psychological health of slaves, noting in particular a mentally disabled "slave personality type" that resulted from repeated physical punishments.[14] More recently, Nell Painter has argued for a more individualized, psychological approach to the study of brutality against slaves, because "denying slaves psychological personhood impoverishes the study of everyone in slaveholding society."[15] Whereas brutality against slaves certainly is an issue that deserves more scholarly attention, Blassingame's and Painter's method of applying modern psychometric standards to slave psychology is problematic, particularly given the paucity of primary sources from slaves themselves, and it sheds little light on how constructs of able-bodiedness and disability operated in slave society as a whole.

Studies of nineteenth-century health that emphasize the social framing of disease and medical practices provide a glimpse of how ideas about illness, debility, and physical defects were constructed and how histories of the health and medical treatment of African Americans both before and after Emancipation have placed slightly more emphasis on disability.[16] Felice Swados and Richard Shryock were among the first scholars to question the romanticized myth that the Old South was a healthy environment for slaves; as Swados claimed, "the popular conception of the slaves as a sleek, robust, hearty group, enjoying a high degree of welfare on the old plantations, is false."[17] Relying mainly on research in Southern medical journals and plantation records, many late-twentieth-century historians of slavery have emphasized this point but, like most of their primary documents, focus rather narrowly on slave mortality—particularly on information about epidemic diseases and survival rates—rather than on morbidity, as well as on white healing practices and perspectives on slave diseases.[18] Todd L. Savitt's *Medicine and Slavery* examines a wider perspective as well as a wider variety of health issues—including endemic and epidemic diseases, living and work conditions, injuries, and the combined use of "white" and "black" medical therapies—for slaves in antebellum Virginia.[19] Although he highlights issues of disability, Savitt takes a biomedical approach to issues of health and slaves' bodies that largely discusses disabilities (from poor living conditions, injuries, old age, reproductive issues, or insanity) only as medical pathologies and focuses almost exclusively on available treatments, or the lack thereof, for disabling conditions.[20]

Two more recent studies in particular have touched on the cultural construction of disability in slaves and provide very useful models for further research. Sharla M. Fett's *Working Cures: Healing, Health, and Power on Southern Slave Plantations* (2002) is a medical history of slavery that builds on Savitt's work but focuses more on power dynamics and cultural communications about health and disease between slaves and their masters. Focusing primarily on Virginia and the Carolinas, Fett argues that slaves were not passive recipients of abusive white medical traditions; slave healing involved a variety of struggles over authority and practice. Slave communities developed a rich healing culture "that worked to counter the onslaught of daily medical abuse and racist scientific theories."[21] In other words, slaves created a collective countervision of health and healing to oppose the "white" medical view that "translated slave health into slaveholder wealth."[22] Although slave healing traditions were necessarily intertwined with issues of plantation control (such as labor and perceived insurrection threats), the existence of a strong healing culture provided a powerful identity for African American slaves and served as a means of resistance and negotiation. In her outstanding analysis of economic assessments of slave "soundness," Fett argues that "the objectification of black health under slavery was . . . not simply a matter of persons reduced to physical bodies but also of minds and personalities subjected to market assessments."[23] White slave traders, masters and physicians supported these ideals of slave worth by requiring and granting guarantees of soundness in market situations and litigation concerning the sale of unsound slaves. However, African Americans had a different image of their bodies and characters that transcended slaveholders' definitions of soundness.[24] Emphasizing the social and economic forces that influenced white notions of slaves' physical worth and disabilities, as well as noting how African American slaves assessed their bodies and soundness differently, Fett illuminates the importance of analyzing the social framing of disability rather than essentializing the concept as pathology.

In addition, Walter Johnson's *Soul by Soul: Life inside the Antebellum Slave Market* (1999) mentions how "unsoundness" in slaves was constructed in sales situations. The book places the culture of the slave market and the "chattel principle," a cornerstone of Southern slavery, squarely in the daily life of slave society and highlights the importance of slaves themselves as historical actors in the market. The visibility of racialized slave bodies was a central aspect of the sale of bondspeople. Constructs of race, especially as a criterion for specific types of work or its associations with temperament, were tools of the trade. According to Johnson, "slaves' bodies were shaped to their slavery" and commodified based on a complex variety of characteristics; indeed, "visible physical coordinates replaced invisible historical identities as the most accessible means for buyers to make their comparisons."[25] However, sellers had to acknowledge the agency of slaves in market encounters and required some participation on the part of the slaves (to perform, tell preplanned stories, or hide ailments from prospective buyers). As a result of this collaboration, slaves could manipulate sales to suit their own purposes and were aware of the physical and "moral" characteristics that buyers sought.[26] Thus, slaves, traders, and prospective buyers participated in a conversation about shared perspectives on desirable and unsound qualities of slaves' bodies. Fett's and Johnson's studies provide glimpses of how concepts about slave soundness and disability were constructed and negotiated in antebellum society, reuniting interpretations of slavery as a potentially traumatizing institution with a focus on slave agency and experience.

Since the 1960s, disability studies scholars have undertaken the project of defining a social concept of "disability" in America, which has been, in the words of Gail Whiteneck, "not a simple linear progression but . . . many interactions."[27] Following the linguistic turn of the 1980s and 1990s, disability theorists like David T. Mitchell, Sharon L. Snyder, Lennard J. Davis, and Simi Linton have accepted the term *disability*—rather than signifiers that identify individuals with impairments, such as *handicapped, invalid,* or *crippled*—to denote the connection between individuals with different sorts of physical or mental impairments and the social, cultural, and environmental responses they face. In other words, disability arises not from disabling conditions themselves but from the complicated web of personal experiences, cultural assumptions, attitudes, discourses, and reactions to those conditions.[28] However, this social model of disability has been slower to catch on in the traditional discipline of United States history. As Paul K. Longmore and Lauri Umansky point out, there has been a conspicuous absence of disability as a category of analysis in history, despite the fact that disabilities function "as personal yet also public experience, social problem, and cultural metaphor."[29] One roadblock in the history of disability has been the prevalence of the medical explanation of disabilities as pathologies, existing only in impaired individuals rather than larger social structures. This view renders individuals with disabilities as passive victims of their impairments rather than as historical actors in their own right. Not surprisingly, the history of disability has been explored mostly in histories of medicine, special education, or rehabilitation, in which people with disabilities are identified primarily as "afflicted" patients who passively submit to physicians to improve their conditions, or as parts of isolated minority groups usually defined by institutions.[30] However, more historians in recent years have identified that disability is a construct that operates at all levels of society, not just in a deceptively discrete medical sphere that has already been deessentialized in histories of health and illness, and historical actors (including individuals with disabilities) at any given time attribute different meanings to bodies, minds, and perceived categories like "normal," "disabled" or "defective" in American culture.[31]

Issues of able-bodiedness and disability are particularly salient aspects of nineteenth-century African American slavery because they are so intimately linked with racialization and social status. Historically, disability and bondage both signified the subjugation of human bodies, and like race, gender and class, disability has been a powerful construct that marks bodies as social "Others" and disrupted cultural understandings of the "orderly body."[32] This raises important questions about how disability was constructed for a group of people whose role in society was strictly limited by their labor status and race. Not only is disability, as Catherine J. Kudlick has noted in her splendid review essay, "on par" with race, class, and gender as a category of analysis, but it actually works in tandem with race, class, and gender to create ideas about normalcy and difference.[33] Furthermore, historical analyses of race and disability as social constructs share similar methodological problems. As historian Barbara Fields points out, although race is more of a construct than a biological reality, "Americans, including many historians, tend to accord race an ahistorical, almost metaphysical, status that removes it from all possibility of analysis and understanding."[34] Longmore and Umansky have indicated historians have tended to "privilege" disability as a fixed physical element, overlooking the social and cultural factors that influence ideas about disability. It is therefore imperative to identify how concepts of race and disability have historically influenced each other, and have worked with discourses about identity, power, and difference in American history.

For decades, disability history scholars have noted significant interactions between race and disability and how both categories are culturally constructed.[35] As early as 1969, for example, Leonard Kriegel drew a parallel between Uncle Tom and Tiny Tim, arguing that, although physical impairments themselves were not "imposed from outside," social responses to disabled individuals created an inferior condition that mirrored the condition of African Americans.[36] More recently, David Mitchell and Sharon Snyder argue that many studies of racism emphasize the social construction of race while maintaining a view of "disability as the default category of 'real' human incapacity" and integrate an emphasis on disability into the world of Paul Gilroy's "Black Atlantic," arguing that disability and race were "mutual projects of human exclusion" in the modern era.[37] The connection between racial identity and disability identity is also apparent in primary evidence; for instance, there was close connection between ex-slave narratives and disability narratives, both of which gained wide readership in the mid-nineteenth century. As Ellen Klages has noted, works like S. Helen deKroyft's 1849 *A Place in Thy Heart* and Mary L. Day's 1859 *Incidents in the Life of a Blind Girl* (which inspired the title for Harriet Jacobs's famous 1861 memoir of her experience in bondage) utilized many of the same conventions as ex-slave narratives, including sentimental language, direct appeals to readers, testimonials and authenticating evidence, and claims of independence.[38] However, whereas many scholars in disability studies have noted the complicated relationship between disability and race constructs, and even between disability and African American slavery specifically, surprisingly few published studies of disability, race, or slavery analyze the issues that arise from this relationship.[39] In his research on constructs of able-bodiedness during the Reconstruction era and the experiences of disabled freedpeople during and after Emancipation, Jim Downs calls attention to this absence in the historical canon and provides an excellent discussion of the discursive elements behind constructs of disability.[40] However, because he focuses solely on the event of emancipation and its aftermath, Downs' research does not explore the lives of African Americans with disabilities within the "peculiar institution." Thus, there have been virtually no published studies of disability constructs and experiences among African Americans who lived in slavery, an institution that affected millions of people and had an overwhelming impact on the economy, culture, politics, social hierarchies and race relations in United States history.

This book seeks to participate in what disability studies scholar Julie Anderson promoted as "a wider dialogue between the history of disability and mainstream history."[41] By framing slave disability in a variety of settings—medical, social, cultural, and personal—we can identify how a variety of participants negotiated and contested meanings of disability in slaves as bodies, property, and significant challengers to power dynamics in the antebellum South. I do not intend to imply that all African American slaves had the same experiences with bondage or disability—assessments of a slave's abilities, value, and defects were influenced by a wide variety of factors, including skin color, age, gender, skills, geographic location, and the needs of owners—but for methodological reasons I have concentrated primarily on plantation slaves in several specific regions of the southern United States. The concept of the plantation régime is somewhat outmoded in the historiography of African American bondage, but is a useful frame of reference for identifying sources that illuminate disability among slaves. Although the majority of slaveholders in the nineteenth century had smaller farms and/or businesses and owned fewer than ten slaves, the majority of bondspeople lived on large plantations for at least part of their lives, and large planters (those who owned more than fifty slaves) were more likely to leave detailed slaveholding records that exist in archives today.[42] Wherever possible I include discussion of slaves on smaller farms, skilled tradespeople, urban or domestic servants, and hired-out laborers, but the bulk of my primary evidence focuses on slaves on larger plantations.

In addition, although I attempt to incorporate a more transnational perspective on slavery into the study, my analysis of primary evidence centers primarily on African American slavery and the Second Middle Passage of internal slave trade that developed in the United States after the international slave trade closed in 1808.[43] By adopting this focus I intend neither to suggest that United States society was completely cut off from the rest of the slaveholding world in the nineteenth century nor to disregard the importance of an Atlantic perspective. As scholars like Paul Gilroy, Ira Berlin, Stephanie Camp, and Edward Baptist have rightly noted, a narrow, isolationist vision of slavery in the United States overlooks significant connections between slaveholding societies in the Atlantic world, as well as the existence of larger communities and conflicts within the African diaspora that remained even after slavery was abolished in the New World.[44] There are many intercultural elements in the history of slavery in the United States that raise significant questions about the complexities of the Atlantic slaveholding world: ships traveling international routes were important sites for discourses on freedom, resistance, and identity for American slaves like Frederick Douglass and Denmark Vesey, news of the slave revolt in Saint-Domingue drove some masters in the United States to more extreme disciplinary measures and displays of violence towards their bondspeople, and ex-slave narratives published in the 1840s and 1850s were printed widely in Europe in a number of different languages, including French and Gaelic.[45] Although such complex connections are important, and I attempt to incorporate them into my discussion wherever possible, I have chosen to center my study mainly on the United States in the nineteenth century to recognize important changes that influenced constructions and experiences of slaves with disabilities.

David Brion Davis, along with Ira Berlin, has argued that many histories of slavery in the American South portray the institution as static and ingrained since the colonial era, but in the first half of the nineteenth century the institution underwent a number of significant and rapid changes that influenced constructs and assessments of slave bodies and disability.[46] For instance, huge increases in cotton production in the nineteenth century and the prevalence of very specific methods for cultivating, harvesting, and processing cotton had a significant impact on the bodies of plantation slaves involved in the industry. Westward expansion, coupled with the closure of the international slave trade, led to the creation of a massive domestic trade centered in the lower Mississippi Valley, which altered market practices and values as well as perceptions of "desirable" qualities. The spread of slaveholders into the "old Southwest" also profoundly changed slave demographics in the United States; whereas the overwhelming majority of bondspeople had lived in the coastal states of the "Old South" in 1790, more than half of the slave population in 1860 lived in states further south and west.[47] Moreover, the slave population that remained in the Old South became significantly older, as slave mortality rates declined and prospective planters moving west purchased younger men and women to begin new plantations.[48] All of these factors combined to make issues of slave disability particularly prominent in the first half of the nineteenth century. By adopting this periodization I do not wish to ignore the significant changes in the slaveholding economy or the social climate and opinions about slavery that underwent major transitions after the 1830s, but instead I wish to call attention to important similarities and trends in ideas about slave disability prior to the Civil War.

This study relies heavily on primary sources from Southern slaveholding states, but we must not assume that a deep cultural divide existed between the South and the rest of the nation. As Berlin and Davis have pointed out, both free and slave states were enmeshed in a "slaveholding republic" by the nineteenth century. Individuals living in free states and territories encountered bondage in a variety of ways: journeying to the South, reading "eyewitness" accounts of slavery in abolitionist literature and ex-slave narratives, participating in a national economy that was fueled by slave labor and productivity, and observing slaves traveling through free states with their masters, particularly after passage of the federal fugitive slave law in 1850.[49] Furthermore, people across the nation participated in similar discourses about able-bodiedness and disability, and the experiences of other groups of people—including working-class whites, immigrants, and free African Americans—influenced discourse about disability in slaves. For instance, rates of mental illness among free African Americans in the northern United States were an important part of the debate about African American "defectiveness" in the nineteenth century, particularly after the 1840 census was published. In some cases, such as medical discourse and legal proceedings, observers explicitly distinguished between slaves and other groups to argue that certain conditions were more or less "disabling" for African Americans in bondage. More comparative studies of disability experiences in different groups, especially minority or socially marginalized groups, would be an important addition to disability history literature, but is beyond the scope of this research.

Evidence of slave disability is simultaneously everywhere and nowhere in the primary record for the antebellum United States. On the one hand, issues of slave disability were extremely important in a variety of arenas in nineteenth-century society, including medical and scientific discourse about the "innate inferiority" of African Americans, discussions of slaves' ability to perform labor, market assessments of slaves' value, court cases concerning fraudulent sales or liability for injuries to bondspeople, and abolitionist rhetoric. On the other hand, ideas about disability were often firmly entrenched in American culture and thought, and observers rarely called attention to their assumptions about disability in the documents they created. Furthermore, although many free white people in the nineteenth century discussed slave bodies and their supposed defects in primary sources, the largest group of people affected by issues of slave disability—slaves themselves—left very few documents describing experiences and observations of disability in their own voices and are often unnamed and marginalized in the primary source canon. Therefore, I have attempted to incorporate a wide variety of primary material into my research of slave disability and maintain a focus on what historian Daniel Wickberg has described as the "reading of absence." In Wickberg's view, histories of socially marginalized or oppressed groups necessarily rely on secondhand primary evidence—such as legal records, tax rolls, or plantation diaries—to document the lives of those who did not, for a variety of reasons, create their own records. In order to avoid false generalizations, it is crucial to read such sources with an eye toward what kinds of information were omitted as well as what is present, as there are "intentions and meanings in their documentary absence."[50] This technique not only allows us to identify marginalized perspectives but also provides a method to "read" ideas about disability in many different kinds of sources.

Free individuals directly involved with the institution of slavery recorded their observations of slave disability in a variety of published and unpublished documents. Masters, traders and overseers made categorical assessments of bondspeople with disabilities in plantation journals and work logs, slave sale records and auction advertisements, warranties and bills of sale, as well as personal correspondence. These sources contain morbidity and mortality data for individual plantations, records of labor losses incurred from disabling physical or mental conditions, and speculations and appraisals of "sound" and "unsound" property; however, they also disclose assumptions about able-bodiedness as well as emotional reactions to disabilities in slaves. Physicians who treated bondspeople on plantations or utilized disabled slaves as medical specimens for new therapies or medical education provide discussions of slaves' disabling conditions and racial theories of able-bodiedness in published journal articles, textbooks, and domestic advice manuals as well as in correspondence with their patients' masters and personal memoirs, some of which, like J. Marion Sims' autobiography, were published posthumously. Furthermore, Southern court records—proceedings, depositions, and judges' opinions—provide evidence of expectations for slave labor, behavior, and physical and mental soundness.

We can also find glimpses of disability constructs in popular culture sources, including newspapers, pro- and antislavery periodicals, novels and short stories, printed ex-slave narratives and interviews, speeches, pamphlets, song lyrics, and lithographs.[51] This is particularly evident in abolitionist sources created in the decades preceding the Civil War, which sought to provide authentic, "unvarnished" glimpses into the atrocities of slave society; of course, sources advocating for one perspective on the slavery debate often exaggerated their positions and evidence. Abolitionist literature from white and black authors alike included many graphic descriptions of slaves' debilitated and disfigured bodies to emphasize the cruelty of the institution, citing Southern court records, runaway slave advertisements in newspapers, "eyewitness" accounts of life in the South and testimony from bondspeople who had fled to the northern United States, Canada, or Great Britain.[52] Reading and comparing these kinds of documents with attention to absences, contradictions, and subtle differences in language or content provides a number of interesting and significant clues about how nineteenth-century observers—white and black, Northern and Southern, pro- and anti-slavery—assessed disability in African American slaves.

Primary documents that provide perspective from slaves themselves are among the most important for my research but are also the most complicated to utilize. The most pressing issue for slave sources is the question of authenticity; because most African American slaves were illiterate by law, and those who were not had few opportunities to write or correspond, many surviving antebellum slave sources involve a degree of perspective or intervention from nonslaves. Fugitive slave narratives, for instance, became very popular in the 1840s and 1850s, as publications from ex-slaves like Frederick Douglass, William Wells Brown, Samuel Ringgold Ward, Josiah Henson, Solomon Northup, Moses Roper, and William and Ellen Craft enjoyed wide readership and multiple printings in the northern United States and Great Britain.[53] These narrators sought to present the experiences of African Americans in bondage to an unfamiliar, free, and largely white audience and to authenticate the abuses of slavery, fantastic tales of escape, as well as ex-slaves' claims to independence and able-bodiedness.[54] However, antislavery activists were engaged in most aspects of the writing and publishing process; John Blassingame has argued that most abolitionist editors of ex-slave narratives were largely honest and dedicated to presenting the "unvarnished" truth of their subjects, but it can be difficult to ascertain where the slave's account ends and the editor's interpretation begins.[55] Slave narrators had to rely on amanuenses, financial backers and editors—mostly white abolitionists—to record and print their stories, and some elements of ex-slave narratives, such as dialogue, direct appeals to readers, editorial supplements, and "literary flourishes," were clearly embellishments from their collaborators.[56] For this reason, calling fugitive slave narratives "autobiographies" has been problematic for literary scholars.[57] Other kinds of antebellum accounts of bondage—such as interviews and depositions of former slaves—present similar issues, because slaves' accounts were recorded or reprinted with obvious influence from interviewers and editors. A few slaves composed letters to slaveholders or family members and mention disability in a number of different ways, from a wife inquiring politely after a husband's chronic rheumatism to elderly servants who describe their infirmities to plead for more support from masters.[58] However, because most letters had to be dictated to someone who was not a slave, and presumably had power over the individual composing the letter, it is likely that content and expression in even the most personal communications between slaves were mitigated.[59]

Former slaves' vernacular histories of bondage, primarily those collected by the federal Works Progress Administration (WPA) employees in the 1930s and which are available through the Library of Congress's *Born in Slavery: Slave Narratives from the Federal Writers' Project, 1936–1938* database, can also illuminate slave perspectives on disability but present a number of methodological difficulties.[60] One issue is the seven-decade span between emancipation and the recording of the oral memoirs. Interviewees were enslaved as young children and often talked about stories they remembered hearing from older family members, not about their own direct experiences, and some scholars have questioned the reliability of those memories after so many years. Furthermore, although many WPA interviewers attempted to record ex-slave testimony verbatim, there are inconsistencies between handwritten and typed transcripts of interviews, including dialect changes. Historians like John Blassingame have also noted that the race of interviewers—most of whom were white and from the same area as the interviewees—influenced the tone of accounts of slavery, how former slaves depicted their owners, and discussion of topics like conjure and trickster tales. WPA interviews are also a particularly challenging source for studies of antebellum slave disability. Jerrold and Karen Hirsch have noted that, although disability issues appear in a number of oral histories collected for the Federal Writers' Project, interviewers did not explore disability as its own category of experience or personal identity, and former slaves were more likely to discuss disabilities they had acquired in old age, long after emancipation.[61] Thus, it is important to maintain a view toward what kinds of information are omitted from interview records and how oral memoirs compare to other kinds of published and unpublished sources from different perspectives. In the chapters that follow, I attempt to bring these different kinds of sources and perspectives together to highlight the complex, and sometimes contradictory, constructions of African American slavery and disability in the antebellum United States.

Part I
Bodies

2 The Dual Stigma of Race and Disability in Antebellum America

Phineas T. Barnum, the most renowned showman and "trickster" in American popular culture, began his career in 1835 with the exhibition of an elderly African American woman named Joice Heth. Billed as a 161-year-old slave who had nursed an infant George Washington, Heth was a spectacle for her extreme superannuation and debility; she was "totally blind from age, and so infirm as to be unable to do any labor."[1] Visitors were invited to examine, and even touch, Heth's body, and listen to her sing or relate anecdotes of life with the Washington family. Her biggest source of appeal, however, was whether or not she was genuinely as old as Barnum claimed. Barnum's graphic descriptions of Heth emphasized her decrepitude, both to provide a reason for her immobility to spectators—in a counterintuitive marketing ploy, he occasionally implied she was an India-rubber puppet performed by a ventriloquist—and to authenticate her astounding longevity. As Barnum described her in his 1854 autobiography,

> She was apparently in good health and spirits, but former disease or old age, or perhaps both combined, had rendered her unable to change her position; in fact, although she could move one of her arms at will, her lower limbs were fixed in their position, and could not be straightened. She was totally blind, and her eyes were so deeply sunken in their sockets that the eyeballs seemed to have disappeared altogether. She had no teeth, but possessed a head of thick bushy gray hair. Her left arm lay across her breast, and she had no power to remove it. The fingers of her left hand were drawn down so as nearly to close it, and remained fixed and immovable.[2]

Less than two decades after Joice Heth made her first appearance in Barnum's Museum, patients of the New York State Lunatic Asylum established a blackface minstrel troupe called the Blackbird Minstrels, staging elaborate performances for their fellow patients, staff members, and even the outside community. Minstrelsy was part of the asylum's program in dramatic therapy, which employed popular comic minstrel routines "as instruments of cure" as well as a disciplinary safety valve to manage patients' emotional

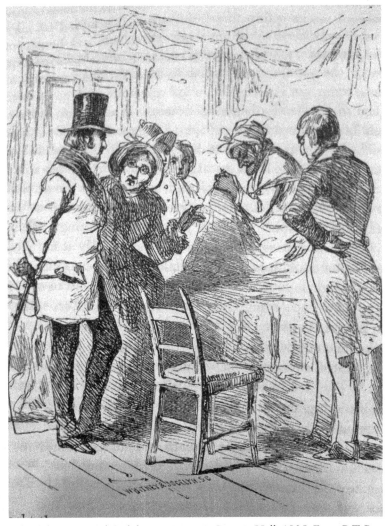

Figure 2.1 The Joice Heth Exhibition, Boston's Concert Hall, 1835. From P. T. Barnum, *The Life of P. T. Barnum, Written by Himself* (London: Sampson Low, Son, 1855), 158.

energy.[3] One 1854 performance, which apparently depicted "in pleasing contrast the 'lights and shadows' of negro life," included songs and "fancy negro dance" with male and female performers, violin solos, a comically indecipherable lecture delivered by "Dr. Snowball," and a routine with "a 'real hanimal'" elephant that "Barnumized [the audience] in the superlative degree." As Ella, a reviewer for the asylum's patient newsletter *The Opal*, commented, the program "contained a rare combination of the ludicrous, burlesque and unique," and "presented to the children of Asylumia a novel and laughter-provoking view of the varieties in human kind."[4]

These two distinct events highlight the complex intertwining of race, slavery, stigma, and disability in nineteenth-century American discourse. P. T. Barnum's Joice Heth exhibit was the launch for the nineteenth-century freak show, an important arena for discourse about the "defectiveness" of racial Others. Whereas Barnum's presentation invited a variety of reactions from spectators, the "grotesque" physical effects of Heth's extreme age were linked directly to her life as a slave; she represented a racial, social, and physical "Other" in American culture, and the exhibition of her "uncertainly real" body invited viewers to read her disability as a function of her race.[5] Around the same time, American blackface minstrelsy—an art form mythically inspired by the dance of a disabled slave—presented a related caricature of the "disorderly" and uncontrolled slave.[6] For patients at the New York State Insane Asylum, donning cork and grease to stage blackface performances provided an opportunity not only to thumb their noses at authority figures and the society that stigmatized their condition but also to ridicule and compare themselves favorably, as "free" (if disabled) whites, to the disabled, racialized Others they portrayed.

This chapter analyzes layers of meaning that were ascribed to race and disability, two socially constructed concepts that were entangled and mutually constitutive in the nineteenth-century United States. Discourse on race and disability was certainly not limited to slaveholding states; just as the notoriety of Joice Heth and blackface minstrelsy spread throughout the nation, so did discussions and portrayals of disabled slaves. Many nineteenth-century writings associated physical and mental disabilities with weakness and dependence, immorality, dishonor, and the grotesque, and these associations influenced discussions of African American bodies in slavery, which bore the "dual stigma" of race and disability. A number of antebellum observers—particularly planters, "racial scientists" and physicians writing in medical journals and domestic advice manuals—claimed Africans' innate physical and mental limitations made them unfit to live in any environment other than bondage in a warm, humid climate.[7] At the same time, antislavery publications, memoirs, speeches, and songs emphasized that the institution of slavery was inherently disabling for African Americans and that independence could confer able-bodiedness to all slaves crippled by their bondage. It is difficult to ascertain how enslaved African Americans conceptualized ability and disability, but folkloric evidence, ex-slave narratives, and postbellum memoirs and interviews provide glimpses of slaves' perspectives. In many cases, slaves shared assumptions about impairment and weakness, but slave perceptions of disability could be influenced by the possibility of self-control or resistance, and bondspeople actively negotiated meanings of disability with each other and with their masters. Thus, although different observers had different ideas about the origins and permanence of the disability of "blackness" or slavery, the stigmatized social constructions of race and impairment often coexisted in complicated and dynamic relationships in antebellum social and cultural discourse.

Analyzing assumptions about, or even the mere existence of, disabilities in an historical context is a thorny issue. One cannot essentialize the physical or mental conditions that are often equated with impairment, or define disability simply as any number of chronic (but not immediately fatal) diseases or disorders that impair an individual's ability to function in their ascribed social roles, without appreciating the fact that impairment is a historical construction contingent on social, cultural, and physical environments. Many disability studies scholars have noted a shift in metaphorical meanings of "disability" in nineteenth-century United States mainstream culture. Prior to this time period, concepts of disability centered on the supernatural, with "defective" or "monstrous" bodies viewed as ill-fated omens or evidence of divine judgment.[8] After the American Revolution, new concepts of normal and abnormal bodies as parts of a natural spectrum began to emerge. The idea of normal bodily integrity became equated with the usual, or not deviating from the common type, and the existence of abnormal, or disabled, bodies was viewed increasingly as a phenomenon of the natural world; in this worldview, "freaks" or "sports" could be understood as "natural" aberrations rather than supernatural monsters.[9]

However, the notion of disability still carried a lot of negative associations in the post-Revolutionary United States. As historian Joan Burbick has argued, the language of American independence and democracy was strongly linked with ideas of a controlled, healthy, and "able" body. Metaphors about the health of the "national" body focused on literal and metaphorical representations of specific body parts and their functions, privileging in particular the brain, heart, nerves, and eyes,[10] and the decrease or loss of physical abilities was associated with American fears of dependence and immorality. Thus, individuals with disabilities were imagined as parts of the natural world but were still constructed in opposition to normal bodies: the "normal" was represented as moral, independent, and usually male, whereas the "abnormal" carried associations with immorality, weakness, reliance, and femininity. It is unsurprising that, as Cindy LaCom has noted in her analysis of disability and sexuality in nineteenth-century literature, disabled characters—particularly females—began to appear regularly in novels around this time period and were often constructed in opposition to "healthy" bodies.[11] Able-bodiedness was also intimately linked with concepts of honor and the prerogatives of "mastery" in the antebellum South, including refinement, land ownership, and authority over human chattel. As historian Kenneth S. Greenberg has argued, disfiguring marks, especially on the face, and crippling impairments had a very significant meaning in the culture of Southern "honor" in the nineteenth century. Any sort of physical mutilation—with the exception of battle wounds—was considered a mark of dishonor for all men, regardless of social class or standing. At a time when an individual's character was often read on their external body, a scar "spoke for itself" as a mark of bad character or dishonor, regardless of how it came into existence.[12] Thus, honor, respect, and independence were intimately associated with a normalized view of the able body, while physical impairments and disfigurements often carried stigmatizing associations in nineteenth-century American culture.

The concept of stigma as a shared experience is useful for studying meanings of disability in the past, and how those meanings interacted with assumptions about race. In 1963, Erving Goffman defined three different types of stigma that serve to debase individuals who fall into the category: physical and mental defects, "blemishes of individual character," and tribal associations, such as race.[13] African American slaves faced stigma in all three categories in the antebellum culture, which constructed them as racial, social and sexual Others;[14] thus, one could argue successfully that the status of slavery, by Goffman's definitions, was itself a significant stigmatizing "disability" in the United States South. As disability studies scholar Douglas Baynton has pointed out, "race and disability intersected in the concept of the normal, as both prescription and description." By attributing labels of "defective" or "disabled" to racial Others, Baynton argues, concepts of disability have been used to represent and/or justify the oppression of entire groups of people.[15]

Many antebellum ideas about African American able-bodiedness were intertwined with concepts of racial inferiority and the natural "defectiveness" that accompanied darker skin. "Racial" science—including analysis of biological difference and the innate inferiority of nonwhite peoples—was a primary focus of study in the antebellum United States, particularly for proslavery apologists. Anthropologists like Louis Agassiz applied a polygenesis theory of Creation to explain the separate evolution of black and white races, while physicians and scientists like R. Dunglison, Samuel George Morton, H. A. Ramsay, Samuel Cartwright, and Josiah Clark Nott utilized anatomical and physiological measurements of perceived racial groups to identify static categories of difference. For example, in 1853, Samuel Cartwright, a prominent New Orleans physician who wrote extensively about the health and biology of African Americans, published an essay that purported to answer the questions of a Northern and British physician about the peculiarities of the "Negro constitution."[16] Cartwright described his use of a spirometer and observations of the liver and lungs of black cadavers to prove that African American slaves consumed less oxygen than white people, which made their movements much slower. This was an echo of an argument made by George Washington decades earlier; Washington argued that, given the naturally slow gait and motions of his slaves, it would be detrimental to drive them to work at the "brisker" pace appropriate for a white laborer.[17] Some observers emphasized the inferiorities of African Americans' intellect. Thomas Jefferson, for instance, wrote in his 1800 "Notes on the State of Virginia" that, although "in memory they are equal to the whites," slaves were "in reason much inferior . . . and that in imagination they are dull, tasteless, and anamolous [sic]."[18] More than fifty years later, Tennessee physician A. P. Merrill noted that enslaved children often seemed witty and intelligent, but "they lose all signs of uncommon talents as they advance in years, and sometimes even become noted for their dullness."[19] Such supposed "childlike" mental incapacity and crude emotional sensitivity, for some white observers, meant that African American slaves were less likely to be troubled by mental illness or alienation and therefore would suffer less from the emotional upheavals that accompanied bondage, such as separation from loved ones.[20] The end result of many of these studies was to illustrate the inherently primitive and inferior characteristics of darker races, which in turn served to justify social and racial hierarchies in the United States, particularly the institution of slavery in the Southern region.[21]

The causes and curability of racial differences were a matter of debate in antebellum scientific discourse, but many observers seemed to agree that miscegenation, or interracial reproduction, created particularly unhealthy characteristics. Most observers claimed "that a mulatto is not a negro any more than he is a white man";[22] in many aspects (particularly intelligence and skin color), mixed-race individuals were viewed as intermediates between white and black, but in physical endurance, sensitivity to pain, reproductive capacity, and the overall hardiness of their constitutions, they were far more fragile and unhealthy than either group.[23] In 1843, Josiah Nott, an Alabama physician who wrote extensively on slave health matters, published an article in the *American Journal of Medical Sciences* that claimed mulattoes as "hybrids" between the "distinct species" of Anglo-Saxons and Negroes, were "intermediate in intelligence between the whites and blacks . . . [but] less capable of endurance and . . . shorter lived than the whites or blacks."[24] Furthermore, Nott claimed that mixed-race women were "particularly delicate" and prone to reproductive dysfunctions that made them "bad breeders and bad nurses."[25] Although New York statistician Samuel Forry disagreed with this idea in 1843 by citing the high number of mulattoes born in the West Indies,[26] many other Southern physicians shared Nott's perspective. H. A. Ramsay, a physician from Georgia, opined that "the mulatto is more subject to *nervous disorders* than the negro, and he possesses a peculiar *constitutional erethism* . . . [he] is less *robust, more delicate, punier,* and *more capricious,* than the negro." Ramsay also argued that mixed-race individuals were more difficult to treat, and more likely to resist medical treatment, than whites or African Americans.[27] Merrill, writing in the *Memphis Medical Reporter*, concurred but noted that mixed-race individuals were better suited to skilled labor. In his view, "feeble as they generally are in their constitutions, they often become prosperous, trustworthy and skillful in their several occupations, which are nearly always other than agricultural pursuits."[28] However, although mulattos were deemed less suited to plantation labor, the idea that their skin color and racial pedigree made them congenital, dependent servants was largely unquestioned.

At the same time, many writers concerned with the constitutional health of slaves deduced that African American bodies were innately "disabled" for freedom or prosperity, echoing the Aristotelian argument that inherent inequalities in human strength and intelligence made some individuals "born servants," unfit for independence. This argument gained particular prominence during and immediately after the Civil War,[29] but it had circulated in American slave society for decades prior to the 1860s. Josiah Nott, for instance, claimed that African Americans were not "sufficiently enlightened to qualify . . . for self-government"[30] and warned of the possibility that the colder climate of the North "freezes their brains as to make them insane or idiotical."[31] One major source of evidence for the argument that African Americans were naturally unfit for freedom in the North came from the results of the 1840 national census, the first census to consider the number of "insane and idiots" as well as the number of the blind, deaf and dumb among both slave and free populations. Harvard-trained physician Edward Jarvis, president of the American Statistical Association, compared the seemingly low number of blind, deaf, and "insane" African Americans among the slave population with the much higher number among blacks in the free North to point out that independence had a deleterious effect on black bodies, while slavery protected African Americans from debility. In his 1844 publication *Two Lectures on the Natural History of the Caucasian and Negro Races*, Josiah Nott cited some examples from the 1840 census, noting that "among the slave population in Louisiana, the insane and idiots number 1 in 4,310; in South Carolina 1 in 2,477; in Virginia 1 in 1,299; but what a different picture is presented at the North—in Massachusetts there is . . . 1 insane or idiot, in 43; and in Maine, 1 in 14!!!!!"[32] The census data were cited widely by prominent proslavery advocates in the 1840s, particularly South Carolina senator John C. Calhoun, but a number of prominent Northerners—including Harriet Beecher Stowe, John Quincy Adams, statistician Samuel Forry, and physician James McCune Smith—publicly refuted the discrepancies in the American Statistical Association's calculations. Some Northern towns apparently had registered all "colored" inhabitants as "insane," and Jarvis falsely reported numbers of insane, blind, and deaf free blacks that were higher than the total of African Americans in certain areas, an action that critics interpreted as an expression of proslavery sympathy.[33] Nonetheless, despite the discovery of Jarvis' fraud, an official correction of the census data was never published, and the argument that slavery was more beneficial to slave's health and able-bodiedness continued to resonate. As disability historian Douglas Baynton has pointed out, even Samuel Forry, a vocal critic of the use of unreliable census data to compare the health of free and enslaved African Americans, did not challenge the central argument that slavery might protect African Americans from disability or that racial differences "disabled" them from the conditions of freedom.[34] Proslavery Virginia minister Thornton Stringfellow, writing as late as 1856, noted that the proportions of blind, deaf, or mentally ill African Americans were two to four times higher in Northern regions, asking "can any man bring himself to believe, with these facts before him, that freedom in New England has proved a blessing to this race of people, or that slavery is to them a curse in the Southern States?"[35] Such evidence indicates a variety of white observers concluded that African American bodies were inherently "disabled" to live in free, Northern society.

Although Cartwright and others argued that "Negroes as a race can neither do as much work nor continue at it as long as the whites,"[36] they indicated that African Americans were inherently better suited to labor in a warmer, more tropical climate than Caucasians. In this instance, innate racial inferiorities of intellect and constitution were supposedly adaptive to the physical environment of the slaveholding South, and provided slaves with an advantage that white Europeans did not have.[37] Medical student William L. McCaa, observing slaves living near South Carolina's Wateree River for his 1822 thesis, noted "there is something peculiar in the constitution of the black man which enables him to enjoy health in an atmosphere where his master dare not venture."[38] Many observers noted that African slaves had a stronger natural resistance to infectious diseases like malaria and yellow fever as well as to constitutional diseases, like phthisis.[39] Although African American slaves had higher mortality rates than whites in the antebellum South, some observed that bondspeople who reached adulthood were more likely to live longer because bondage was beneficial for slaves' health.[40] McCaa noted that the "noxious" swamp air of the region, which seemed to cause fevers among Caucasian inhabitants, "is to them a prop in the decline of life."[41] Barnum, writing about Joice Heth after her death in 1836, implied that the "fact" that Heth had lived for so long in bondage, then died shortly after her arrival at Barnum's American Museum in New York, was because African Americans thrived in a warm, southern climate under the protection of their masters.[42] Furthermore, some observers believed that slaves were less susceptible to *opprobria medicorum*, or "diseases which destroy the pleasures of the studious and the wealthy," such as gout, apoplexy, and consumption as well as mental illness and emotional disorders.[43] Furthermore, Merrill noted that those of African descent required less sleep and had "greater insensibility to pain," two characteristics that were ideal for the plantation work routine and hard physical labor.[44] Cartwright also noted that African Americans thrived on the diet and physical exercise that bondage provided and did not, like their masters of European descent, "become dyspeptic and feeble" with age, or suffer from "sanguineous" ailments that caused general debility.[45] People of African descent, according to Cartwright, also had a peculiar foot structure—known in French as *l'allure déhanchée*—and a hinged knee, which were conducive to carrying heavy burdens and bowing low in a servile manner.[46] Indeed, in his estimation, people of African descent are naturally weak-willed, but "their strong muscles, hardy frames, and the positive pleasure that labor in a hot sun confers on them, abundantly qualify them for agricultural employment in a hot climate."[47] Furthermore, Cartwright concluded from his observations of slaves' pulmonary functions that "as a necessary consequence of the deficient aeration of the blood in the lungs, a hebitude [*sic*] of mind and body is the inevitable physiological effect; thus making it a mercy and blessing to negroes to have persons in authority set over them."[48] The image of the black body and its peculiarities that emerges from such observations is one that is singularly fit for bondage and physical labor in a warm climate, such as the American South or British West Indies.

Assumptions about the connections between disability and enslavement did not solely originate from proslavery voices, and many abolitionists relied on powerful images of disability (real and metaphorical) to represent the institution of slavery. It is unsurprising that the metaphor of slavery as disability had tremendous power in an antebellum culture influenced by a sentimental objection to pain and suffering as well as a strong work ethic that scorned weakness and dependence.[49] Indeed, it was an interaction with a disabled slave that led Kentucky evangelical minister John G. Fee to devote his career to abolition.[50] As scholar William L. Andrews has argued, "metaphors do not simply adorn arguments for persuasive purposes. Metaphors *are* arguments. Their success depends greatly on the capacity of the reader to accept and explore the creative dialectic of the semantic clash until new meanings emerge from the debris of old presuppositions."[51] White and free black Northerners alike could conceptualize the effects of blindness, scars, broken or crippled limbs, and the inability to speak as devastating disfigurements and dependencies. The fear of disability, defect and helpless reliance that accompanied enslavement was a strong impetus for the moral outrage that many Northern abolitionists aroused in their readers and listeners.

Alongside graphic and emotional descriptions of the physical suffering and disabilities of African American slaves, abolitionist rhetoric placed the blame for such physical and emotional devastation squarely on the institution itself and emphasized the uplifting aspects of freedom, claiming that emancipation would free African American bodies from the devastating, horrific impairments of bondage. Like other reform movements of the time, abolitionism was dedicated to Enlightenment ideas of self-improvement, as well as the capitalistic free labor system of the North. Once the arbitrary inequalities that impaired African American slaves were removed, many antislavery advocates argued, former slaves could enter free society as independent, hard-working (and by implication, able-bodied) citizens.[52] Nestled in this idea was a celebration of normal bodies in free society and a conviction that healthy, able bodies were necessary for "proper" citizenship and social progress.[53] However, these arguments coincided with other powerful ideas about the inherent defectiveness of African Americans and the socially devastating dependence of persons with disabilities. Indeed, as Douglas Baynton has noted, "by the mid-nineteenth century, nonwhite races were routinely connected to people with disabilities, both of whom were depicted as evolutionary laggards or throwbacks ... placed in hierarchies constructed on the basis of whether they were seen as 'improvable' or not."[54] Free black intellectuals in the North, such as New York City minister and editor Samuel Cornish, reflected this opinion when expressing disgust for the popularity of minstrelsy, which degraded African Americans and suggested that their "monkeyfied manners" were innate rather than imposed by the institution of slavery.[55] While many nineteenth-century reformers interpreted persons with disabilities as "suffering humans trapped within defective bodies,"[56] some abolitionists—particularly free African Americans—presented the idea that slaves could be rescued from their physical and emotional impairment through emancipation, education, and the fruits of free labor.[57] As abolitionist author James Redpath concluded from his travels in the South, "no complaints are ever made of the indolence or incapacity of the negroes, when they are stimulated by the hopes of wages or of prerogatives which can only be obtained in the South by hard work. It is the *slave*, not the *negro*, that is 'lazy and clumsy.'"[58] Furthermore, a piece in published in the Massachusetts Anti-Slavery Society's 1840 annual report made a direct appeal to President Van Buren, addressing arguments that slaves were not ready for freedom: "He is weak and unable to move. Why is he so? Because your dominion has palsied him. Will any man, who pretends to a jot of philosophy, deny that it is *slavery* that has disabled the slave?"[59]

The notion of former slaves, "crippled" and weakened by their bondage, living as public burdens certainly would have been an uncomfortable prospect to a largely white Northern public. Reverend Jermain Wesley Loguen, an abolitionist speaker and himself a former slave, indicated in his autobiography that the vitality of fugitive slaves was an important issue to the audiences abolitionists hoped to reach:

> The public eye is turned towards them, and public feeling extended to them as they pass through northern thoroughfares. Crippled as are their minds, and scarred as are their bodies by lashes and wounds, they present a sample of a strong and hardy and bold race—whose manly qualities the severest tyranny cannot subdue. It may be doubted whether, in like circumstances there is another people on the face of the earth who could preserve their nature less impaired or subdued.[60]

Loguen's remark combines assumptions about the disabling aspects of slavery with the idea that Africans were, by nature, stronger and hardier than white Europeans. Like a bracing tonic, according to some abolitionist rhetoric, emancipation (and by extension, introduction into a free labor system) immediately would confer fitness and vitality to black slaves temporarily "unfitted" by the peculiar institution. There is evidence that former slaves themselves internalized ideas about their able-bodiedness as freedpeople. In his autobiography, John Thompson described his reactions to reading an abolitionist speech by John Quincy Adams published in an 1830 newspaper: "little did Mr. Adams know, when he was uttering that speech, that he was 'opening the eyes of the blind'; that he was breaking the iron bands from the limbs of one poor slave."[61] Oral narratives of former slaves describe elderly slaves tossing away their walking sticks, and paralyzed slaves standing up to praise God, when they were emancipated.[62] Freed slaves, though saddled with physical, social, and emotional impairments in their bondage, could overcome those debilities as free individuals. This argument had particular salience in the antebellum North and served to assuage fears of a dependent class of "disabled" former African American slaves.

Even in antislavery rhetoric and literature, the enslaved body was often represented as a disabled, racialized Other and used as an object of both pity and revulsion.[63] Frederick Douglass, for instance, described the experiences of abused and disabled female slaves to represent the horrors of the institution and the hypocrisy of "Christian" slaveholders in *Narrative of the Life of Frederick Douglass, an American Slave*. His cousin Henny, "a lame young woman" who had sustained crippling burns as a child, was subjected to horrific beatings at the hands of their master before her eventual abandonment. Douglass uses very graphic language to describe the whippings Henny endured, objectifying her physical characteristics—her crippled, burned hands, naked shoulders, and "warm red blood"—and presenting her as a body rather than as a person.[64] An abolitionist song entitled "The Blind Slave Boy," widely published in England and the United States, utilizes blindness to indicate the vulnerability of slaves and evoke sympathy from listeners. The song describes an auction in which an enslaved mother is sold away from her young, blind son, who was picked up by another buyer for one dollar. In this example, both the enslaved boy and his mother are "disabled" by the condition of their bondage; the boy because of his blindness and the mother by her inability to halt his or her own sale:

> O! None like a mother can cherish the blind!
> . . . For the slave-owner drives her, o'er mountain and wild,
> And for one paltry dollar hath sold thee poor child!
> . . . Blind, helpless, forsaken, with strangers alone,
> She hears in her anguish his piteous moan,
> As he eagerly listens—but listens in vain,
> To catch the loved tones of his mother again![65]

This lyric reinforces the marginalization of both the disabled and the enslaved as "wretches" forsaken by loved ones and society in general. The construction of blindness as an utterly hopeless condition, particularly when paired with bondage, is also expressed in an article from *The North Star*, in which Reverend President Hitchcock describes an encounter with an unnamed blind slave in the Mid-Lothian coal mines of Virginia, whose "eyes had been entirely destroyed by a blast of gunpowder many years before, in that mine . . . There he stood, an old man, whose earthly hopes, even at the best, must be very faint; and he was a slave—and he was blind—what could he hope for on earth?"[66] In both of these descriptions of blind slaves, the authors take for granted that the blind are unloved (and unlovable), consigned to lives of despair and isolation. While antislavery mouthpieces certainly invited a number of reactions to their accounts of cruelty and graphic portrayals of impairment and disfigurement, they also firmly entrenched the disabled black slave as a social and cultural Other who could direct Northerners' moral outrage without questioning the divide between normal and abnormal bodies.

When comparing such evidence to cultural sources from African American slaves themselves, however, there are indications that slaves did not internalize the metaphor of disability as weakness or dependence. Historian Stephanie Camp has noted that enslaved African Americans had very different relationships with their bodies than did free individuals, and did not necessarily define their social roles by their physical abilities or the "soundness" of their bodies as market commodities. Instead, the enslaved body—weakened, exploited, and often disabled—could be a site of endurance and transcendence.[67] This is particularly evident in animal tales collected by folklorists in the deep South. As Charles Joyner and Lawrence Levine have pointed out, animal folktales and trickster stories often involve "weak, relatively powerless creatures who attain their ends through the application of native wit and guile rather than power or authority."[68] Physically weak characters, such as Bruh Rabbit, accepted and overcame their physical limitations, relying instead on their cunning and patience to maintain dignity and prevail in conflicts with stronger, "abler" characters.[69] One "Uncle John" tale, collected on Hilton Head Island, South Carolina, even implies the moral superiority of slaves, represented by a physically weakened creature:

> An "ol' man servan" named Uncle John was asked by his master while hunting ducks, "why is it de Devil is always after you, an' de Devil never worry me?" Uncle John answered after his owner had "shot into a covey of ducks" and ordered him to "hurry, an' ketch de wounded duck fus'!" Completing his task, Uncle John said, "Now, 'ketch the wounded duck firs'," an' dat is jus' what de Devil say. Say ketch me, because I'm scramblin' to get away f'om him, an' you are de dead duck. De Devil already got you, sah."[70]

Furthermore, African American slaves conceptualized health and physical wellbeing as a spiritual and community issue rather than as a matter of individual soundness, and felt a strong obligation to care for disabled individuals, such as the blind and elderly.[71] Some slaves with disabilities, such as musical prodigy "Blind Tom" Bethune, were even revered in slave communities; according to one nineteenth-century biography, his fellow plantation slaves regarded Tom "as a spirit from another world, and he was treated with the utmost tenderness by the people of color."[72] Spirituality also could be an important element in a "disabled" slave's self-perception. Abolitionist Wilson Armistead remarked on the extraordinary religious faith of disabled bondspeople, identifying it as evidence of slaves' intelligence and reason in a "helpless" state. For instance, in his "vindication of the moral, intellectual, and religious capabilities of the coloured portion of mankind,"

Armistead described the "Faith of a Poor Blind Negro," who was no longer able to read her Bible and was attended by "a respectable looking White girl" who read to her. The slave did not lament her loss of sight, because "by and by, when I get on Zion's hill, I shall see as well as any body [*sic*]."[73] Armistead also described a man named Maquaima, "a Negro Slave stolen from Africa, and who, when old and blind, was discarded in a helpless state." In Armistead's estimation, Maquaima's belief that "'the prospect of eternal happiness . . . infinitely overpays all my sufferings'" was evidence that he was "possessed of an intelligent and reflecting mind."[74] Similarly, African American teacher Charlotte Forten, who traveled from the North to educate Gullah freedpeople in the Sea Islands during the Civil War, described the remarkable faith of an elderly man named Maurice; he had been blinded after his master hit his head with a loaded whip, and felt "great distress" after losing his sight, "but den I went to see de Lord; and ebber since I know I see in de next world, I always hab great satisfaction."[75]

Nonetheless, African Americans were not immune to discourse about the humiliation and weakness ascribed to disability in the nineteenth century. Patrick Rael's intellectual history of Northern free black politics notes that, while the free black bourgeoisie challenged notions of white supremacy and racial inequality, their emphasis on uplift and respectability did not subvert or transgress mainstream values and social assumptions about the ability to participate in free society.[76] Furthermore, as scholars Elaine Scarry and Lennard J. Davis have noted, the disabling physical and emotional effects of slave labor were important to the identity and identification of slaves.[77] In her study of African American female writers, Carla Peterson observes that the women she studies often suffered from vague, undiagnosed illnesses, and hypothesizes that such ailments were internalizations of the concept of black women as "disorderly" bodies.[78] Slaves also seemed to have anxieties about growing older, according to historian Leslie J. Pollard's historical analysis of aged African Americans; despite the respect for the elderly that was common in slave communities, many may have dreaded their loss of abilities, not to mention their dependence on slaveholders and others to sustain their health, and the possibility of being cut off from support systems and necessary medical attention.[79] Furthermore, as scholar David Brion Davis has noted, "like all humans, slaves were sensitive to privilege, status, and inequality,"[80] which in the slave's forced lifestyle was linked with their physicality and ability to labor.

These perceptions of disability are evident in printed ex-slave narratives; for instance, in 1840, fugitive James Curry related the story of a slave debilitated by overwork, who felt emasculated by his weariness and loss of strength. When this slave passed by a field on the plantation where he had once worked, he remarked to Curry, "'When I went there to work, I was a man, but now, I am a boy. I could then carry several bushels on my shoulder, but now I cannot lift but one to it.'"[81] The man described in Curry's tale seems to have conceptualized his personal identity with his physical strength and ability to work; the extreme labor that had debilitated his body—made him a "boy" rather than a man—also affected his self-esteem. Furthermore, James L. Smith, the man who was crippled by a fractured knee as a child, identified that disabling moment as a central part of his memory and identity; his postbellum memoir opens with a recounting of the incident that resulted in his injury, and he notes that after the Civil War he visited Hog Point, the plantation where he had grown up, to visit "the very spot where I was made lame."[82] His "lameness," therefore, was a crucial aspect of how he viewed himself, both as a slave and as a free man. Other ex-slave narratives indicate that able-bodiedness was important to slaves' identities because it enabled them to resist the terms of their bondage, and conceptualize themselves as independent. For a young Frederick Douglass, his ability to best the strength of Mr. Covey, a slave "breaker" hired to discipline Douglass, was a pivotal point in the development of his identity—describing the incident in his autobiography, Douglass equates his physical prowess in his struggle with Covey to his blossoming self-perception as an independent man:

> I was *nothing* before; *I was a man now.* [The victory] recalled to life my crushed self-respect, and my self-confidence, and inspired me with a renewed determination to be a *free* man. A man without force is without the essential dignity of humanity. Human nature is so constituted, that it cannot *honor* a helpless man, though it can *pity* him, and even this it cannot do long if signs of power do not arise.[83]

Similarly, Harriet Jacobs implied that her physical ability was important because it allowed her to escape from a sexually abusive master. Using the pseudonym Linda Brent to publish her autobiography, Jacobs describes being bitten by a reptile while she was hiding from her master, and notes that "the dread of being disabled was greater than the physical pain I endured," implying that a disabling reptile bite could inhibit her ability to flee, but she could withstand any amount of pain if she could continue in her escape.[84] It is possible that these narratives—published for a largely white audience, and often with the editorial influence of a white amanuensis—may depict disability in this light more to reflect assumptions about disability than to portray how the slave narrators really imagined their own able-bodiedness. However, it is clear that while slaves did not assess disability in terms of soundness the way that slaveholders did, ideas about their able-bodiedness could be an important part of their identity and how they presented themselves as free individuals.

Other escape narratives indicate that some slaves would not protect others with physical impairments if it compromised their own freedom. Harriet Tubman, the "Moses" of the Underground Railroad and herself a "disabled" slave, had strict rules for escape expeditions, and claimed that "if any man gave out, he must be shot . . . is he was weak enough to give out, he'd be weak enough to betray us all, and all who had helped us."[85] During one of his attempts to find his family in Maryland, runaway slave Charles Ball met "a dark mulatto, small and slender in person, and lame in one leg," who had also escaped his bondage; the man was resting in a shelter he had made, and invited Ball to share his food, although Ball was anxious that such an encampment was too risky for a successful escape. In Ball's words, "he then proposed to join me, and travel in company with me; but this I declined, because of his lameness and great want of discretion."[86] Furthermore, James L. Smith described his 1838 attempt to flee with two other slaves named Zip and Lorenzo. Because of Smith's lame leg, he could not keep pace with his companions:

> At last Zip said to me . . . "we shall have to leave you for our enemies are after us, and if we wait for you we shall all be taken; so it would be better for one to be taken than all three." So after he had advised me what course to take, they started, and in a few minutes left me out of sight. When I had lost sight of them I sat down by the road-side and wept, prayed, and wished myself back where I first started.[87]

Smith's example indicates that, despite general ideas about illness as a community issue and slaves' responsibility to help each other, some African American bondspeople assumed that those with physical impairments were weak and burdensome. While slaves with disabling conditions certainly attempted to negotiate the terms of their bondage, some had some negative images of the nature of disability and its impact on slaves' ability to resist their bondage through self-defense or escape.

Significantly, these mentions of disability in escape narratives indicate that, despite masters' attempts to "correct" disobedient slaves by disabling or weakening them, physical impairments did not prevent slaves from attempting to escape or fighting back against authority figures. As John Hope Franklin and Loren Schweininger have pointed out in their analysis of runaway slave advertisements, "the profile of a runaway reveals a diversity in origin, appearance, language, skills, color, physique, gender, and age," and even slaves described as feeble, scarred, crippled, and elderly ran away from their slaveholders.[88] Runaway advertisements contain numerous examples of slaves with considerable impairments who attempted to flee. For instance, Ralph, a thirty-two-year-old Virginia man, ran away from his master in 1808 despite "an iron clog on his leg,"[89] and a Cobb County, Georgia, jailor reported that he had caught a slave named Jupiter who was "very lame, so that he can hardly walk."[90] Bob, a New Orleans slave who absconded in 1840, had an amputated leg and escaped using a crutch; another man from New Orleans, Davis, fled his master in 1829 and remained at large for over four months, despite the fact that he dragged his left leg when he walked.[91] Furthermore, fugitive slaves with disabilities, like Smith and Tom Wilson, eventually succeeded in their escapes from bondage despite their physical impairments. However, slaves with physical impairments also resisted the terms of their bondage by fighting back against their masters in other ways.

For instance, Smith, then a "lame" house servant, once managed to get himself away from his mistress while she attempted to administer a whipping.[92] In 1842, Kentucky fugitive Lewis Clarke, giving a speech in Brooklyn, reported the story of a more extreme example of a disabled slave's resistance:

> I remember one old slave, who was the most abused man I ever did see. His master had knocked and kicked him about till he had hardly a sound joint in his body. His face was all smashed up, and his right leg was broken to pieces . . . When he got old and a cripple, he wan't [*sic*] worth much, and his master would like well enough to get rid of him. He didn't like to drown him; but he thought he'd contrive to make him drown his self. So he drove him into the water for a punishment, and kept throwing stones at him to make him go further in. The slave turned round, and held his hat so as to catch the stones. This made the master so mad, that he waded in with a whip, to drive him further. The slave was a strong, stout fellow, by nature; and cripple as he was, he seized hold of his master, and kept ducking him, ducking him, without mercy. He said he meant to drown him; and I believe he would, if the neighbors hadn't come and saved him.[93]

All of these examples suggest that slaves not only participated in discourse about the meanings of impairment but also that some "disabled" slaves refused to see their physical conditions as a sign of weakness and could actively resist their bondage.

Images of enslaved bodies that bore stigmatizing symbols of disability were a prominent feature of antebellum American culture—thousands of Americans flocked to observe Joice Heth's decrepit body, and even more delighted in watching the contortions of blackface minstrels—and illuminate the complex interconnections of race, slavery, and disability in American discourse. Disability, like race, bore significant stigmas in the young American republic; antebellum observers often described racial difference in terms of physical or mental inferiority (and vice versa) and established divisions between "normal" and "defective" that were defined by skin color as well as physical and mental ability. According to many prominent proslavery advocates, particularly in the American South, the black body was biologically defective: intellectually stunted, physically weakened in the North American climate, prone to savagery and vice, and incapable of assimilating to a "civilized" culture or competing with the "superior" intelligence of Caucasians. Thus, Africans needed the controlling, domesticating effects of slavery in a hot, humid climate to survive and were "disabled" from living a free, Northern society. Some abolitionists and freed slaves, on the contrary, argued that the institution of slavery debilitated and weakened the bodies and minds of African Americans and claimed that emancipation could confer able-bodiedness and productivity onto even the most "wretched" slaves. While these viewpoints often argued directly against each other, and arrived at opposing conclusions about the role of African Americans in American society, both perspectives relied on common assumptions about the weakness, dependence, and deviance of disability and linked the concept of disability with race in a dual stigma that arced through antebellum discussions of slavery. Slaves themselves—able-bodied and disabled alike—had their own assumptions about disability and negotiated meanings of impairment with their own bodies, their masters, and each other. However, in all of these arguments and opposing viewpoints, concepts of race, bondage and disability were intimately linked and mutually constituted.

3   Sources of "Unsoundness" in African American Slaves

On 28 April 1838, George J. Kollock rebuked an overseer at his Retreat plantation on the Little Ogeechee River in Georgia for flogging a slave named Grace. According to his account, the overseer administered two whippings to Grace that day, one "for covering Corn bad" and "a second time for insolance [*sic*]," but Grace incurred "an accidental cutt clost [*sic*] to her eye," which Kollock seemed to believe was the intentional result of the overseer's violent correction. In his journal entry for that day, the overseer took umbrage to Kollock's reprimand, and noted that "when the owner takes the part of the negro against the overseer . . . it never failes [*sic*] to . . . Ruin the negroes, & make the owner a bankrupt."[1] However, Kollock's primary concern with the punishment may have been the potential damage to his slave's vision rather than to his overseer's temper. Slaves with eye problems were certainly concerning to Kollock; he owned at least one blind slave, a man named March, and was always careful to note eye disorders in his plantation records. For instance, in his "Plantation Work by the Day" log at Retreat, Kollock usually listed only a slave's name and the word "sick," but on 13 March 1849 he noted that Ginny was "sick with her eye."[2] On Kollock's Ossabaw Island plantation in 1855, "1 Gon Blind" appears in the daily work log for 23 April, and "1 Blind" was mentioned daily for three subsequent days.[3] The fact that these slaves were set apart from other "sick" laborers in plantation logs indicates that Kollock, for any number of personal or financial reasons, was particularly worried about threats to the soundness of his slaves' vision in the daily management of his plantation, including routine punishments from overseers.

Like Kollock, many slaveholders—even those who may have believed the institution of slavery was beneficial to African Americans—recognized that the circumstances of slave life could be hazardous to the bodies and minds of their bondspeople. Although it is difficult, if not impossible, to estimate a percentage of slaves who were considered disabled or "unsound," it is clear that disabling conditions were common among bondspeople in the antebellum South. Meager subsistence, unsafe work conditions, repetitive stress injuries, corporeal punishment, and abuse—physical, sexual or emotional—could cause physical and mental conditions among African American bondspeople that rendered slaves unsound in the eyes of the slaveholding class. The prevalent risks to slaves' health and able-bodiedness made a significant impact on discourse about slave soundness, a complex calculus for the economic value of human chattel based on a variety of medical, physical, psychological, and aesthetic factors. Although slaves could perform any number of different tasks based on age, gender, skin color, and character as well as on their physical strength, skills, or work environment, masters expected to have control—physical and psychological—over every one of their bondspeople, and assessing "soundness" was, in essence, an elaborate system for determining the controllability of an enslaved body. In determining sources of unsoundness, and discussing conditions that they considered disabling in human chattel, slaveholders betrayed their own assumptions about disabilities, the culture of mastery, and control over the labor, behavior, appearance, and physical function of their slaves. A variety of plantation record books, slaveholders' diaries and correspondence, estate inventories, runaway advertisements, medical publications, and ex-slave narratives contain assessments of unsound slaves and indicate why certain conditions were considered so disabling for African Americans in bondage.

In discussions of disability in slaves, many scholars utilize the nineteenth-century concept of soundness, a term used by the slaveholding class to indicate an individual slave's overall state of health and, by extension, his or her character and worth in the marketplace. As historian Sharla M. Fett has noted, the concept of soundness was rooted at the intersection of medicine and the Southern political economy and provided slaveholders with a language to determine the physical condition of their human chattel in terms of market value and productivity. Sources of soundness or unsoundness were individual characteristics of a slave's body, mind, or character, and discussions of a slave's soundness emphasized that those characteristics were not mitigated by the slave's job or environment; a slave with unsound qualities could be judged unsound in any situation.[4] Juriah Harriss, a professor of physiology at Savannah Medical College who published several articles on the assessment of slave soundness in the late 1850s, made a clear statement of what circumstances could, in his opinion, render a slave "unsound":

> I believe no disease will constitute unsoundness, unless it is of a *chronic* or *constitutional* character, *and incapacitates the negro for the performance of the usual duties of his calling, viz: hard labor, or tending to shorten life; or an acute disease of such a character as will probably leave as a sequence, a chronic affection, which will more or less incapacitate the negro for manual labor; or again an acute disease, which will render the negro liable to subsequent attacks of the same affection."* . . . There are some deformities which should constitute unsoundness. These may be congenital or accidental. Any deformity which materially diminishes the value of the negro, or disables him for the performance of

such labor as is usual for him to perform, or prevents the execution of natural functions which are necessary to the preservation of health or life, should constitute unsoundness."[5]

This statement highlights several significant points about how antebellum white authorities viewed soundness in slaves. The primary considerations in assessing a slave's able-bodiedness were ability to perform manual labor, "face value" as a commodity, and, finally, individual health; as Harriss indicates, the general health and well-being of slaves was lowest on the list of priorities in assessing their soundness. Indeed, the existence of disease alone did not necessarily render a slave unsound, but conditions that were considered uncontrollable, unpredictable, or not "expedient" to treat were disabling for African American slaves. For instance, Harriss noted that a slave with an amputated leg might be considered "healthy," if not "sound."[6] Furthermore, certain diagnoses, such as epilepsy or syphilis, could make otherwise healthy slaves "unsound" because there was no way to predict when symptoms would reappear, even in well-treated patients; thus, the concept of soundness encompassed conditions that were unseen as well as those that were visible.[7] Southern physicians, slaveholders, and traders utilized a number of clues to predict the soundness of slaves. For instance, skin color was viewed as an important indication of African Americans' overall health and vitality; "the blackest negroes were always the healthiest," whereas gray or flaky skin could signal poor physical or mental health in a slave.[8] However, the calculus of soundness was not as codified as Harriss (and Fett) indicate; in essence, the assessment of soundness was a system for determining how predictable and controllable slaves were, but it was influenced by a variety of other factors, including "character," appearance, physical ability, longevity and reproductive capacity as well as individual masters' aesthetic concerns and emotional reactions to their human chattel.

Because "soundness" was such a broad and complicated designation, it is extremely difficult to speculate on the number of African American slaves who fell into the category of disabled or "unsound" in the antebellum United States. Abolitionist Theodore Dwight Weld tried to make a statistical estimate of slaves with disabilities—including "the old, the worn out, the incurably diseased, maimed and deformed, idiots, feeble infants, incorrigible slaves, &c."—in his propagandist masterpiece *American Slavery as It Is*, claiming at least 100,000 African American slaves could fit this description in 1839 but admitted there was no way to make a firm assessment. Weld employed proportional data gathered from Northern states and an 1838 census of Chatham County, Georgia, to guess that the number of "lunatics" must be higher among slaves than the white population, particularly given "the dreadful physical violence to which the slaves are subjected, and the constant sunderings of their tenderest ties." Similarly, Weld claimed a total of 1,300 blind and 1,600 deaf and dumb slaves based on proportional data from Northern state censuses but without any clear indication of how he drew those conclusions for Southern slave populations.[9] In 1951, medical historian William Dosite Postell attempted to quantify physical and/or mental impairment among adult African American slaves by examining succession records, which included inventory appraisals of human chattel, in various Southern counties. According to his analysis, "disabled" slaves comprised between 4.1% (in Adams County, Mississippi) and 9.6% (in Montgomery County, Alabama) of all slaves included in the succession records;[10] however, this was obviously not a complete survey of all Southern communities, and only examined one kind of source. Furthermore, because definitions of "soundness" were not set in stone and individual slaves could move between the categories of "sound" and "unsound" throughout their lifetimes, a statistical analysis of disability among slaves at any given moment in time probably would not be meaningful for a study of the antebellum period more generally. What is significant to note is that, first, the forced lifestyles of the majority of slaves—plantation laborers—were highly conducive to ailments and conditions that could render them "disabled," and second, slaves with disabling or "unsound" conditions were common enough in the southern United States to warrant a lot of discussion in private and published antebellum sources.

While most slaveholders and overseers often referred to disabled and chronically ill slaves with such vague labels as "sick" or "unsound," a close reading of plantation journals provides a glimpse into the lives of plantation slaves with perceived disabilities, and how their owners assessed those conditions. Work rolls often indicated the ages of slaves and any notable skills or defects and rated their utility on the plantation by a calculus of "hands" (full hand, half- or quarter-hand, etc.). Many slaveholders were not explicit in their description of health problems that made slaves miss days of work, but these documents can indicate slaves with chronic ailments or conditions that would make them seem "disabled" in the eyes of their masters. Estate inventories are also particularly useful sources for identifying the types of disability that occurred among African American slaves, and were considered significant in the eyes of slave traders, masters and prospective buyers. All slaves, not just the ablest or most "likely," were appraised for estate inventories, and any source of unsoundness had to be disclosed at auctions. These documents indicate a wide range of health conditions and impairments, although some conditions were linked more closely to age or gender. Runaway slave advertisements, which often emphasized "peculiar marks" (such as scars, brands, and physical deformities) and easily recognizable defects (including stammering, missing body parts, or abnormal gait) are also a good source to examine how antebellum observers visualized abnormal or stigmatizing characteristics in slaves.[11]

It is important to note that slaves themselves did not consider their bodies in the same terms of soundness as the slaveholding class. Many primary sources from bondspeople that discuss disability emphasized the disabling aspects of slavery, particularly the effects of corporeal punishment and abuse, but they also indicate that slaves sometimes attributed chronic illnesses and impairments to conjurers in antebellum slave communities. As medical student William McCaa observed, "you can enquire of none of the negro's [*sic*] who cannot point out to you some 'old witch' on the plantation."[12] Data from ex-slave interviews in the 1930s indicate some former slaves believed that those suffering from conditions like blindness and chronic or incurable disease had been "fixed" by a conjurer or root worker; in this respect, slaves considered sickness and disability a matter of human interaction, not individual affliction. Conjurers—who were often identified as having "disabled" or abnormal bodies themselves—held a special place in slave society; scholar Elliott J. Gorn notes that "many root workers lived on the margins of slave society as old, irascible, or physically deformed individuals," but their powers were often respected and feared by slaves and white masters alike.[13] For instance, in his 1892 memoir, Frederick Douglass described a man named "Uncle" or "Doctor" Isaac Copper, who was "both our Doctor of Medicine and our Doctor of Divinity"; according to Douglass, "where he took his degree I am unable to say, but . . . one qualification he certainly had. He was a confirmed cripple."[14] This description indicates that Copper's disability conferred upon him a supernatural knowledge or skill that inspired reverence from his community. Similarly, in another postbellum memoir, former slave William Wells Brown described a conjure man named Dinkie, who awed his entire community:

> Dinkie, a full-blooded African, large in frame, coarse featured, and claiming to be a descendant of a king in his native land, was the oracle on the "Poplar Farm." At the time of which I write, Dinkie was about fifty years of age, and had lost an eye, and was, to say the least, a very ugly-looking man . . . Everybody treated him with respect. The whites, throughout the neighborhood, tipped their hats to the old one-eyed negro, while the policemen, or patrollers, permitted him to pass without a challenge. The negroes, everywhere, stood in mortal fear of "Uncle Dinkie."[15]

Secondary literature on slave conjurers often focus more on their healing powers, but while hoodoo healers supposedly had the power to *cure* debilitating conditions like blindness or fits, they were also believed to *cause* them in some cases. As Gorn notes, "many bondsmen deeply feared being conjured into sickness or even death by their enemies. They related stories of friends or family members blinded, crippled, even driven insane" by hoodoo workers in slave communities.[16] Southern physicians also observed that slaves believed some chronic illnesses like rheumatism and "neuralgic pains" could be the product of witchcraft and complained that this belief aggravated health problems and debilitating conditions because slaves were less likely to seek "regular" medical attention for ailments they attributed to conjure.[17]

Despite such different perspectives on the meanings of "unsoundness," injuries, illnesses and disorders that were considered disabling for slaves were common in the American South; indeed, as one runaway slave remarked in 1838, "there was hardly a day that some of the slaves did not get crippled or killed."[18] Many slaves subsisted on meager diets and a dearth of basic necessities like adequate clothing and shelter. In addition, the strain of plantation labor, unsafe work conditions, and physical, sexual, and psychological abuses took their toll on the bodies of slaves; many slaves experienced disabilities resulting from physical stress, in addition to injuries from work and punishment. All of these factors could also have a negative effect on women's capacity for childbearing and caused high rates of miscarriage and infant mortality. Of course, not all disabilities that African American slaves experienced were the direct result of their bondage; however, the circumstances of slave life and labor certainly could aggravate physical or psychological impairments, which then compromised the ability of slaveholders to perceive or maintain control over their human chattel. These issues were significant considerations in determining the soundness of African American bodies in bondage.

Viewing slave health through the lens of contemporary medical knowledge, it is clear that regular circumstances of slave life and labor could cause a number of health problems and defects, particularly functional losses that impaired the utility of bondspeople. A number of historians have noted that slaves' poor diet caused a number of vitamin deficiency diseases such as rickets, pellagra and scurvy, which could cause stunted growth as well as "dirt-eating"[19] (known as *cachexia Africana*), sight impairments, and recurring diarrheal illness. In addition to their deficient diet, many slaves also did not have access to proper clothing or shelter, particularly in the winter, and recurring respiratory illnesses and frostbite were common.[20] Evidence of poor diet and overexposure is common in runaway slave advertisements from the first half of the nineteenth century. For instance, Daniel Meaders's collection of runaway advertisements in Alexandria and Richmond, Virginia, from 1801 to 1820 includes many mentions of "bowlegged" or "bandy-legged" slaves, whose bones were likely deformed from dietary deficiencies as well as descriptions of slaves who had lost fingers or toes to frostbite.[21] The conditions of slave labor, including overwork and repetitive motions, also caused a number of different health problems that resulted in disability. Hernia, or "rupture," was very common among African Americans in the South, and although they could be treated surgically or with the use of a truss, hernias could permanently impair the "usefulness" of slaves.[22] Some believed rheumatism—a more expansive disease category in the nineteenth century that could arise from infections or arthritis—to be less common in warm climates, but the disease appears frequently in descriptions of slave health problems and often incapacitated its victims.[23] Other occupational impairments are frequently mentioned in medical literature, plantation records and slave appraisals, particularly sore fingers, aneurysms, and swollen or "sore leg," a very common problem that was not necessarily chronic but could debilitate slaves for long periods of time.[24] In one extreme case, physician T. P. Bailey of North Santee, South Carolina, described a twenty-year-old woman named Betty, who had "for several years past suffered from pain and inflammation of the fibula of the left leg . . . the leg is misshapen and enlarged . . . she is a times totally incapacitated for work, the irritation being so great as to cause fever and painful swelling."[25]

In addition, injuries—especially head trauma, burns, fractures, and loss of limbs—were common causes of slave unsoundness and were mentioned often in estate appraisals, plantation journals, and runaway slave advertisements. Even minor injuries could result in weeks of convalescence for plantation laborers. South Carolina planter Thomas W. Peyre had two slaves that were "laid up" for nearly a full month each for cuts on their feet,[26] and Juriah Harriss noted that seemingly minor concussions could impair mental function and vision as well as cause paralysis or convulsive disorders, all of which were viewed as permanent disabilities.[27] Burns were a frequent occurrence; as ex-slave Moses Grandy explained in his memoir, the lack of adequate bedding forced slaves to sleep too close to unprotected fires to stay warm, and "their legs are often in this way blistered and greatly swelled, and sometimes badly burnt."[28] Severe burns could result in "great and distressing deformity" from muscular contractions, extensive scarring, and gangrene.[29] Runaway slave advertisements occasionally included graphic descriptions of the effects of such burns. For instance, a notice in the *Winyah Observer* in 1852 identified a fugitive slave named Gabriel as "a bright mulatto aged about 22 yrs . . . has a contraction of 3 fingers on the right hand occasioned by a burn when quite young."[30] Similarly, in 1811 the *Alexandria Daily Gazette, Commercial and Political* advertised Ben, a twenty-five-year-old runaway, who had "a remarkable scar in one of his hands, occasioned by a burn when young; it has caused a contraction of his thumb, and a part, or all his fingers on that hand."[31]

Fractures were also common on plantations, and could be the result of a number of different occurrences, including horse kicks, malfunctioning farm equipment, industrial accidents with mills or threshers, and the repetitive plucking of cotton bolls.[32] Many fractures were improperly treated because of the limited compassion and/or medical knowledge of planters and overseers or because physicians could not respond to a summons from a remote plantation in time, and therefore resulted in permanently deformed limbs.[33] For example, James L. Smith, a slave in Virginia, was disabled as a boy after he fractured his knee carrying a heavy piece of timber. His master was initially reluctant to treat Smith's knee; as a result, long after the accident, a physician told Smith's mother and owner that "as it had been out of joint so long it would be a difficult matter to break it over again and then set it." Smith's leg subsequently became infected and "broke in seven places," which resulted in permanent "lameness."[34] An 1815 advertisement in the *Richmond Enquirer* described a runaway named Doctor, noting that "he has once had his right arm broken, in consequence of which, his arm is smaller & shorter than the left one, and stands a little crooked."[35] Slaves with missing limbs and extremities—from surgical amputations, accidents, punishments, or frostbite—were frequently reported in estate inventories of slaves and runaway advertisements.[36]

Any perceived loss of function—from chronic or recurring illnesses as well as missing or defective limbs—could be considered disabling for slaves because it represented a significant labor deficit. Masters of slaves with chronic health problems were responsible for providing care for their ailing bondspeople, and those slaves could be a significant drain on plantation resources if they were unable to work for long periods of time. The deformity or absence of a limb did not necessarily render a slave completely useless in the eyes of a master. At an 1860 public auction in the Chalmers Street Mart of Charleston, for instance, a fourteen-year-old slave named Scipio was described as a field hand even though he had "one hand off,"[37] and a member of the "Gordon Gang" of slaves belonging to South Carolina planter Edmund Ravenel included a forty-year-old man named Aaron who was a carpenter, but had lost an arm.[38] However, fractures, burns, and other injuries almost always considered disabling, or unsound, to some degree, because they were accompanied by the threat of compromised or lost function.

One particularly common disability among Southern slaves—and one that aroused a lot of concern from slaveholders—was blindness. "Sore eyes," which some historians have attributed to a vitamin A deficiency but could have also arisen from infections or allergies, was a widespread complaint on plantations in the United States and West Indies alike,[39] and although physicians and masters attempted to treat their affected bondspeople with such measures as linen bandages and warm water or milk poultices, the condition often resulted in loss of vision.[40] Of course, not all cases of blindness among slaves were acquired from environmental hazards or deficiencies; there were certainly cases of congenital blindness, most notably the musical prodigy "Blind Tom" Bethune, a Georgia slave who began performing across the South before he was ten years old.[41] However, damage to the eyes was a very common problem for African American slaves. New York statistician Samuel Forry claimed that the higher ratio of blind individuals among the "colored" population revealed in the 1840 census "may be reasonably referred to their severer labor and greater exposure, to their greater improvidence, and less advantage of medical aid."[42] Mentions of sore eyes are common in plantation journals across the South; for instance, in 1844 Louisiana planter Bennet H. Barrow noted that his "hands seemed to be in fine humour & all well—Excepting Demps with sore eyes." Although a physician treated Demps's eyes over the next two months, Barrow feared that his slave would "loose [*sic*] his sight."[43] Several estate auctions in Charleston also indicate the importance of disclosing eye defects. For instance, a "prime gang of 158 Negroes," belonging to the late T. Bennett Lucas and sold in 1860, included a forty-year-old laborer named Hester with a "defect in one eye," and Robert, a twenty-three-year-old bricklayer, was described as "blind one eye."[44] The loss of vision, whether congenital or acquired, was a prominent cause of "unsoundness" or disability for antebellum slaves. Not only could blindness prohibit a slave from performing certain kinds of duties, it could also prohibit a slaveholder from instructing or disciplining the slave in the same ways he used for other bondspeople. Sensory defects were also easier to exaggerate or feign than an injury or loss of limb function, so it is probable that slaveholders would be concerned about malingering. All of these factors made blindness a particularly undesirable source of unsoundness in a slave.

Another concerning cause for unsoundness was infertility and reproductive dysfunction in African American women. Uterine prolapse, vesicovaginal fistula, irregular menses and amenorrhea, and miscarriage—while common for women of various ethnicities and social classes in the nineteenth century[45]— were observed to occur more often among African American slaves than other women. Common reproductive problems, especially uterine prolapse, were viewed as permanent afflictions; self-described "Professional Planter" Dr. Collins noted that, although "falling down of the womb" did not always impair a female slave, "even in the mildest cases, it seldom admits of a perfect cure."[46] As South Carolina medical student Perry F. Pope lamented in his dissertation on the management of slaves, "Prolapsus Uteri is quite a common disease . . . at present we are only able to assist and mitigate."[47] As a result, evidence of a fertility problem almost always rendered a female slave unsound and was an important issue for disclosure to prospective slaveholders. Female slaves who could not get pregnant were at risk of being sold or traded, and women who experienced even benign reproductive problems aroused concerns; for example, Juriah Harriss noted that the existence of ovarian cysts always constituted unsoundness in a female slave, even if they did not seem to affect her fertility.[48] This is evident in several different estate auction advertisements from Charleston, which identify a variety of reproductive issues in female slaves for sale, including "prolapsus" or "tendency to prolapse," "fib[rous] tumor of womb," "menstrual derangement," and "breeds fast & looses [*sic*] children."[49] As historian Jennifer L. Morgan has noted, female slaves were ascribed the "dual value," and performed the dual role, of producing both crops and more laborers, and slaveholders were particularly alarmed when their bondswomen experienced problems with their reproductive systems.[50] Historian Elizabeth Bankole has indicated that these problems arose from using women as "breeders," but it is also likely that nutritional deficiencies, external injuries, overwork during pregnancy, and difficult deliveries also affected slave women's reproductive capacity.[51] Although some antebellum slaveholders believed that the root of slaves' infertility was sexual promiscuity, many were certainly aware that the conditions of slavery could adversely affect the reproductive capacity of bondswomen and warned against forcing pregnant women to perform "kinds of labour which require extraordinary exertions."[52]

Psychological and neurological conditions also affected assessments of the slave soundness. Although some antebellum observers—using the misinterpreted results of the 1840 census as evidence—argued that "hard working" slaves were less susceptible to the disappointments of a more "refined" life and thus less likely to be afflicted with nervous disorders than their white masters,[53] there are many cases of bondspeople identified with a variety of psychological and neurological disorders.[54] In 1953, William Dosite Postell examined antebellum probate records from different counties and parishes in Alabama, Georgia, Mississippi, and Louisiana and determined that of the 31,170 slaves mentioned in these records, 391 were identified as suffering from some type of mental affliction; the records used such terms to describe them as *simpletons, imbeciles, crazy, deranged, insane, "subject to spasms"* or *fits,* and afflicted with paralysis, palsy, and spinal injury. However, Postell acknowledges that slaveholders and overseers inconsistently applied these labels, and because of these irregularities the prevalence of nervous disorders among African American slaves was probably much higher than his statistical analysis indicates.[55] Moreover, Todd Savitt has pointed out that the majority of individuals with mental disorders, white and black, were not institutionalized in the mid-nineteenth century, and these slaves were just incorporated into plantation life; indeed, "the lines separating mental soundness from temporary and total insanity were necessarily hazy."[56] However, any personality, emotional, or neurological disorder was viewed as important for disclosure in slave sales and could be assessed as a cause of unsoundness, particularly if it affected a slave's ability to work or to be controlled by his or her master. As Juriah Harriss noted in 1859, any slave afflicted with a nervous illness could be unpredictable and potentially dangerous:

> The negro may eat his meals *regularly* and *heartily,* and so long as he does not present any outward manifestation of disease, other than mental, his is in the eyes of the law "healthy." He may be idiotic—utterly unable to execute the orders of his owners, or even worse, a raving maniac, requiring not only the time and attention of the purchaser, but perhaps of sound negroes, to prevent his doing an injury to the immediate family of the owner or his slaves; or setting fire to the premises.[57]

This was particularly true in the case of slaves who experienced *fits,* a term used to describe a variety of convulsive disorders—particularly epilepsy—in the nineteenth century. Individuals assumed to have epilepsy might experience fits on a regular basis (for example, at lunar changes) or live for months or years without any evidence of the disorder. Many observers also saw a clear "alteration betwixt insanity and epilepsy";[58] some primary evidence merely records the coincidence of the two conditions without drawing conclusions about their causal relationship, but others indicate a belief that recurring fits could lead directly to a violent type of mental instability known as *furor epilepticus.* The fearsome appearance of epileptic fits, which were incapacitating, unpredictable and presumed to be largely incurable, as well as the association between epilepsy and violent behavior made epilepsy a particularly concerning cause of unsoundness in even seemingly healthy African American slaves and was viewed as an "illness serious enough to keep the

Negroes indoors" when it occurred.[59] The loss of labor, and difficulty in controlling slaves with nervous ailments made mental and neurological disorders a significant cause of unsoundness in African American slaves.

Even old age—which some slaveholders defined as fifty years of age and over, but which was often influenced by the presence of an infirmity—was a significant cause of unsoundness for slaves. Many plantation records refer to elderly slaves as "Old," "Aunt/Uncle," "Granny," "Nurse" or "Mammy," which served as honorific titles in the slave community[60] and may have differentiated slaves with the same given name. However, these titles seem to appear more frequently as indicators of a slave's age and also of their labor capacity. On Isaac Ball's Limerick plantation in South Carolina, for instance, there were a number of slaves identified as "Old" in plantation records from 1815, and all of them were over the age of fifty.[61] On Bennet H. Barrow's Louisiana plantation, a slave named "Old Betty" died in 1836 at the age of 65.[62] There appears to have been a difference in value between slaves considered "old" and "aged" or "superannuated," which generally referred to slaves over the age of 70.[63] In some estate sales, slave auctioneers often listed older slaves simply as "aged" or "infirm," an indication of more general debility. Elderly and superannuated slaves were more likely to experience health problems that disabled them for service, including failing eyesight, rheumatism, paralysis, and, to a lesser extent, dementia; also, as historian Leslie J. Pollard argues, older slaves generally required more medical attention, which decreased their investment value and reduced their chances of receiving the care they needed.[64] Thus, despite the respect that elderly slaves garnered from masters and fellow slaves alike, age was an important factor in assessments of a slave's health and able-bodiedness.[65]

In many cases, doctors treated slaves with acute conditions that threatened to cause permanent physical or mental impairment, particularly if the enslaved patients were valuable or productive laborers. Occasionally, physicians opted for surgical interventions in the treatment of potentially disabling conditions, preferring a more "heroic" approach to even seemingly minor problems. John Douglass, a doctor in Chester, South Carolina, described surgical interventions he performed on slaves for a variety of problems, including fractures and skull injuries that resulted in chronic "mental derangement" and symptomatic convulsions.[66] Antebellum Southern physicians also performed surgical removals of tumors in enslaved patients, such as a slave woman in Georgia who had an abdominal growth that seemed to endanger her health after the delivery of her fifth child. The woman had lived with the tumor for fourteen years, and four healthy pregnancies, before it "was attended with more pain and general derangement of the system."[67] Following a successful surgery, a report in the *Oglethorpe Medical and Surgical Journal* lauded the procedure, noting that "this may be heroic surgery, but it was duty, and should have been done long ere this."[68] Juriah Harriss noted that seemingly benign tumors or polyps could become severe problems affecting the value of slaves if they were ignored or improperly treated; "when a small point of the disease has been allowed by neglect, or interference of quacks, to spread, ulcerate, and infect surrounding glands, it becomes a permanent cause of unsoundness."[69] Some doctors made the decision to *create* a physical impairment in a slave in order to treat a potentially life-threatening problem. Physicians in the antebellum South were frequently called upon to perform dangerous procedures—particularly amputations of injured or diseased limbs and extremities—on injured or ailing bondspeople, in the effort to mitigate or reverse a disabling condition such as a severe compound fracture or a malignant tumor. For instance, T. P. Bailey performed two amputations on Hector, a forty-year-old slave who was caught in a large mill wheel in 1859.[70] On the Araby Plantation in Louisiana's Madison Parish in 1843, a slave named Anthony was injured in a gin, and his owner, Natchez planter Haller Nutt, called a physician after Anthony's hand "assumed a very bad appearance fingers withering away and the whole hand sluffing." The physician immediately suggested removal of Anthony's entire arm, which was performed eight days after the accident.[71] One physician in Florida, Richard Jarrot, even attempted to amputate the leg of a 102-year-old man with gangrene of the foot, even though "his great age and weak condition rendered the operation perilous;" Jarrot's report of the case indicates that the slave was still active and productive, despite his age, which may have contributed to his master's decision to seek treatment and the physician's decision to amputate as a last resort to save the man's life. Unfortunately, the patient developed pleurisy and died soon after the operation.[72] The sheer number of amputations performed in Southern practice was concerning to one correspondent to the *Virginia Medical Journal*, identified as "Senex," who criticized that many surgical procedures, particularly on slaves, were in fact unwarranted:

> The most cruel and heartless operations . . . that a surgeon executes, are those designed chiefly for éclat or self-laudation; and there is too much reason to believe that many, nay very many of the operations of the present times are of this description. It is by no means uncommon "now a days" to hear of amputations of the limbs, especially the lower, for ulcers, not involving the bones, nor possessing very questionable or menacing characters.[73]

Senex's article clearly indicates that amputations, including those that created disability in slaves, were common practice in the antebellum South, and the fact that the author used a pseudonym to make the critique may imply that opposition to such practices for enslaved patients was unpopular. From the abundant evidence of surgical interventions that physicians applied to slaves with severe injuries—and the descriptions of procedures that Senex's dissent provides—it is clear that Southern physicians had the authority to decide upon more risky therapeutic interventions, even those that could create impairment, in their treatment of slaves. Some physicians even argued that the loss of a limb was less disabling for African American slaves than for free white laborers. For instance, in an 1839 issue of the *Southern Medical and Surgical Journal*, medical student W. H. Robert wrote an account of surgical amputations performed by Louis Alexander Dugas, a founder of the Medical College of Georgia, over the previous few years. Dugas attended two enslaved boys, both fifteen years old, for "swelling of the knee": Henry, "a mulatto boy" who had suffered for years from an immovable knee joint and a "fistulous opening" in his leg, and Ned, whose "growth had been very much retarded" by the painful ulcers his swelling had caused. In both cases, Dugas resorted to above-the-knee amputations of the patients' affected legs.[74] Although this intervention seems to have been a last resort, at least in Henry's case, Robert assured his readers that the removal of these slaves' limbs was not an extreme measure, or even necessarily disabling. Instead, Robert noted that

> the loss of so important a limb as the leg, should be very differently estimated in the different classes of society. Whilst to the gentleman of fortune it would be a horrid deformity, and the destruction of most of his enjoyments; and to the free laborer, it would, in many instances, constitute the loss of the means of subsistence for himself and his family; it is to the slave a matter of comparatively little importance.[75]

Because slaves were prone to "idleness" and did not need to provide for themselves or their families, according to Robert, the prospect of losing a leg should not trouble them or the physicians treating them. Assumptions about the patients' race and servile status thus influenced Dugas's judgment of the worth of their legs as much as the medical evidence. The student concludes his report by noting "we should hesitate much less to remove a limb, whose affection endangers the life of the patient, if he be a slave, than if he be a free man, and especially a white man."[76]

Many white physicians and slaveholders were proud to report the good treatment they provided to disabled or chronically ill slaves and lauded the institution for providing such care to ailing bondspeople. Slaves with debilitating conditions, according to many boastful Southern physicians, received the best care available to them and could be effectively restored to work for their masters. For instance, Thomas S. Powell, a doctor in Sparta, Georgia, wrote a report for the *Atlanta Medical & Surgical Journal* concerning a slave named Mary, who suffered from a severe knee pain for three weeks. Mary's mistress thought she had just sprained her knee and "applied vinegar and clay from the back of the chimney for several nights" before calling an unnamed "celebrated Thomsonian" to induce vomiting with lobelia. Powell determined that Mary suffered from a synovial inflammation that required no internal treatment, and he successfully alleviated her pain with hot ammonia and vinegar poultices, allowing her to return to field labor.[77] His report of this largely unremarkable case casts doubt on the reputation of the "irregular" physician who attempted to treat knee pain with severe vomiting and further laid up a valuable field slave, and lauds his own ability to treat African American patients successfully and expediently. Others linked their treatment of slaves with chronic ailments more directly to the benevolence of bondage itself. W. H. Robert, in his proud description of Ned's 1837 successful amputation, noted that the surgery would not have cured Ned's debility had he been a free man: "The lad's life had been saved, none of his comforts sacrificed, and he is in the full enjoyment of fine health; nor has his master sustained any loss, for he has made him a cobler [*sic*]. A poor Irishman, whose leg I amputated for a dreadful injury sustained by a rail road car, now wanders about a miserable beggar!"[78] As proslavery author Thornton Stringfellow noted, free laborers, the "slave[s] of money," often had no one to take care of them when they were disabled by illness or injury, and were unable to provide for themselves when they could not work.[79] Therefore, the system of slavery was ultimately more benevolent than the free labor system for its care of laborers with disabilities. In a communiqué to the Executive Department of the State of South Carolina, rice planter Robert F. W. Allston noted that planters did not fail to provide professional surgical attention to debilitated slaves, even when the cost of the physician exceeded the slave's value. Furthermore, "the aged & infirm are not neglected when pain & suffering demand the kindly services of the Physician . . . for continued attendance upon chronic case[s], hopelessly ill—& for years utterly useless."[80] Daniel Colman, overseer for Memerable W. Creagh in Perry County, Alabama, in 1847 and 1848, noted that several disabled slaves of various ages on the Creagh plantation "acquired and received the aid of physicians," even though "they were of considerable trouble to M. W. Creagh on account of their sickness, inability to performe labour [*sic*] and the attention they required."[81]

Despite such praises for the "kindly" care and treatment of slaves, mutilation and injury from corporeal punishment and abuse of African American bondspeople were frequently causes of disabling impairments. Many planters only made oblique or cursory references to punishment in plantation journals and estate inventories; slaveholding society viewed most corporeal punishments as prerogatives of the white ruling class, and they therefore did not warrant much attention in these documents. The explicit and "impolite" descriptive language used in runaway slave advertisements sheds more light on the effects of corporeal punishment and physical abuse of slaves in the antebellum South.[82] Abolitionists used runaway advertisements printed in Southern newspapers to highlight the cruelty that slaves endured, reprinting notices describing slaves with gunshot wounds, cropped ears, whipping scars, and cuts from knives or axes. Indeed, as historian Kenneth Stampp observed, the language of runaway slave advertisements changed as a result of this abolitionist tactic, with more slave injuries identified by vague terms like "scars" or "burns," not "marks of the whip" or "brands."[83] While slaveholders may not have been very explicit in their descriptions of discipline and its effects on slave bodies, corporeal punishment was a significant element of the culture of mastery. Southern slaveholders focused on the external bodies of slaves that had "dishonored" them, and utilized disfiguring and physically disabling punishments for disobedience or running away; as historian Kenneth Greenberg notes, "the body drew a disproportionate degree of attention" in the discipline of slaves.[84] Wayward bondspeople were often whipped and branded with hot irons, had their faces cut, their ears cropped, and their teeth knocked out, all punishments that were highly visible marks of dishonor and "vicious" character.[85] Eugene Genovese has made the persuasive point that, since disfiguring marks and disabling injuries rendered slaves "unsound" and decreased their market value, many slaveholders devised less injurious forms of punishment in the nineteenth century;[86] however, the sheer volume of accounts of violent physical abuse of slaves indicates that there were emotional and cultural factors beyond financial concerns involved in the punishment of slaves. Disabling punishments could serve other purposes, such as physically preventing a slave from further disobedience, or creating a permanent sign of that slave's dishonor and the master's rightful retribution.

The most common form of physical punishment was whipping, which masters and overseers applied to slaves of both genders and all ages.[87] As fugitive slave John Brown described it in 1855, the whip was a feared instrument of violence, designed "to 'whip down' savage bulls, or unruly cattle." In most cases the whip was only used to "lick" a slave's skin, cutting the flesh and raising a scar without causing any permanent physical damage.[88] However, there is also evidence that whipping led to psychological problems, shock, and infection, and could create permanent impairments like muscle damage in slaves.[89] Moses Grandy described a whipping he had received at the hands of a "severe man" named Jemmy Coates, who had hired a young Grandy to work in his cornfield:

> Because I could not learn his way of hilling corn, he flogged me naked with a severe whip made of a very tough sapling; this lapped around me at each stroke, the point of it at last entered my belly and broke off . . . I was not aware of it until on going to work again it hurt my side very much, when on looking down I saw it sticking out of my body . . . the wound festered, and discharged very much at the time, and hurt me for years after.[90]

While most slaveholders would have argued that permanent disability was only a minor risk and not the purpose of the whip, disfigurement—not to mention terrible pain—certainly was an intention. The presence of whip scars was often noted in sales of slaves and runaway slave advertisements, and a slave whose "back was well marked with stripes"[91] was often assumed to have a bad or vicious character.

Another particularly mutilating punishment was branding, particularly searing initials into skin on the face or near the genitals. According to abolitionist propaganda, there were many indications that the main purpose of branding was to humiliate the slave by creating a permanent disfigurement. One 1853 British abolitionist tract, lamenting the frequency of slave-branding, listed runaway slave advertisements that mentioned bondspeople with letters branded on specific parts of their bodies, including a mother with the letter "M" branded on her cheek who was ashamed of the scar and "kept a cloth over her head and face, and a fly bonnet on her head, so as to cover the burn." Another example was Molly, a teenaged slave with the letter "R" on her left cheek and the inside of both thighs.[92] The location of Molly's brands were an overt sign of the slaveholder's domination over her sexualized body, and seemed designed to violate and demean her womanhood as much as punish a perceived transgression. Theodore Weld also cited several advertisements in his 1839 *American Slavery as It Is* that described very specific branding injuries. For instance, Weld notes that R. P. Carney of Clark County, Georgia, placed a notice in the *Mobile Register* on 22 December 1832 for a slave named Pompey, who was "branded on the left jaw." In another example, Micajah Ricks of Nash County, North Carolina, advertised a runaway slave in the *Raleigh Standard* on 18 July 1838, noting that "a few days before she went off, I burnt her with a hot iron, on the left side of her face, I tried to make the letter M."[93] The locations of brands on the face, the most visible part of the body and the one most associated with individual character, indicates that main motivation for branding was to dishonor a slave, even if it meant devaluing the bondsperson for resale. This was the case for James Smith, a slave in Virginia and Georgia, who had attempted multiple escape attempts after his wife was sold away. After one failed flight, Smith's overseer took him to a Richmond jail where he stayed for several months awaiting a sale before he came into contact with his master again. Smith's interviewer, Henry Bibb, described this encounter in 1852:

> His master came after him with the spirit of a demon. After having him stripped and most unmercifully flogged, a hot iron was applied to his quivering flesh on one side of his face and back of his neck, which left stamped, in letters of flesh and blood, the initials of his master's name. A few days after this punishment, he was sold at public auction.[94]

The fact that Smith's master chose to brand Smith *after* he had already been taken away to be sold, a decision that certainly would have diminished Smith's market value, indicates that Smith's disfigurement held a deeper meaning for his owner beyond mere punishment. As a result of his repeated escapes, Smith had "dishonored" his white master, and was forced to carry the branding scar as a reminder of that dishonor and his master's retribution.

Other punishments were intended to weaken or disable disobedient slaves. Slaves who possessed more strength than white authorities, and could therefore fight back, were a threat to the slaveholding class as a whole; several examples from ex-slave narratives indicate that disabling punishments were meted out to those who used their physical abilities to resist authority figures. Some slaves sustained fractures from beatings that caused permanent impairment.

For instance, Josiah Henson, a black overseer reputed to be the inspiration for Harriet Beecher Stowe's Uncle Tom character, was beaten by a white overseer and several slaves in retaliation for shoving the white man at a party; he received two broken shoulder blades and one broken arm, and lost full motion of both arms as a result.[95] Tom Wilson, who escaped to Great Britain and told his tale to the *Liverpool Albion* in 1858, noted that in addition to the severe whippings he received for resisting punishment, his overseer had once "cut [his] right arm across the middle, and then had it stitched up. He did that, he said, to weaken me, because I was too strong in the arm."[96] In many cases, weakening punishments were used on runaway slaves. Dr. Collins, a "professional planter" in the British West Indies, described the logic of such punishments in his guide to the treatment of slaves in the sugar colonies, noting that escape was an involuntary "habit" for some slaves. In Collins' opinion, "if they are long prevented from indulging that disposition, by external restraint, they may, in time, lose their muscular propensity, and contract a better habit of remaining at home."[97] While not all slaveholders recognized the disease construct of *drapetomania*, a compulsion to run away, many masters utilized punishments that impaired troublesome slaves from escaping, particularly attaching irons to their legs.[98] Some ex-slaves described being "hobbled" with leg irons to prevent repeated escape attempts. For instance, Israel Campbell, who along with two others tried to flee from a plantation near Vicksburg, Mississippi, noted that, in addition to whipping all three runaways, his master "had a piece of iron weighing seven pounds put around Barry's ancle [*sic*], six pounds around Lucinda's and six around mine, to cripple us."[99] Robert Smalls, a personal servant from South Carolina, described a sixty-pound leg weight, fastened around both feet, that would prevent a slave from even walking for days. After the weight was removed, "he attempts to lift his foot [and] his leg flies up and he can not get along."[100] Some masters shot escaping slaves to dissuade or disable them from continuing their flight. Theodore Dwight Weld cited a few instances of this, including runaway advertisements for a Mississippi woman named Mary, who "has a *scar* on her back and right arm near the shoulder, *caused by a rifle ball*" and a man from Maryland, Elijah, who "has a scar on his left cheek, apparently occasioned by *a shot*."[101] Bennet H. Barrow also described shooting a potential runaway named Jerry on his plantation in a journal entry from 16 August 1841:

> Jerry has been sherking [*sic*] about every time since Began to pick cotton. after Whipping him yesterday told him if ever he dodged about from me again would certainly shoot him. this morning at Breakfast time Charles came & told me that Jerry was about to run off. took my Gun found him in the Bayou behind the Quarter, shot him in his thigh.[102]

Barrow's description of this occurrence is significant, not only because it is one of few direct references to corporeal punishment in slaveholders' documents, but also because he was following through with a threat he had made if Jerry continued to "dodge" him; there is no implication that Jerry had absconded from the plantation in the past, just that he was prone to avoiding his master to get out of work. By shooting Jerry in the thigh, Barrow almost certainly disabled him and threatened his life to prevent any future escape attempts, as well as to exercise his authority over a troublesome slave.

A multitude of primary sources indicates that disabilities were a common occurrence among the slave population, and many common sources of unsoundness in human chattel were connected to the circumstances of slavery. Slaveholders utilized the designations of *sound* and *unsound* to assess the abilities and defects of their bondspeople's bodies; however, there was no single system for assessing the physical, mental, or moral soundness of any slave. The term reflected a wide variety of concerns about enslaved bodies, included economic and labor incentives, esthetic preferences, and the need for masters to control their human property. Slaveholders ascribed the term *unsound* to a number of physical and psychological conditions they observed in slaves—including chronic debilitating illnesses, fractures, burns, missing limbs, blindness, reproductive disorders, psychological or cognitive impairments, neurological problems, old age, whipping scars, and debilitating injuries resulting from abuse—and while the meaning of the term *unsound* was never precise, the concept of soundness carried a lot of weight in the minds of planters. This is why it is particularly significant that George J. Kollock described his slave Ginny as "sick with her eye," as opposed to just "sick," in 1849; his account of her potentially disabling condition set her apart from his other bondspeople, and his particular concern for her eyes, rather than just her general health, seems to indicate a more complex reaction to the threat of unsoundness.

Part II
Property

4   Labor and Expectation in the Lives of Slaves with Disabilities

In the mid-1830s, Samuel G. Barker, a Charleston attorney and slaveholder, composed a detailed list of 87 slaves, presumably laborers on South Mulberry plantation, in his estate book. The list identified Barker's bondspeople by their names, dates of birth, and gender, but he also included brief descriptions of their skills and remarkable characteristics, categorized each person according to their "hand" rating, and noted if they were considered "diseased" or "useless." Among the slaves identified as useless were Old Stephen, who "rakes trash"; Old Betty, a nurse and midwife; Peggy, who "cooks for negroes"; Bess, a twenty-three-year-old "feeble" woman who "can cook"; and Old Minda, a "first rate midwife and nurse."[1] The fact that this estate book lists the jobs of elderly and disabled slaves, including one considered "first rate," directly alongside its categorization of those slaves as "useless" is intriguing; it is clear that Barker was using the useless in his plantation's labor system. Like Barker's estate inventory, records from other plantations provide evidence of slaves described as "useless," even as they list the duties that those slaves performed. For example, in an 1825 chart from Edmund Ravenel's Grove plantation in South Carolina, male and female slaves are listed as either "prime" half-hands, "old" half-hands, children, or "useless"; the column of "useless" women includes a cook named Mary, a nurse named Cotto, and Sary, a blind woman who minded poultry.[2] The contradictions embedded in these impersonal charts raise important questions about how white slaveholders assessed the worth and utility of those slaves, and what kinds of treatment "useless" disabled laborers received at the hands of their masters and overseers.

Barker's and Ravenel's seemingly unproblematic use of the word *useless* to categorize slaves with disabilities indicates they had a clear idea of what the term meant to them, but there were many different reasons a slave might be considered useless in antebellum society. In his 1839 compendium *American Slavery as It Is*, Theodore Dwight Weld—uses the term *unprofitable* to describe slaves with disabilities, indicating that he reduced slaveholders' interest in their slaves to economic considerations alone.[3] "Useless" could also denote a failure to live up to expected duties for a particular social role; in the case of slaves, this might be their ability to perform manual labor, gain a profit, or merely to be disciplined and controlled by their masters. On a more personal level, slaveholders could have used the term to describe a slave who failed to live up to the master's individual expectations for behavior, physical appearance, and performance. Tensions between goals of production, profit, control, and the expectations and emotions of planters created a number of surprising contradictions in the ways slaveholders assessed disability and uselessness in their human property. This tension is evident not only on Southern plantations but also in other types of slave "labor," which could include a variety of tasks. Disabled African American slaves, like their able-bodied counterparts, performed a wide variety of functions and were used for many different tasks, even serving as specimens for medical research and experimentation.

Although the number of white "planter aristocrats" with large plantations in the South was small, the majority of African American slaves, at one time or another, lived on large plantations and participated in plantation labor systems. The term *planter* did not have a single meaning in the antebellum South—in some cases, it was synonymous with *farmer* and did not indicate the number of slaves owned—but by the early nineteenth century, when the majority of farmland in the eastern South was cultivated and most larger estates had been established, the term came to refer to slaveholders with large or multiple estates and at least twenty slaves. As historian James Oakes has noted, the ideal of the large plantation—a profitable, efficient model of mastery and production—influenced slaveholders' identities and organization of labor systems, even if they did not own as much land or as many slaves as planter aristocrats.[4] Most planters in the antebellum South planned labor schemes based on a "hand" system, a measure of proportional function that could be used to rank different slaves within any specific job category. However, "hand" designations could also be used to assign slaves to different duties according to the level of physical demands. In general, a person who was able to perform the expected amount of a full day's labor for an adult, able-bodied male slave was assessed to be a "full" hand. Full hands did the bulk of hard field labor, while three-quarter, half, and quarter hands—including "elderly" slaves over the age of fifty or sixty, pregnant women, or individuals with physical or mental impairments—were occupied with less strenuous tasks.[5] These fractioned ratings allowed slaveholders and overseers to distribute work equitably to bondspeople as well as to attempt to impress a sense of duty on them, while taking their individual abilities into account. The overriding principle of plantation management was the discipline of the enslaved labor force, which was managed hierarchically by white overseers and white or black drivers, but different positions and ratings had different rules for obedience and command.[6] House slaves, for instance, may have been rated full hands, or "prime" in market terms, but performed a very different kind of work. Domestic tasks were generally less strenuous—largely indoors, with less physical strain—but also involved more direct supervision from white masters and less interaction with other slaves. Eugene Genovese has argued that, although domestic labor was more comfortable and house servants often viewed themselves as "elite" in the slave community, many slaves preferred the relative independence, social interaction, and physical satisfaction of work in the fields.[7]

In assessing the roles of slaves with disabilities on plantations, it is important to consider categories of difference within the specific economic system of slave labor. Estate inventories, plantation records, and ex-slave narratives indicate that slave community hierarchies and plantation management schemes were very fluid in the antebellum South, and it was very common for slaves to change jobs and status during their lifetimes. Slaves with disabilities performed a variety of necessary duties, such as cooking, sewing, gardening, and minding children and livestock. However, as the example of Samuel G. Barker indicates, slaveholders assessed "useless" slaves with disabilities in contradictory ways, even on a single plantation roster. This evidence, as well as accounts of the devaluation and abuse of slaves with disabilities, indicates that there was more to slaveholders' judgments of impaired slaves than their ability to perform labor. Proslavery observers often argued that slaveholders had an economic incentive to protect the lives of their human chattel. Physician and slaveholder Richard D. Arnold, for instance, wrote in 1849 that "a planter loses so much capital by the death of every one of his operatives & hence to save his capital is to save his negroes."[8] However, there are many examples of slaves with disabling conditions—even those with jobs that were vital to the running of a plantation—who were subject to corporeal punishment, neglect, and even murder, because of their impairments.

Although many planters strove for efficiency and maximum output in the design of their labor schemes,[9] communities of bondspeople were constantly in flux as births, illness, sales and deaths occurred on a regular basis, and the structure of labor had to be fluid to accommodate these changes. Given that a slave was expected to labor for his or her entire lifetime, a slave's hand rating and place in the plantation labor system were subject to change, and many slaves were, at one point, evaluated as less than a full hand. For instance, Maryland slave Charles Ball, describing his experiences on a large South Carolina plantation in the early nineteenth century, noted that of 263 slaves in that community, only 170 were "full hand" field workers; "the others were children, too small to be of any service as laborers . . . old and blind persons, or incurably diseased." Of those, "the most handsome and sprightly" were chosen to serve as house servants for the white slaveholding family,[10] while the others were utilized in other capacities. Such a labor scheme was not uncommon in the antebellum South, since slaveholders considered their human chattel to be lifetime investments and placed them to work for as many years as possible. Philip D. Morgan's study of the poor in the United States points out that lifestyle changes in a working population necessitated the existence of different jobs;[11] similarly, systems of slavery had to account for regular demographic changes and the broad range of bondspeople's physical characteristics and abilities. In most cases, criteria such as chronological age, gender, or physical condition did not arbitrarily determine what kind of work a slave could or could not do, and an individual slave was expected to perform whatever kind of labor of which he or she was capable. The major reason for this system was that slaveholders wanted to exert the maximum amount of work possible from their human chattel; as Leslie J. Pollard has noted, "slave masters quite simply expected slaves to wear out, that is, to use every ounce of their physical energy in the furtherance of the masters' economic well-being."[12] However, plantation labor schemes were not under the absolute control of slaveholders and overseers; slaves themselves, by setting their own work rhythms and demonstrating the range of their abilities, were in a position to negotiate—often successfully—the amount of labor that a slaveholder could expect of them.[13]

Plantation records—letters, journals, memoirs, and inventories of slave "gangs"—are a useful primary source to demonstrate the wide range of duties that slaves of different ages and abilities performed; whereas "taskable hands" were often not described in detail, slaves with impairments or restrictions on their abilities received more attention in plantation records. In many cases, disabled slaves were employed in a variety of tasks that did not involve field labor, such as gardening or minding children and animals. They were also utilized as house servants, and performed other duties such as nursing and cooking. Some slaveholders assigned trusted older male slaves to be drivers for field laborers, positions that rewarded faithful bondsmen but that also capitalized on the slave community's respect for its older members.[14] Old Handy, a slave on the Ball family Limerick plantation, was listed as a driver for slaves working on roads in 1811 and 1812,[15] and Paul, a "very trusty" driver on Samuel G. Barker's plantation, was categorized as a full hand despite his being older and "diseased" from a hernia, or "rupture."[16] A journal from the medium-sized Rockingham Plantation in Brunson, South Carolina, included a list of "not all taskable" slaves on the plantation in 1828 and 1829, including a driver, a "Nurs," a gardener, dairy workers, stock and poultry minders."[17] Elderly or disabled slaves regardless of gender also worked in plantation kitchens and watched children; John G. Clinkscales, a white teacher raised on a plantation in Abbeville, South Carolina, recalled a slave named Dick, who was disabled after a childhood episode of typhoid fever and served as "boss of the pickaninnies."[18] Indeed, the wide variety of duties necessary for the successful management of large plantations ensured that there were a number of different jobs for slaves with disabilities.

Some planters felt that specific, "simple" duties were particularly suited to slaves with physical or mental impairments.[19] As Louisiana planter Haller Nutt complained in an 1843 journal entry, overseers sometimes erroneously assigned "hearty strong negros [*sic*]" to tasks "which could be done equally as well by some feeble hand or cripple."[20] However, the jobs that disabled slaves often performed were not necessarily easy; for instance, Northerner Emily Burke's memoir of life as a female seminary teacher in Georgia in the 1840s discusses how strenuous the tasks of elderly or disabled house servants were. In Burke's view, "the task of the cook was the most laborious" of all house servant positions, since cooks had to rise early, prepare lots of meals, and perform strenuous tasks like grinding meal or meat and gathering firewood.[21] The job of watching over plantation nurseries—which could include children from one week old to five years old—was also difficult for elderly women. As Burke notes, "it is no small task for two or three of these females, themselves in a second infancy, to rock the cradles and attend to the wants of twenty or thirty young children."[22] Furthermore, old age or physical impairment did not automatically preclude a slave from being assigned to hard labor. On the Ball family's Limerick plantation in South Carolina, an 1807 crew assigned "to work on the roads" included several "old hands past muster" like Old Billy, Old Handy, and Old July.[23] Additionally, in an undated broadside advertising Barnwell estate executor Louis B. DeSaussure's auction of Sea Island slaves in Charleston, sixteen-year-old Richard is described as a field hand even though he had "lost one eye,"[24] and in 1849 Louis Manigault purchased a fifty-five-year-old slave named Moses whom he described as "prime," an indication that he was a full-hand laborer despite his age.[25] In some cases, slaves with disabilities performed duties that seem surprising; Charles Ball recalled a blind slave who drove the breakfast cart to slaves working in the cotton fields, and South Carolina planter Edmund Ravenel's "Gordon Gang" of slaves included a one-armed carpenter named Aaron.[26] Some feeble or disabled slaves also worked away from plantations as hired-out laborers or tradesmen. Anderson Henderson, a slave belonging to North Carolina planter Archibald Henderson, had been hired out to work in hotels in Wilmington in 1849 and continued in this job even after an improperly healed sprained ankle necessitated his use of a cane. As Henderson described in an 1857 letter to his masters, "I haul Baggage with a one horse Wagon about Salem and that sutes [*sic*] me Better than walking or Toating [*sic*] Trunks up and down Stair cases in a Hotel as I used to doe [*sic*]."[27] For some slaves with disabling conditions, learning a skilled trade seemed like a better alternative than field or house labor. In a letter from slave Nancy Venture Woods to her master (presumably John Haywood) in 1825, Woods asks that her grandson Virgin be trained as a tailor or shoemaker, because he was impaired by "a hurt he has had in his ancle [*sic*] which he still feels at times."[28] James L. Smith, the fugitive slave who had become disabled in childhood, "was not very profitable on the plantation," and after his mother died he was trained in shoemaking and placed to work in a shop in Heathsville, Virginia.[29] These examples indicate that slaves with perceived disabilities were employed in a wide variety of duties—and not necessarily easy or expected ones—in and out of plantation labor systems in the antebellum South.

The plantation records of lawyer and cotton planter George J. Kollock provide a good microhistorical example of the various roles that slaves with disabilities fulfilled in plantation labor systems. Between 1836 and 1861, Kollock owned three plantations in Georgia—Retreat, Rosedew, and

Ossabaw Island—where he grew Sea Island cotton and corn. The number of his slaves fluctuated during this time period; Kollock began planting at Retreat with thirteen slaves and six "hires," but by 1850, after selling Retreat and Rosedew, he cultivated 800 acres on the south end of Ossabaw Island and had increased his workforce to seventy-two slaves. The Kollock family resided near Clarkesville, Georgia, and between 1849 and 1861 overseers at his Ossabaw Island plantation wrote detailed journals that noted slave births and deaths, rates of work performed, sick days, allowances, and daily tasks.[30] It is apparent that almost all of Kollock's bondspeople had jobs, regardless of their age or impairments. The overseer's journal from 1855 refers to slaves rated as half- or quarter-hands doing "household" work; for example, half-hands Grace and Juno are listed as a cook and a nurse, respectively, and Lee, rated as a quarter-hand, is described as a gardener. Furthermore, some slaves described as "old" in daily work logs—such as Old Ned and Old Mary—were rated as full hands and presumably worked in the cotton fields or cornfields.[31] The only one of Kollock's slaves who seemed to do no work at Ossabaw Island was Patty, a "cripple" who first appears in the 1855 journal. Details of Patty's impairment and the circumstances under which Kollock acquired her are unclear, but she is the only person not given any rating in the journal. Furthermore, she never appears in daily work logs or sick lists, and did not receive any new clothing in 1855.[32] This may indicate that Patty was deemed unfit to perform any job on the plantation and thus would not warrant the overseer's attention if she became ill. We may also infer that Kollock and his overseers did not think she would need new clothing, as did most of the other slaves, because she was not subjecting her clothes to the wear-and-tear of daily labor. However, Patty seems to have been the only one of more than seventy slaves at Ossabaw Island who did not perform some duty on the plantation, which is evidence that elderly and disabled slaves were indeed put to work despite their impairments.

The overseer's journals for Kollock's Ossabaw Island plantation allow us to trace the career of one disabled slave, a blind man named March, to demonstrate the utility of slaves with debilities. At the time Kollock was consolidating his assets on his new plantation, March was rated to be a "quarter hand," with no indication of what jobs he was expected to perform at that time. In the 1850 and 1851 journals, March is not included in tallies of cotton pickings by weight, unlike most other male slaves on the plantation, and is never mentioned by name in daily work logs or sick lists.[33] However, the 1855 journal notes that March had two sick days, one in January and one in July, indicating at that time he performed some sort of work for which an absence was noteworthy.[34] In 1858, March was listed as one of the "hands that went to bring back [the] boat" that had carried a few slaves "to town" for Christmas,[35] and in early 1859, overseer H. Jarrel composed a letter to Kollock, indicating that March wanted his master to measure bushels of corn he had shelled.[36] This evidence of March's work at Ossabaw Island, though fragmentary, offers a glimpse at the role of a disabled slave on a cotton plantation. In 1850, when the plantation was young and the labor system not fully realized, a slave like March would seem relatively unimportant to his master and overseers and not warrant much attention. His blindness may have prevented him from the hard field labor necessary to establish the new plantation. There is evidence that eye problems could keep field slaves from working on Kollock's plantations; on 23 April 1855, the daily work log lists one slave who had "Gon Blind" and remained so for three subsequent days, unable to perform any sort of work.[37] However, while Kollock certainly seemed concerned about the effects of blindness in his slaves, after several years it seems that March had been assigned to tasks that were important to the running of the established plantation; thus, when he was sick, it merited a notation in the journal because the overseer viewed it as "time lost." Most importantly, the fact that March made an appeal, through the overseer, to his master to view the corn he had shelled indicates he had been assigned to a regular task and might suggest that his performance had accorded him a degree of respect from white authority figures. The experiences of March on Kollock's Ossabaw Island plantation are a good indication of the different kinds of work slaves with disabilities could perform, as well as the fluidity of plantation labor systems.

As Kollock's plantation journals and other sources indicate, the successful management of a large plantation involved a variety of different tasks performed by enslaved workers. The volume of jobs to be done, as well as their various physical or mental requirements, ensured that slaves with any number of perceived disabilities could be consistently employed. While many of the tasks performed by impaired slaves were considered less strenuous or "simple," they were not necessarily easy, and were certainly not negligible. Thus, slaves with disabilities were often vital to the management of a successful, efficient plantation. However, despite the different kinds of important work that elderly or impaired slaves performed on plantations, slaveholders often assessed slaves with disabilities to be useless, either overtly—as in the rosters of the Barker and Ford-Ravenel plantation records—or more subtly. Plantation records, estate inventories and appraisals, and insurance policies provide documentation that slaves with physical and mental disabilities were often devalued in the eyes of slaveholders and subjected to a number of abuses—including punishment, neglect, and even murder—at the hands of masters and overseers.

This evidence calls into question arguments that slaveholders were primarily benevolent, or that they always followed economic incentives to protect their human chattel. The decreased value of economically productive yet disabled or unsound slaves could result from a variety of motives beyond economic rationality or humane sentiment, including repulsion, prejudice against disability, or even frustration and impatience. The devaluation of disabled slaves despite their utility on plantations is evident in estate inventories. Although William Dosite Postell claimed in 1953 that "unsound" slaves were often appraised at or near market rates in estate inventories,[38] Sharla Fett has argued more recently that appraisals for elderly and impaired slaves, despite their skills or labor histories, were usually very low.[39] For example, slaves belonging to

Charles Carroll, a Chesapeake Bay planter and the last signer of the Declaration of Independence to die, were appraised in the early 1830s; nineteen of his human chattel were described as extremely old, crippled, or diseased and were appraised at one penny apiece.[40] In an 1854 appraisal of Alabama planter D. L. McDonald's estate, a woman named Rachel, aged 65, was valued at fifty dollars, one-third the value of Amey, woman only five years younger.[41] Also in 1854, the estate of Bennet H. Barrow included a forty-three-year-old blind slave named Temps or Demps who was appraised at fifty dollars, the same price as infants; other male slaves in their forties were valued between $700 and $950.[42] Given this practice, it is possible that slaveholders who considered their disabled slaves "useless" were concerned with their resale values rather than the labor they were actually capable of performing.

The devaluation of elderly and impaired slaves is also apparent in life insurance policies, which became increasingly popular among slaveholders in the 1850s. Todd Savitt has pointed out that insurance companies, part of a newborn industry in the early nineteenth century, did not sell many policies for white people in the South but slaveholders became more interested in purchasing life insurance for their bondspeople, particularly for slaves involved in dangerous work, such as mining or construction.[43] In 1860, the North Carolina Mutual Life Insurance Company had 1,699 slave policies, compared to their 501 policies for free white individuals.[44] The growing popularity of slave life insurance concerned Alabama physician Josiah Nott, who argued that the types of labor that insured slaves performed had the potential to be debilitating, and African American slaves were by nature unlikely to take care of themselves. In an 1847 article in *DeBow's Review*, Nott warned that a life insurance policy would tempt "unfeeling masters" to allow elderly, injured and disabled slaves to suffer and die:

> Such individuals will not show any increase of kindness during sickness, should their interest be opposed to humanity. As long as the negro is sound, and worth more than the amount insured, self-interest will prompt the owner to preserve the life of the slave; but, if the slave became unsound and there is little prospect of perfect recovery, the underwriters cannot expect fair play—the insurance money is worth more than the slave, and the latter is regarded rather in the light of a superannuated horse.[45]

Life insurance companies that sold policies in the South certainly took these issues into consideration, and regulations for slave life-insurance policies were stricter than those for free white people. For instance, companies limited the maximum amount of insurance based on the value of the slave; usually, a slaveholder could only hold insurance at half the market value of the insured slave, although there are some policies where the insured amount was more than half the market value. In 1860, the Charter Oak Life Insurance Company insured a thirty-four-year-old Savannah house servant named Mary for $600 for one year, although her market value was estimated at $900.[46] Most policies also restricted the time limit for which a slave could be insured (usually no longer than a five-year term), required medical examinations of slaves before and during the term of insurance, and charged extra premiums for older slaves or those employed in dangerous labor.[47] The North Carolina Mutual Life Insurance Company's 1849 cost schedule for $100 slave insurance policies, for example, indicates that premium costs skyrocketed for older slaves. The premiums began with $1.18 per annum for ten-year-olds, and increased at a rate of five cents per annum for every year of a slave's life up to age forty one. After a slave reached fifty years, premium rates increased twenty cents per annum, and ended at $5.10 per annum for a sixty-year-old.[48] Many policies also included broad exclusionary clauses for slaves; Mary's policy from Charter Oak, for instance, included exceptions for suicide and suicide attempts, mob violence, insurrection, kidnapping or escape, travel to the free states, as well as "the neglect, abuse, or maltreatment of the owner or any one two [sic] whom she shall be entrusted."[49] Thus, despite Nott's warning, there does not seem to be much evidence that slaveholders intentionally abused or neglected disabled slaves to collect on insurance; as Savitt argues, "each of these means of protecting the company's liability also protected the slave's life."[50] However, restrictions on antebellum slave life insurance—particularly health examination requirements and increased premiums or caps on insurance of older bondspeople—indicate the lower value that elderly and debilitated slaves held in the eyes of slaveholding society, regardless of the kinds of work they performed.

The management of elderly slaves was a difficult issue for planters and a prominent element in the slavery debate, with Southerners highlighting the care and affection shown to older slaves as an indication of the institution's overall benevolence. Although some planters manumitted elderly slaves who could no longer work, most elderly slaves remained on plantations with their families, and their masters provided for them until they died.[51] Several letters from older slaves to their masters exist in which the slaves requested relocation or additional sustenance, appealing to their owners' sympathies and emphasizing their own faithfulness. For instance, in 1824 a Virginia woman named Phillis asked her masters, Mr. and Mrs. St. George Tucker, if she could move to be with her children, since "old age And infirmity Begains to follow me . . . [and] I know From my heart that you and Mistress would never See me suffer."[52] Charleston cobbler Samuel Robertson wrote to his mistress, Louisa Lord, in 1857 to request a larger monetary allowance, since he was "getting old & sick unable to Move about as I Once did," and could not subsist on his own; Robertson mentions his faithful service to Lord several times in the letter.[53] Proslavery observers remarked that slaveholders were often attached to their aged bondspeople, calling them "Uncle" or "Aunty," providing them with their own homes and gardens to raise vegetables, having ministers come specifically to visit them, giving them small presents, and attempting to make them happy.[54] For instance, in a letter to South Carolina planter Vardry McBee, William Irvin noted that he wanted to send back Old

Jinny, a slave he had sold to a woman named Jane Lytle for $150. Jinny was unhappy with Lytle; according to Irvin, "she evidently wishes to live with you & surely she ought to be gratified." Irvin recommended that McBee pay "what ever [*sic*] she is worth to you" for Old Jinny, and implied that he would settle the difference; the clear intent of the transaction was to satisfy the wishes of Jinny.[55] Pennsylvania businessman Francis Cope Yarnall, in his 1853 publication *Letters on Slavery*, gave the example of a master telling an elderly slave named "Uncle" Bob to "remember you're old & cant do as much work as you once could . . . you mustn't strain yourself."[56] Some slaves also described such good treatment of the elderly. One elderly slave in Williamsburg, Virginia, composed a letter to her daughter in 1858, noting that "I have every kindness shown me, & have no wish which is not gratified."[57] In his WPA memoir, former slave Bill Simms recollected that old slaves who could no longer work were set up in their own cabins, and provided for until they died.[58] These accounts, however, are unique in the canon of primary evidence from slaves, and quite possibly were mitigated by the white individuals who transcribed the slave's voice onto paper.

In many other accounts, slaves with disabilities were subjected to abuse than kind, benevolent treatment at the hands of their owners. Impaired slaves could be punished for their inability to perform certain tasks or to work as effectively as others; slaves with physical or mental limitations often worked more slowly than others and had more trouble with the physical demands of plantation labor, thus potentially affirming the stereotype that African Americans were inherently "lazy" in the minds of white authority figures.[59] Philemon Bliss, an Ohio minister who had lived near Tallahassee, Florida, in the mid-1830s, noted that "the most common cause of punishments [for slaves] is not finishing tasks";[60] this was certainly the case for slaves who could not complete their work as quickly as masters and overseers wanted because of a physical impairment. Old age or disability did not necessarily stay the whips of slaveholders; Frederick Douglass recalled watching one of his former masters, Colonel Lloyd, "make old Barney, a man between fifty and sixty years of age, uncover his bald head, kneel down upon the cold, damp ground, and receive upon his naked and toil-worn shoulders more than thirty lashes at a time" for unsatisfactory performance.[61] To be certain, evidence from abolitionists and ex-slave narratives should not be taken as objective accounts of reality, but their discussion of the abuses that slaves with impairments faced provide a useful counterpoint to proslavery accounts of kind benevolence. There are many other examples of slaves who faced neglect when age or disability prevented them from working.[62] Less profitable slaves often received reduced rations from masters; Harriet Jacobs recalled an elderly, "faithful" servant whose mistress denied him an allowance of meat, claiming "that when niggers were too old to work, they ought to be fed on grass."[63] Historian Deborah Gray White notes that many masters were indifferent to the needs of elderly, unproductive slaves, and left the responsibility for their care to the slave community.[64] Some slaveholders sold their worn out slaves, usually in private transactions and for a considerable bargain, to relieve themselves from the burden of caring for their disabled property.[65] Henry Bibb, an escaped slave who established the first black newspaper in Canada, composed a series of letters to his former master, Albert G. Sibley, and chastised him for selling Bibb's aging mother after promising her liberty; Bibb's mother was forced to work for six years as the chief cook in a Bedford, Kentucky, hotel, which left "her constitution . . . completely broken" and rendered her unable to care for herself.[66] Others manumitted their elderly and disabled chattel and sent them to Southern cities, effectively abandoning them to a life with no financial or community support. In Frederick Douglass's memoirs of slavery, he describes his cousin Henny, who had been disabled by a severe burn in childhood and "was a constant offense" to their master, who "seemed desirous of getting the poor girl out of existence." After severe beatings did not improve Henny's productivity, their master attempted to give her away to his sister, but ultimately "set her adrift to take care of herself" despite her impairments. In Douglass's view, this abandonment was the ultimate cruelty of human bondage; slaveholders held "with tight grasp the well-framed and able-bodied slaves . . . who in freedom could have taken care of themselves," but abandoned those who were "helpless."[67] Emily Burke, who left New Hampshire to teach at a Georgia female seminary in 1840, described an asylum in Savannah, where "old and worn out" slaves "left without any sort of home or means of subsistence" often ended up; however, in Burke's estimation, life in the dreaded institution was "next to having no home at all, and those who avail themselves of the comforts it affords only do it when every other resource for the means of subsistence fails them."[68] Increasingly strict legislation against manumission in the later antebellum years largely precluded the practice, protecting elderly or infirm slaves while also preventing them from becoming public charges.[69] There were, however, slaveholders who bent these laws; Louisiana planter Bennet H. Barrow noted in his diary in 1842 that "Uncle Bat. told my boy to turn old Demps loose & let him go. been runaway for some months . . . he shall not stay in this neighbourhood." Apparently, Demps, an "old & cripple" man, had been treated badly by his owner[70] and probably welcomed the chance to flee; from his master's perspective, however, allowing Demps to escape was an expedient, no-strings-attached method for freeing himself from the burden of a disabled slave without formal manumission or any provisions for the slave.

More commonly, slaveholders abandoned elderly and disabled bondspeople unable to perform labor without sending them away from the plantation. When the usefulness of slaves ran out, particularly due to old age or blindness, they were sent to rooms or cabins in the woods to live alone and fend for themselves, separated from slaveholding families and the slave community.[71] In 1813, a woman named Mary Woodson wrote to the mayor of Alexandria, Virginia, to relate the story of a disabled slave who was abandoned by her master to live alone in a single room. According to Woodson, the slave, "the property of on[e] Posten in whose service she was burnt almost to death before Easter," had been isolated in a single room "without a change of clothing, or one single necessary of life, or comfort."[72] This theme of abandonment is prominent in ex-slave narratives and abolitionist publications describing the treatment of elderly relatives and community members. For instance, Moses Grandy recalled the fate of his mother, who, like many other feeble bondspeople, was "sent to live in a little lonely log-hut in the woods" when she could no longer work on the plantation:

> As far as the owner is concerned, they live or die as it happens; it is just the same thing as turning out an old horse. The children or other near relations, if living in the neighbourhood [*sic*], take it by turns to go at night, with a supply saved out of their own scanty allowance of food, as well as to cut wood and fetch water for them . . . the aged inmate of the hut is often found crying, on account of sufferings from disease or extreme weakness, or from want of food and water in the course of the day: many a time, when I have drawn near my mother's hut, I have heard her grieving and crying on these accounts: she was old and blind too, and so unable to help herself. She was not treated worse than others: it is the general practice.[73]

Similarly, abolitionist Philo Tower described meeting a superannuated and blind woman whose master had consigned her to live alone in a shanty and gave her no provisions, except corn. The woman told Tower that she did not have adequate clothing, and "suffer[ed] a good deal from cold in the winter;" she also had no one to bring her water and was too feeble to carry it herself. Her twelve children had all been sold—at a profit of at least $6,000, according to Tower's estimate—and the lonely woman, who had spent seventy years laboring in the cotton field, essentially waited to die.[74] Like Frederick Douglass, Tower viewed this treatment as a significant example of the inhumanity of slavery. Stories of abandonment of the elderly and disabled were common in abolitionist propaganda and described in such a way to arouse the pity and horror of readers, but there is ample evidence to suggest that tales of neglect were not antislavery fabrications.

In a few extreme cases, American slaveholders or overseers reportedly murdered elderly and disabled slaves for their inability to perform satisfactory labor. Abolitionist journalist James Redpath, on one of his travels to the South, talked with an elderly male slave who had witnessed the murder of an ailing girl in Georgia. Her overseer was frustrated that the girl was "lagging behind" and ordered her "to mend her gait"; when the girl replied that she was "so sick I kin hardly drag one foot after the other," he struck her on the neck. The girl "was taken up insensible, and lingered till the following morning."[75] On Haller Nutt's Araby Plantation in 1843, the planter reported several slave deaths that resulted "from cruelty of overseer," including Tom, who was "beat to death when too sick to work."[76] Although the murder of a slave was technically illegal, there are examples of slaveholders who escaped responsibility for killing their disabled slaves. According to Emily Burke, an "old feeble woman" was sold to a new master and made to work in the fields for the first time in her life. After sustaining a severe beating, "she was scarcely able to supper her weight upon her feet" and could not wield her hoe to the satisfaction of her master; he "gave her a blow to the neck, and she fell dead at his feet." Several days later, physicians performed a postmortem examination and determined that the slave had been murdered, but her master had left the plantation and could not be found. Eventually, "the excitement died away, and as it was only a poor old slave when the cruel tyrant did return the whole matter was nearly forgotten."[77] Similarly, in his journal, Sea Islands planter Thomas B. Chaplin described the murder of Roger, a disabled slave who had belonged to neighboring planter James H. Sandiford, in February 1849. Chaplin had been called to examine the body of Roger to determine if his death should be prosecuted and was horrified by what he saw: "there was the poor Negro, who all his life had been a complete cripple, being hardly able to walk & used his knees more than his feet, in the most shocking situation, but *stiff dead*. He was placed in this situation by his *master*, to punish him, as he says, *for impertinence*." Apparently, Roger had been late in returning with oysters, and received a beating from Sandiford; later, Roger was overheard telling another slave "that if he had sound limbs, he would not take a flogging from any white man." Sandiford shackled Roger in wet clothing in an open outhouse overnight, where he died not from exposure, but from strangulation from the chain around his neck after Roger "slipped from the position in which he was placed." Roger's death was deemed to be accidental, even though Chaplin felt "the verdict should have been that Roger came to his death by inhumane treatment to him by his master."[78]

All of these examples, which appeared in published abolitionist propaganda as well as private plantation records, indicate there was certainly a broad spectrum of the treatment of slaves with disabilities. However, it is clear that devalued slaves, particularly those who were no longer able to perform hard labor, received worse treatment at the hands of masters regardless of the duties they performed or had performed in the past. Although elderly and disabled slaves' experiences ranged from kind treatment to being ignored or mistreated, planters were probably more likely to be indifferent, if not overtly hostile, to the needs of useless bondspeople who were unable to do the work their masters expected or desired.

There is also substantial evidence that some masters sold or hired out slaves with disabilities for medical research. Some Southern physicians utilized enslaved subjects to attempt new techniques or therapeutic interventions, "borrowing" or purchasing sick and impaired slaves for empirical treatment to "cure" conditions that the slaveholding class considered disabling.[79] African Americans were certainly not the only population to undergo such therapies; experimental remedies that seem harsh by today's standards were common for patients of all races in the mid-nineteenth century. Some doctors experimented on themselves, their friends and family members, and during the Civil War, doctors used soldiers to test new diagnostic measures and treatments.[80] However, physicians in the antebellum South—possibly acting on the belief that

African Americans were less susceptible to pain than whites[81]—frequently used slaves with disabilities or incurable illnesses as experimental subjects. The most notable example of "disabled" slaves used for experimental therapies were Alabama physician J. Marion Sims's 1849 surgical trials for vesicovaginal fistula, for which he performed multiple procedures on several female slaves over the course of three years. As Sims noted, the condition was presumed to be entirely incurable, but slaveholders had frequently asked Sims to do something to help their bondswomen even after he had refused, claiming that their cases were hopeless.[82] Vesicovaginal fistula patients suffered extreme pain from the constant flow of urine and feces from their torn vaginas; he described his first subject Anarcha's life as "one of suffering and disgust. Death would have preferable. But patients of this kind never die; they must live and suffer."[83] The women lived under Sims's care and assisted him in the "little hospital in his yard," experiencing painful surgeries without anesthesia on their hands and knees, as well as the agony of sepsis and the repeated reopening of their fistulas after failed attempts; Sims performed a total of thirty operations on Anarcha before he perfected his technique using silver wire sutures to close the fistula.[84] The legacy of Sims's vesicovaginal fistula cure is certainly controversial. Some give him credit as the "father of American gynecology" and a humanitarian who went to great lengths to treat "social outcasts" with an abominable disorder; many others have described his treatment of his patients as brutal and degrading, the ultimate example of medical abuses toward slaves.[85] Regardless of these judgments of Sims's achievement, it is clear that the close relationship between medical practitioners and slaveholders enabled Sims to undertake such trials on disabled slaves.[86]

Southern physicians also used enslaved African Americans—supposedly biologically distinct, but close enough to Caucasian bodies—to test remedies for chronic diseases and for surgical demonstrations, with the goal in mind that successful treatments they discovered also could be used for white patients. For example, Georgia physician Crawford Long, credited as the first doctor to perform surgery using sulfuric ether as anesthesia,[87] experimented on both white and black subjects in 1842. The first application of ether on 30 March 1842 was for the removal of "two small tumours" from the neck of James M. Venable, presumably a white man because Long identified him with a first and last name. His third operation, made on 3 July 1842, was to amputate the toe of an enslaved boy near Jefferson, and "was performed without the boy evincing the least sign of pain."[88] Furthermore, Long described two patients on whom he "could satisfactorily test the anaesthetic power of ether" by performing multiple procedures, with and without ether. One of these cases is described as "a negro boy" who had two fingers amputated; the other case, involving the use of ether in one of three "tumour" removals, does not mention the race of the female patient but implies that she was white. Both patients, according to Long, "suffered" their operations without ether but experienced no sensation under anesthesia.[89] Long's example indicates that Southern physicians believed the use of enslaved individuals as experimental subjects could help doctors treat patients of all races.

Some bondspeople with disabilities were sold outright to physicians or hospitals to be used as nontherapeutic specimens, such as clinical subjects in medical education. Occasionally, local physicians would refer white masters to hospitals for extended care for their slaves,[90] but there is also evidence that hospitals and medical schools actively solicited for enslaved subjects. Indeed, African Americans comprised a significant number of educational patients for medical students in the antebellum South.[91] According to Todd Savitt, African American bodies "did not seem to differ enough from Caucasians to exclude them from extensive use in Southern medical schools . . . Blacks were considered more available and more accessible in this white-dominated society."[92] In 1838, an advertisement in the *Charleston Mercury* asked for "fifty negroes . . . considered incurable by their respective physicians"; a person identified as "Dr. S." offered to pay "the highest cash price" for slaves affected with a variety of physical and psychological disorders, including scrofula, apoplexy, and confirmed hypochondriasm.[93] Other newspaper advertisements asked for sick or injured slaves to serve as test patients at medical school infirmaries, with treatment fees waived if the slaves had to be sent home.[94] Slaves were also utilized as subjects for surgical demonstrations in medical schools. For example, four out of five eye surgery demonstrations conducted by Professor Dugas, of the Medical College of Georgia, reported in the June 1838 issue of the *Southern Medical and Surgical Journal*, were performed on enslaved patients.[95] Northern antislavery activist William Goodell found this practice abhorrent, referring to the advertisement in the *Charleston Mercury*, argued that "assortments of diseased, *damaged*, and disabled negroes, deemed incurable or otherwise worthless, are *bought up*, it seems (cheap, no doubt, like old iron), by medical institutions to be experimented and operated upon."[96] Senex, the pseudonymous critic of surgical malpractice in the *Virginia Medical Journal*, specifically criticized the practice of performing unwarranted surgeries on slaves as medical school demonstrations. According to Senex, a "mutilated son of Africa" was presented to a Virginia medical college with an ulcer on his shin, secondary to a burn, and was subjected to the extreme remedy of amputation:

> The man seemed to be about one or two and twenty years of age; and represented his general health, at the time of the operation, to have been very good. He also informed the writer that the ulcer was not painful at the time the limb was amputated, nor had it ever been so after the burn became an ulcer . . . he believed that his leg was cut off just to let the students see the operation, and to bring the doctor, as well as the medical college with which he was connected, into notice.[97]

In addition, slaves with congenital birth defects were frequently studied as fascinating, unusual phenomena, and objectified for the scrutiny of medical professionals. Some doctors collected deceased African American "specimens," such as stillborn fetuses and skeletons,[98] and some examined living medical "oddities" among the slave population, publishing their findings in prominent medical journals. For instance, correspondents to the *Western Lancet* in 1845 were interested in determining how common certain impairments or deformities, such as cleft palate, were among African Americans, and invited their readers to post any known cases.[99] In 1857, an article in *The New Orleans Medical & Hospital Gazette* described a "double-headed" monster born "of a slave mulatress" in Jeanerette, Louisiana; the accompanying illustration depicts an otherwise "perfect" child with two heads, three eyes, and two cleft palates.[100] To be sure, unusual medical phenomena were published regardless of the subject's race, but as Todd Savitt has pointed out, many case studies in Southern medical journals, particularly reports of deformities involving genital organs, involved African American subjects. As historian Marie Jenkins Schwartz has noted, severely disabled children born on slave plantations were considered "worthless" as future laborers; placing a disabled slave—dead or alive—on display for medical examinations was one way for masters to earn money from "defective" chattel.[101] Thus, while slaves themselves regarded children born with severe disabilities as cultural omens or signs,[102] white physicians focused on faulty congenital development, conducting detailed (and often invasive) examinations of enslaved "monsters" regardless of their subjects' privacy or feelings.

The case of Millie-Christine McCoy, conjoined twins born to "a very stout negress . . . of large frame and pelvis"[103] in North Carolina in 1851, is a good example of how physicians viewed disabled slaves as medical curiosities and regarded their bodies primarily as specimens, not individuals. From the time Millie and Christine were newborns, many physicians were fascinated by the anatomical and physiological development of these "two strange lumps of humanity";[104] they were "remarkably sprightly and healthy children, of natural size," but were joined back-to-back at the sacral bones and experienced profound difficulties in locomotion and muscular development as they grew. Many physicians who examined the infant twins were particularly fascinated with their reproductive organs and anus, as well as with their mother's pelvic girdle, and conducted intimate physical examinations of all three women. P. Claiborne Gooch, writing in *The Stethoscope, & Virginia Medical Gazette*, lauded the birth of "The Carolina Twins" as a boon for the scientific study of "monsters":

> It is sincerely to be hoped that these little phenomena may be spared, and that they may both live to enjoy life, to exhibit a most curious example of nature's freaks, and to afford illustrations of physiological laws which are as yet unknown, or at least, unsettled. We recommend to all medical men to lose no opportunity of visiting them, and it will be a gratification of no idle curiosity to examine them carefully . . . Health and long life to the NORTH CAROLINA TWIN SISTERS.[105]

THE HISTORY

OF THE

CAROLINA TWINS.

SOLD BY THEIR AGENTS FOR THEIR (THE TWINS) SPECIAL BENEFIT, AT 25 CENTS.

SOLD BY THEIR AGENTS FOR THEIR (THE TWINS) SPECIAL BENEFIT, AT 25 CENTS.

TOLD IN "THEIR OWN PECULIAR WAY"

BY "ONE OF THEM."

PUBLISHED AT THE

BUFFALO COURIER PRINTING HOUSE.

Figure 4.1 Millie-Christine McCoy, c. 1869. From Millie-Christine [McCoy], *The History of the Carolina Twins: "Told in Their Own Peculiar Way" by "One of Them"* ([Buffalo]: Buffalo Courier Printing House, [1869?]), courtesy of the Carolina Digital Library & Archives, www.docsouth.unc.edu.

James P. Smith purchased the infant twins for $6,000 and began exhibiting them publicly when they were fifteen months old. At one point, the girls were kidnapped by a man who "gave private exhibitions to scientific bodies, thus reaping quite a handsome income off of 'two little black girls' whom he had stolen away."[106] When they were three years old, they were billed as "Celebrated African United Twins" in Barnum's American Museum in New York City and toured throughout the United States and Europe, following in the tracks of Chang and Eng Bunker, the "original Siamese twins." Scholar Joanne Martell has noted that Millie-Christine McCoy was seen as more of a "marvel" because the twins were more impaired in their movements than Chang and Eng.[107] Millie-Christine grew into adulthood, and in an 1869 pamphlet entitled *The History of the Carolina Twins*: *"Told in Their Own Peculiar Way" by "One of Them,"* described her travels and experiences as an exhibited "freak." A poignant poem concludes the pamphlet, and highlights the life of the "defective" twins as a medical spectacle:

> It's not modest of one's self to speak,
> But daily scanned from head to feet
> I freely talk of everything—
> Sometimes to persons wondering . . .
> Two heads, four arms, four feet,
> All in one perfect body meet;
> I am most wonderfully made,
> All scientific men have said.[108]

The true authorship of this poem is unclear, but it is significant that all published accounts of the Carolina Twins, even their own autobiography, describe them as specimens and invite "medical" and "scientific men" to examine their bodies as a medical curiosity. Millie-Christine McCoy is a significant example of the objectification of "defective" black bodies for medical study and publication in the slave South. There were few social or ethical barriers regarding the treatment of enslaved patients, experimental subjects, and medical "displays"; as scholars Michael W. Byrd and Linda A. Clayton have noted, "physicians in America performed on a medical stage where there was little scrutiny or concern when Blacks . . . were concerned."[109]

In antebellum labor systems, there were a number of different jobs and skill levels required of slaves, and disabled slaves were certainly no exception. Despite the evidence of disabled slaves' utility in labor systems, many white observers categorized them as useless and accorded them lower markets in estates and insurance policies. The fact that planters like Samuel Barker and Edmund Ravenel would use the term *useless*, even as they described the duties that useless slaves performed, illuminates a fascinating and underexplored contradiction in assessments of disabled bondspeople. Based on evidence in plantation work logs, correspondence, and estate inventories as well as published sources, it is clear that, although individuals with disabilities could do a number of jobs that were necessary to the running of plantations, many slaveholders devalued their disabled slaves in estate appraisals and insurance policies and subjected them to a number of abuses, including punishment, neglect, and even murder. In addition, many doctors, taking advantage of the social and racial inequalities in the South, utilized African American slaves with disabilities and chronic illnesses as subjects for experimental therapies and medical education exercises, and seemed to take no issue with indiscreet examinations of "medical oddities" among the enslaved class. The contradiction of using the "useless" in the antebellum slave economy calls into question the assumption that planters only ascribed to economic motivations in their assessments of their human property. A variety of functional and psychological factors beyond task and productivity—including issues of control and discipline, ideas about disability, and emotional reactions to "disorderly" enslaved bodies—were at play in how planters assessed the utility and performance of slaves with disabilities.

5 Disability, Value, and the Language of Slave Sales

In 1859, slaves belonging to the estate of prominent Georgia planter Major Butler were offered for public auction at Savannah by his grandson, Pierce Butler. The sale, one of the largest slave auctions from a single estate in American history, took place at a race track and included 436 men and women of all ages, with a variety of skills, attributes, and defects. For several days before the auction, the bondspeople were made available for buyers to inspect by "pulling their mouths open to see their teeth, pinching up and down to detect any signs of lameness, making them stoop and bend in different ways that they might be certain there was no concealed rupture or wound; and in addition to all this treatment, asking them scores of questions relative to their qualifications and accomplishments."[1] New York journalist Mortimer Neal Thompson, writing under the pseudonym Q. C. Philander Doesticks, posed as a prospective buyer to attend the huge event, taking extensive notes about the slaves offered for auction and the transactions. The sales of two similar young men, Guy and Andrew, caught Thompson's attention as a telling example of the horrific impersonality of the "chattel principle." Guy, a "prime young man," "sold for $1,280, being without blemish; his age was twenty years, and he was altogether a fine article." Andrew, the very next person offered on the auction block, was Guy's "very counterpart in all marketable points, in size, age, skill, and everything save that he had lost his right eye," a defect which brought Andrew's price down to $1,040. Thompson sarcastically surmised that, based on the result of these transactions, "the market value of the right eye in the Southern country is $240."[2]

This cutting observation of the sadness inherent in the Southern trade in human commodities, recorded by a Northern journalist for an abolitionist publication, brings to light the complicated role of defect and disability in calculations of value of African American bondspeople brought to auction in the antebellum South. The auction block is a particularly significant site to assess antebellum meanings of slave disability. After the closing of the international slave trade in 1808, the internal slave trade, or "second middle passage," became the only legal avenue for masters to purchase new human chattel, and sales were a central, and often devastating, part of the slave experience.[3] As the institution of slavery spread westward with settlers and planters, slave sales—particularly in major centers like New Orleans, Richmond, and Charleston—flourished. On the surface, the commodification of bodies in the growing slave market seemed to render human beings into cold, objective, dollar terms; however, the translation of human into chattel, and "value" into "price," was never a simple matter, particularly for slaves with disabilities. Nineteenth-century slave sales relied on a more complicated language—involving descriptions, physical signs, comparisons, performances, and compromises—to assess the value of disabled bondspeople. Assessments of slave soundness in the market, just as in determinations of slave's productivity, involved a complicated web of ideas about physical fitness and esthetics, fears of disease or slave resistance, and expectations for specific performance from prospective bondspeople; the slave sale was a place where slaveholders, traders, buyers, and slaves themselves constantly negotiated meanings of "sound" able-bodiedness and "unsound" disability, all using the complex language of the market.

A number of scholars have done significant and superb research on the culture of slave markets, and the complexities of human commodification in the antebellum South. These studies indicate that assessments of slave soundness and unsoundness in sales situations were subjective, if not idiosyncratic, and were influenced by a variety of factors and experiences. In their discussions of economic assessments of slave soundness in antebellum markets and courtrooms, Sharla M. Fett and Ariela J. Gross have noted that white idealizations of slave bodies centered on concepts of social, mental, and moral worth that were linked to physical characteristics, including gender, skin color, physical condition, attractiveness, "likeability," and disability or defect. Thus, slave bodies were objectified according to the economic motivations of their white masters, but the existence of soundness guarantees and litigations over allegedly fraudulent sales indicates overriding concerns among the master class about the soundness of slaves and how that soundness would be determined at market and at court.[4] Furthermore, Walter Johnson's *Soul by Soul* places the culture of the market and the "chattel principle," a cornerstone of Southern slavery, squarely in the daily life of slave society. The commodification of African Americans on the auction block represented white idealizations of black slaves, and "the purposes that slaveholders projected for slaves' bodies were thus translated into natural properties of those bodies."[5] Gender, chronological age, types of work they were expected to perform, and even skin color and physical attractiveness were factors that determined assessments of slaves' able-bodiedness and, consequently, their value. Most importantly, Johnson highlights the role of slaves as historical actors in the slave trade; sellers relied upon a degree of cooperation from their human wares—to perform, tell preplanned stories, or hide ailments from prospective buyers—and had to acknowledge the agency of slaves in sales encounters. As a result of this necessary collaboration, slaves, aware of slaveholders' perspectives on desirable qualities of human chattel, could use their sound or unsound bodies to manipulate sales to suit their own purposes.[6] Michael Tadman's study of slave speculation and trade in Virginia emphasizes the different goals that slaveholders and slaves had in sales situations and analyzes how those goals influenced negotiations and performances of soundness in the market. More recently, Daina Ramey Berry and Steven Deyle note the importance of looking beyond price to assess how different perspectives on slave worth influenced market transactions.[7] All of these studies—which discuss soundness at length but do not focus on the sale of slaves who were considered disabled, or unsound—read into the language of the market to uncover a world of contested and negotiated meanings.

The bulk of primary evidence in this chapter is derived from records of estate sales, which were a common occurrence in Southern society and a significant source for the study of the antebellum slave trade. Many slaves who were brought to auction belonged to masters who needed to sell—to secure a loan, divide an estate, or decrease the number of their bondspeople for financial relief—and although planters generally preferred to buy young, strong field hands and fertile women, slaves of all ages and physical abilities found themselves offered for auction, particularly as part of estates.[8] Since estate auctions were often neighborhood affairs, prospective buyers were occasionally familiar with the slaves for sale and knew about their abilities and defects. Otherwise, however, there were few differences between estate sales and other kinds of slave auctions; they were often advertised in the same way as commercial sales, and the sale of slaves from larger plantations often occurred in large public sites (such as courthouses and slave marts), handled by professional auctioneers.[9] Furthermore, estate sales were not as profitable as commercial sales—slaves auctioned in court-ordered sales were often less expensive—but formed a large portion of slave traders' business in most Southern cities.[10] Debates over value and "defect" in slave bodies could also continue after the sales encounter had concluded, and the language of slave sales is evident in breach-of-warranty litigation in many Southern courts. Thus, a number of different voices and concerns participated in conversations about the value of defective or disabled slaves, which allows us to read the language of slave sales from a variety of perspectives.

One primary facet of the language of the slave market was monetary price. Average prices for bondspeople differed by region, and due to the increase in cotton production and closure of the international slave trade, prices for slaves of both genders and all ages generally rose over the first half of the nineteenth century. As John Hope Franklin and Loren Schweininger have noted, young, "able" field hands were sold for lower prices in Richmond markets than in Charleston or New Orleans, and between the early nineteenth century and 1860, values in all three markets increased at least threefold. Generally, young male field hands were the most expensive slaves in the South, while women, children, and disabled—elderly, crippled, scarred, or otherwise impaired—usually sold for lower prices.[11] Many planters and traders prided themselves on their knowledge of the market and their ability to estimate the price of individual slaves based on a variety of criteria, particularly age and ability to perform field labor.[12] For instance, Tyre Glen, a trader from Forsythe County, North Carolina, attempted to create a mathematical scale for the valuation of slaves based primarily on age, reflecting a common economic interest in young adults who were presumably the strongest and healthiest and who were most likely to appreciate in value over the course of their lives.[13] However, at no point in the history of the antebellum slave trade was there an absolute standard or calculus for determining slave prices in antebellum markets. For one thing, circumstances of slave sales varied widely; Walter Johnson has noted that there was no discrete, definable "slave trade" in the antebellum South, and many transactions took place privately, between family members or neighbors.[14] Even in cases of public auction of slaves, a seller's motives for selling could influence prices. For example, slaves brought to market in court-ordered sales—to liquidate an estate or secure a mortgage—were generally sold at lower prices, regardless of their commercial marketability. Furthermore, as Gavin Wright argues in his study of the political economy of the slave South, "the price of slaves did not reflect an observable intrinsic value of slave labor, but an expectation of future returns"; because individual slave owners would have their own expectations of labor and discipline for prospective human chattel as well as of what kinds of burdens they were willing to assume as part of their investments, "the determination of slave prices was essentially a psychological matter,"[15] and prices were attempts to measure buyers' concerns about productivity as well as their emotional responses to prospective bondspeople.

Slaveholders and traders also developed a lexicon of descriptions that enabled them to communicate with each other about desirable qualities, and how slaves with those qualities should be valued. General terms like *prime* (which designated a slave able to labor at the capacity of a full field hand), *sound* (usually indicating a slave free from physical or mental disorders, and without whip scars or other disfiguring marks) and *likely* (which usually described the most desirable slaves in terms of their age, strength, physical condition and appearance, compliance, "likeability," and capacity to produce more capital) appear frequently in newspaper advertisements, planter and trader correspondence, warranties, and bills of sale. Conversely, there were market terms used to describe less desirable slaves, including *unsound, half-* or *quarter-hand*, and *scrub*, which generally described a slave who was not "likely."[16] Slaveholders also referred to more specific traits in their discussions of prospective human chattel, including skin color, breeding capacity, and dental quality, creating an understanding of what kinds of slaves they did and did not want.[17] As Walter Johnson has pointed out, assumptions about desirable and undesirable qualities in slaves could be complicated and not universally applied to all slaves. For example, most light-skinned female slaves were considered "likely," but a light-skinned male slave was much less desirable because potential masters might view him as a flight risk.[18] Nonetheless, the use of such common terms enabled buyers, sellers, and traders to negotiate the sale of individual slaves without face-to-face encounters.

These negotiations are evident in the correspondence between South Carolina slave trader A. J. McElveen and broker Ziba B. Oakes, who founded the slave-jail and trading house known as Ryan's Mart in Charleston. In July 1853, McElveen wrote to Oakes to describe several slaves he looked to acquire and to discuss his assessment of their value. For instance, in his description of a boy with "one of his Big toes knocked off," McElveen indicates an awareness that the defect could drive down his price—he explains to Oakes, "I could not Get one dollar nocked off for that," implying that he himself attempted to use the defect to make a bargain—but claims "I dont think it Should lessen his value he is no 1 Boy in appearance, and I cant By [*sic*] such for less Price here."[19] Conversely, McElveen refused to purchase a twenty-year-old girl for $700 whom he valued at no higher than $675, but he invites Oakes to reconsider that decision because "She is very Badley whipt [*sic*] but good teeth the whipping has been done long Since She is tolerably likely."[20] In both of these cases, McElveen uses common market phrases and specific physical descriptions of slaves to communicate his purchase decisions to Oakes, and invites the broker's opinion, even though Oakes had not laid eyes on the slaves in question. These examples indicate that slaveholders, traders, and purchasers considered a variety of factors in their assessments of the value of slaves for sale, and utilized a set of common terms to communicate with each other about the value and desirability of slaves, particularly those with potentially defective or disabling conditions.

Slaves who arrived at market in traders' gangs or as part of estates were often advertised in broadsides, and the language of these advertisements is a valuable tool to examine how disability influenced market values and the presentation of slaves at auction. Slaves who were sold in commercial gangs were less likely to be inspected thoroughly prior to their sale, and catalogs or broadsides advertising their sale usually provided only cursory information; other advertisements, particularly for estate auctions, included much more detail about individual slaves, such as their names, ages, the type of work to which they were accustomed, and any known or apparent defects.[21] However, the advertisement of such information was a tricky issue for traders selling elderly or disabled slaves.[22] Too much detail about slaves with unsound qualities could preclude their sale, but sellers who omitted information about disabilities risked litigation from buyers who discovered sources of unsoundness after the transaction was over.[23] As there was no arbitrary calculus for ascribing value to human chattel, particularly those with unsound qualities, sellers needed to consider the interplay of such factors as age, visible scars, past injuries, and known disabilities in their descriptions of available slaves. This is particularly significant for estate sale advertisements; when a slaveholder died and his or her estate needed to be divided or liquidated, all slaves that had belonged to the owner needed to be sold, regardless of their value as laborers. Certainly, it was a liability for an estate to include unsound or disabled slaves; for instance, in an undated communiqué to the Orphan's Court of Wilcox County, Alabama, Sheriff Samuel Burnett, administrator of Luke Herrington's estate, noted that "two old negroes . . . who are of little or no value" would be "chargeable" to the estate unless they could be sold.[24]

The valuation of disabled slaves began with estate inventories, often recorded by executors or family members, and these initial appraisals indicate that elderly and disabled slaves were usually valued far less than younger, able-bodied individuals. In the estate of Dr. Joseph Glover, a South Carolina planter who died in 1840, all slaves described with the title "Old"—such as Old Clarinda and Old Peter—were valued at twenty-five dollars or fifty dollars, when all other slaves had appraisals at $100 or more. One man on Glover's Snug-It-Is Plantation, described as "Old Yellow Ben," was valued at one cent.[25] While a seller most likely would have asked higher prices for these individuals, it is clear from Glover's appraisal that elderly slaves were devalued and would not be attractive to potential buyers at market. This general opinion about elderly slaves also appears in the report of an English traveler in the South, who witnessed the sale of two older slaves in a South Carolina market. His account, which was published in a British antislavery tract, notes that the slaves—a husband and wife, offered for sale as a pair— "were almost worn out with stripes and hard usage; and the woolly heads of both were nearly white. The old negro was more than 70, his wife a year or two younger. They were knocked down for 13 dollars . . . they would (commercially speaking) have been dear [as] a gift."[26] Therefore, estate sales included a wide variety of slaves—from infants to the elderly, prime field hands to the infirm—and sellers were faced with the difficult task of making them attractive to potential buyers.

One useful method to analyze how sellers assessed the value of disabled slaves for sale is to compare descriptions of slaves for sale with their assigned prices. In some cases, sellers of estate slaves provided asking prices in their printed broadsides alongside descriptions of slaves offered for sale. For instance, an 1851 estate list of slaves for sale by "Major" Joseph A. Beard, a prominent New Orleans auctioneer, includes a "man, 50, unhealthy, [$]475," as well as deaf thirty-five-year-old man and his wife, who had lost one eye, offered at $430 and $225, respectively. The advertisement also included a twenty-five-year-old woman named Nanny, "hand injured," for $345, and Charlotte, a thirty-year-old woman described merely as "disordered," for $200.[27] Such prices, however, do not reflect any intrinsic worth and do not always correspond with descriptions of abilities and disabilities. An advertisement for slaves belonging to the estate of Luther McGowan, sold in Savannah in 1852, is a good example of how we can read prices and descriptions against each other to ask deeper questions about how the value of slaves with disabilities was assessed in slave sales. The list includes a number of slaves with physical or mental conditions that were worth announcing publicly as known defects; consequently, these individuals were listed at lower prices than more "able-bodied" slaves.[28] Most of the slaves on the list were identified first by the kind of labor to which they were best suited followed by their physical condition; the exception is Bessie, a sixty-nine-year-old woman who is identified as "infirm, sews." This system of identification may have been used to emphasize that most unsound slaves were still able to perform labor despite their defective conditions; a similar classification was used in a Charleston broadside advertising the sale of twenty-five slaves in January, 1860, which listed "Hester, 20, Field hand, prime, one eye lost by accident."[29] Although good eyesight was often considered vital for domestic servants, the loss of an eye may not have been a particularly disabling characteristic for a field slave.[30] Therefore, Hester's missing eye—an obvious, disfiguring condition—was important enough to mention in her sale, but not debilitating enough to preclude her from being considered "prime" for field work, and was noted after her identification as a prime laborer. Conversely, another Charleston estate sale advertisement included a woman listed as "Marilla, 70, Old, gardener."[31] The mention of Marilla's chronological age by itself is an indication that she was elderly; the adjective "old," rather than being a mere redundancy, seems to indicate that Marilla—like Bessie in the 1852 advertisement from Savannah—was considered infirm or senile because of her advanced age. The advertisements for these auctions used this simple classification system to distinguish slaves who were more likely to perform labor in spite of known disabilities and slaves who, despite having some skills or abilities, would be less productive.

However, the different prices assigned to slaves with unsound qualities indicate that sellers (and presumably potential buyers) placed different values on different kinds of disabilities. For instance, the "prime" rice hands on the McGowan estate list were offered at prices between $1,000 and $1,200, whereas those with unsound qualities were offered at much lower prices. However, there was a significant degree of variability among the prices of "defective" rice workers, even those of comparable age. Tom, a forty-year-old rice hand with a "lame leg," is valued at $700, whereas Abel, aged forty-one, with "eyesight poor," is listed at $675, and Theopolis, a thirty-nine-year-old man who "gets fits," is listed at $575. This discrepancy may stem from concerns of potential buyers about a slave's accountability and potential for future labor. On the one hand, a slave with a "lame leg" might work more slowly or be prevented from performing more strenuous kinds of labor, but could still be predictable and controlled with little change in his condition over time. On the other hand, a slave with poor eyesight might be able to perform one task well, but a potential buyer would have to contend with the possibility that his vision might deteriorate further and disable the slave from working at all; furthermore, a slave with a known history of fits could not be considered predictable at all, as epileptic fits could strike at any moment and lead to a more severe infirmity. It is possible to read these kinds of concerns into other descriptions in the list. For instance, Flementina, a thirty-nine-year-old "good cook" with a "stiff knee," is valued at $400, far less than forty-year-old Tom with his "lame leg," possibly because in addition to her disabled knee, Flementina was beyond the optimal age for childbearing. Honey, a fourteen-year-old "prime girl" with "hearing poor" may have been listed $150 lower than "prime" sixteen-year-old Angelina because a slave who had trouble hearing would be more difficult to discipline, and a slaveholder had to contend with the possibility that she could actually hear better than she let on. Examples of descriptions and prices from this advertisement may indicate that, apart from merely considering the kind of labor that slaves were able or suited to perform, traders and buyers were also concerned with how easily disabled slaves could be counted upon and controlled, and whether their known conditions could lead to more severe disability.

In some cases, it is possible to compare different drafts of slave lists for estate auctions to determine which unsound characteristics traders felt they could hide from potential buyers, and what they felt they needed to divulge. As mentioned above, disclosure of disabling characteristics was important for slave traders who wished to avoid litigation, but there was a lot of leeway for sellers to omit undesirable characteristics from estate sale broadsides.[32] Langdon Cheves, a prominent judge and planter from South Carolina who died in 1857, left an estate that included 170 slaves advertised for sale in Savannah on 3 February 1860. Prior to the sale, on 17 January, Cheves's executor composed a handwritten estate inventory list of the planter's slaves. Slaves described as having disabling conditions such as fits, rheumatism, and "running ear" appear

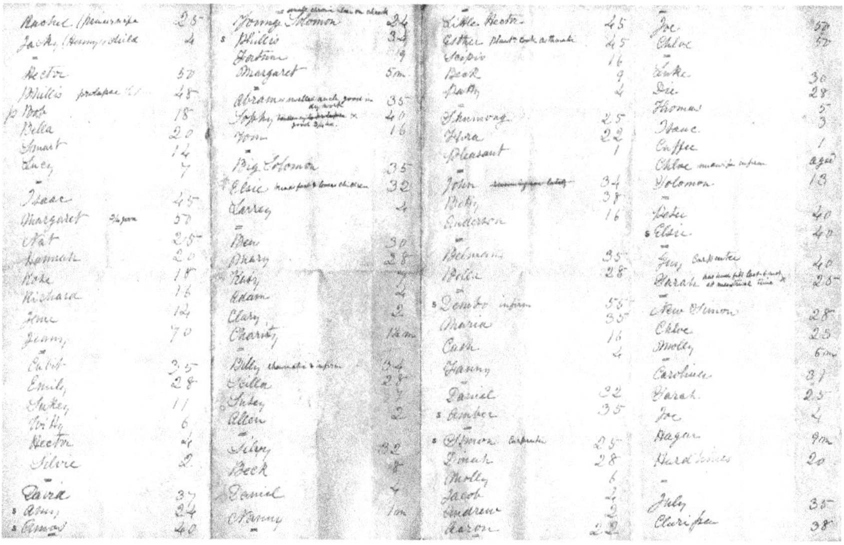

Figure 5.1 Slave inventory. Excerpt of "Negro List of Southfield, Jany 17, 1860," Langdon Cheves Papers, Correspondence January 17–31, 1860 (re: estate?), 12-49-22, used with permission of the South Carolina Historical Society, Charleston.

LIST OF

170 RICE FIELD NEGROES,

BELONGING TO THE ESTATE OF LATE HON. LANGDON CHEVES.

To be Sold at Public Outcry at

SAVANNAH, Ga., Friday, Feb. 3rd, 1860.

The capacity of these negroes may be judged from their ages, which are carefully stated. All defects konwn are duly noted. As a gang they are considered prime.

TERMS:

One third cash, balance in one and two years, secured by bond of the purchaser, mortgage of the negroes and personal security if required. Apply to

J. BRYAN,

Johnson Square, Savannah.

	NAME.	AGE.		NAME.	AGE.
1	Cæsar—Driver,	36	87	Mary,	28
2	Sally,	35	88	Katy,	7
4	Joshua,	14	89	Adam,	4
4	Tyra,	10	90	Clary,	2
5	Frederick,	7	91	Charity,	2 months.
6	Dole,	3			
			92	Billy—infirm.	34
7	Venter—Driver,	55	93	Sylla,	28
8	Maria—prime hospital nurse,	55	94	Sasey,	7
9	Booby,	22	95	Allen,	2
10	Tena,	20	96	Silvy,	32
11	Young Venter,	18	97	Beck,	8
12	Betty,	16	98	Daniel,	4
13	Judy,	10	99	Nanny,	1 months.
14	General,	7			
15	Charley,	1	100	Little Hector,	45
16	Juno,	58	101	Esther—plantation cook, astho-	45
				[matic.	
17	Frank,	38	102	Scipio,	16
18	Elsy,	30	103	Beck,	9
19	John,	10	104	Patty,	4
20	Annie,	7	105	Shumoug,	25
21	Jupiter,	1	106	Flora,	22
22	Mingo,	38	107	Pleasant,	1
23	Thamar,	35			
			108	John—running ear lately.	34
24	Jim—Head carpenter and good	39	109	Betty,	28
25	Dolly, [engineer.	48	110	Anderson,	1
26	Harriet,	12	111	Belman,	25
27	Emma,	10	112	Bella,	28
28	Isaac,	8			
29	Alffy,	6	113	Dembo—infirm.	55
			114	Maria,	35
30	Brister,	35	115	Cash,	16
31	Binah,	32	116	Tunny,	4
32	Mariah,	12			
33	Lucy,	10	117	Daniel,	32
34	Renty,	8	118	Amber,	35
35	Queen,	6			
36	Hannah,	2	119	Simon, Carpenter	25
			120	Dinah,	28
37	March,	25	121	Molly,	6
38	Elsie,	45	122	Jacob,	4
39	Bob,	16	123	Andrew,	2
40	Chloe,	14	124	Aaron,	22
41	John,	38			
42	Rose—has had menstrual de-	30	125	Joe,	50
	[rangement about one year.		126	Chloe,	50
43	Old Quacco,	aged.	127	Luke,	30
44	Esther,	aged.	128	Die,	28
45	Young Quacco,	25	129	Thomas,	5
46	Henry,	23	130	Isaac,	3
47	Bess,	45	131	Cuffee,	1
48	Billy—liable to sore on leg, now	34	132	Chloe—midwife, infirm,	aged.
49	Abby, [healed.	30	133	Solomon,	13
50	Prince,	32			
51	Rachel,	25	134	Peter,	40
52	Jacky,	4	135	Elsie,	40
53	Hector,	50	136	Guy—Carpenter,	40
54	Phillis—prolapsis, ½ hand.	48	137	Sarah—has had fits for last six	25
55	Bob,	18		[months at menstrual time.	
56	Bella,	20	138	New Simon,	28
56	Smar.,	14	139	Chloe,	23
58	Lucy,	7	140	Molly,	5 months.
59	Isaac,	45	141	Carolina,	31
60	Margaret, ½ hand good.	50	142	Sarah,	25
61	Nat,	25	143	Joe,	4
			144	Hagar,	9 months.

Figure 5.2 Slave auction broadside. Excerpt of *List of 170 Rice Field Negroes, Belonging to the Estate of Late Hon. Langdon Cheves. To be Sold at Public Outcry at SAVANNAH, Ga., Friday, Feb. 3rd, 1860*, 43/1037, used with permission of the South Carolina Historical Society, Charleston.

in both versions of the list, but there are other significant differences between the printed broadside for the sale and the handwritten inventory. For example, the wording of the advertisement for Billy, a thirty-four-year-old "prime" slave with a history of sore leg, is changed slightly from the inventory description to sound more appealing; the executor's inventory describes him as having "leg sore 3 times in 9 yrs.," whereas the printed advertisement notes that Billy is "liable to sore on leg, now healed." Other conditions noted in the inventory are simply omitted from the broadside. A thirty-five-year-old slave named Sally was described in the inventory as having "doubtful health lately," and a forty-five-year-old woman named Elsie was described as "delicate," disclaimers that were left out of the printed advertisement. Similarly, the estate inventory noted that another woman named Elsie, thirty-two, "breeds fast & looses [*sic*] children," a fact not mentioned in the broadside, just like thirty-five-year-old Dinah's "slight tendency to prolapse."

It is possible that, because slight reproductive dysfunctions were easy to conceal and perhaps considered less disabling in women who were past optimal childbearing age, the traders in charge of selling Cheves's estate decided to omit Elsie's and Dinah's conditions to avoid alienating potential buyers.[33] A similar phenomenon occurred in the sale of slaves from General James Gadsden's estate in Charleston, first offered for sale in November 1859. At that time, Caty and Hester were both described as having "prolapsus," but when a second auction was held to sell the estate in January 1860, the condition is omitted from their descriptions.[34] These examples suggest slave traders and buyers were aware that certain conditions in individual slaves could be more disabling than others and required disclosure prior to a sale; other conditions, particularly those that were easier to conceal, might not warrant mention in advertisements, especially if they could preclude a sale. Sellers, therefore, artfully used the language of the slave market in advertisements of disabled slaves to both disclose and obscure information about defects that might influence a sale.

Buyers, of course, did not rely on advertisements alone in their decisions to purchase slaves. Before the bidding commenced, buyers usually conducted their own inspections of slave bodies to identify potential causes of unsoundness or to assess for themselves how defective a slave with a disclosed disability actually was. Ex-slave Solomon Northup described the importance of this practice in his published narrative, noting "unsoundness in a slave, as well as in a horse, detracts materially from his value . . . close examination is a matter of particular importance to the negro jockey."[35] In the words of former Georgia slave John Brown, "I dare not—for decency's sake—detail the various expedients that are resorted to by dealers to test the soundness of a male or a female slave. When I say that they are handled in the grossest manner, and inspected with the most elaborate and disgusting minuteness, I have said enough for the most obtuse understanding to fill up the outline of the horrible picture."[36] Such inspections often involved stripping slaves to examine the appearance and function of all limbs and extremities, scrutinizing skin on the back and buttocks for marks of punishment and disease, counting teeth, and conducting simple tests of hearing, vision, and mental competence. Some slaves were questioned directly, or required to walk or dance for prospective buyers.[37] In particular, buyers searched for evidence of disabling injuries or defects—including broken bones, old sprains, illness, internal injuries, and burns—and potential physical signs of "bad character," such as whipping scars.[38] In many cases, female slaves were subjected to additional intimate physical examinations so buyers could assess their reproductive health and capacity for childbearing.[39] Buyers also questioned slaves about their ages and medical histories and used evidence from their bodies and testimonies to assess their conditions and, consequently, their market values.[40] The quality of a slave's teeth, for instance, seemed to have been an important sign for overall health, and slaves with bad teeth were usually considered unsound; as A. J. McElveen described to Ziba B. Oakes in 1856, "the fact is you cannot do much with defective negroes. Bad teeth & old ones."[41] Whip scars were usually interpreted as a marker of disobedience, and could produce lower bids; as a result, slaveholders at market spent a good deal of time examining scars to determine their origin and age, "reading" the scars like a deck of tarot cards to determine how "unruly" the slave would be in the future.[42] Because potential buyers who identified defects in slaves at auction could bargain for a lower price, many paid close attention any and all signs of defectiveness and disability. For instance, the papers of South Carolina planter Robert F. W. Allston include a printed broadside describing slaves from the Nightingale Hall plantation, offered around 1846 by prominent Charleston broker Alonzo J. White, with additional handwritten notes (possibly made by Allston himself) describing defects identified in slaves during a pre-sale inspection. The broadside does not identify slaves by physical description, skills, or ages, but the planter provided his own assessments of the bondspeople for sale, noting those that were "idiotic," "fittyfied," "unsound," "sickly," "shuffling," or "diseased."[43] By conducting their own inspections of human chattel for sale and using on the same language that sellers and traders used, prospective buyers were able to draw their own conclusions about the soundness of individual slaves and added their voices to the conversation of disabled slaves' value.

Given such close attention to slaves' bodies during inspections, as historian Michael Tadman has noted, it would have been unlikely that careful buyers would fail to identify prospective slaves with known physical or mental disabilities. However, some disabling conditions—such as insanity or epilepsy—were not always visible to prospective buyers and traders at the time of sale;[44] therefore, many sellers provided warranties, or "guarantees of health," for slaves, again relying on market language to indicate soundness. Although warranties could be made as oral agreements, many antebellum slave bills of sale contain statements guaranteeing the bodies of human chattel to be "sound Sensible and health and Slaves for Life.[45] On 1 March 1811, for instance, William Guy sold "a negro girle named Silvey" to Samuel Guy and claimed "that She is healthy Sound and Sensable." An

1813 bill of sale, provided by a slaveholder named Garvin, concerned "a Negro Woman Named Sue which Negro I do warant [*sic*] to be Sound."[46] By 1849, traders in Richmond even utilized a preprinted form in sales that included the language of a soundness warranty:

> Received of _____ Dollars, being in full for the purchase of _____ Negro Slave named _____ the right and title of said Slave _____ warrant and defend against the claims of all persons whatsoever, and likewise warrant _____ sound and health. As witness, my hand and seal.[47]

Although most antebellum buyers required warrants of health and soundness in slave sales, guarantees were not foolproof insurance against the unwitting acquisition of disabled slaves. Guarantees of soundness could be fraudulent; Bernard Kendig, a prominent New Orleans slave trader, knowingly sold dozens of "defective" slaves—including habitual runaways and a few with physical impairments—with full warranties. Historian Richard Tansey has noted that Kendig's average gross profit from the sale of these slaves was higher than his sales of fully sound slaves, although he did void the sales contracts and provide refunds on twenty-four defective slaves.[48] In other cases, a physical condition that seemed minor at the time of a warranted sale turned out to be a chronic or disabling problem; such was the experience of Robert S. Mills, a businessman from Cedar Spring, Tennessee, whose newly purchased slave girl who turned out to have a chronic pulmonary problem, possibly asthma. Writing to seller James B. Harris in the summer of 1844, Mills complained of his new slave's worsening condition and his inability to resell her:

> Strengthened by the confidence in the Drs opinion . . . you gave me a sound Bill of sale to the Girl but to my surprise the relieaf [*sic*] was but a temporary one the difficulty of breathing soon returned and continued some days worse than others and some days she seemed to be all most cleare of it but when ever she takes any exercise her breathing becomes so laborious the she cant stand it . . . even to walk any thing like brisk 50 yds . . . I have had had her curfully examined by some of the most experienced our cuntry and unhesitateingly [*sic*] give it as there opinion that her disease is of some several years standing and cant be other wise from the present [symptoms] yet she is going a bout and looks as well as she did when I traded for her and if see [*sic*] was sound I could have sold her several times and could know for a high price say $600 could be had for her if she was sound but I cant give a sound bill of sale to her.[49]

Furthermore, the coverage of a soundness warranty was occasionally a matter of dispute. For instance, historian Jenny Bourne Wahl has noted that some warranties were not intended to cover obvious signs of unsoundness, which a buyer should have recognized at the time of the sale, but included more obscure defects, such as blindness or epileptic fits, that might not be evident in the sales encounter.[50] However, Juriah Harriss, arguing that guarantees of soundness should be implicit in all sales, noted in 1858 that, according to the Supreme Court of Georgia, a guarantee of health was intended to cover only physical conditions, not "mental infirmities."[51] Some conditions, like a history of epileptic fits, precluded slaveholders from providing guarantees of health, and some slaves were sold without warranties for discounted prices.[52] For instance, on 6 August 1853, Emanuel Geiger sold a fourteen-year-old girl named Mariah to Alexander Forsyth for the paltry sum of $200; the bill of sale noted that "said negro girl is subject to falling fits, and I sell her as unsound property, both in body and mind, and without any warranty whatever express or implied."[53] Thus, while guarantees of soundness were common in antebellum slave sales, they were not always included in sales agreements, and did not always protect buyers from acquiring slaves with unseen defects or disabilities.

In some sales, with or without warranty, the transaction of slaves with known or unknown disabilities could last much longer after the initial market encounter if new masters discovered conditions in their human property that compromised earlier sales agreements. In December 1848, Samuel R. Browning, a Louisiana planter, wrote to North Carolina planter Archibald H. Boyd, describing negotiations with a buyer named Edrington over the sale of a group of slaves. Apparently, Edrington refused to pay Browning the $1,500 he had promised for the group because two women, Candis and Rose, were "unsound" and "an Ediot," respectively, and two of the lot had died. By January 1849, Browning agreed to exchange Candis and Rose for two other female slaves for an additional $250.[54] In 1806, Henry Izard, an executor for his father's estate, offered South Carolina planter Timothy Ford a discounted gang of two dozen slaves, "among them are several who from age & infirmities are useless; others are very fine field negroes & some fine children."[55] Ford agreed to purchase all of the bondspeople, even a woman named Willoughby whom he described as "old & Blind, & a crazy old woman,"[56] but complained to seller Henry Izard in 1806 that two slaves he had purchased, a father and son, were misrepresented at the time of the sale. According to Ford, Izard's driver informed him after the sale that "Joe the Son of Sancho was apt to fly the course when pressed to work," and "his father Sancho[,] set down as old but works a little, insists that he can do nothing but eat hominy when it is *ground for him*."[57] Ford is careful not to call Izard's honor into question, noting "I assure myself most confidently that the forgoing [sic] defects if real, were unknown to you," but his missive implies that he could seek redress. The dialogue between Ford and Izard relies on the language of guarantee to discuss the purchase of slaves with disabilities, and indicates that both men shared some assumptions and understandings about the nature of the bondsmen's defective bodies.

Presale inspections also provided slaves themselves with an opportunity to participate in assessments of their soundness and value, entering into a dialogue with traders and buyers using the same language of the market. As Walter Johnson has noted, the market and encounter between a slave for sale and a prospective buyer was a complex process that "demand[ed] a decree of specific performance" from individual slaves;[58] during inspections, slaves had direct contact with prospective purchasers, and every signal they provided—with their speech patterns, answers to questions, facial expressions, physical motions, and emotional states—could influence assessments of their value. Traders were certainly aware that encounters between prospective buyers and individual slaves were crucial in sales. In an 1854 letter, for instance, A. J. McElveen described a sixteen-year-old boy he was considering purchasing, and noted that the boy was "very likely . . . but cant Speake well to white persons." McElveen hesitated to take the slave because he was "fearful the boy will not Sell well on account of his Speech," indicating that, despite the slave's other desirable qualities—including "Good Sense" and "fine teeth"[59]—he would appear unsound and possibly impaired in a face-to-face encounter with a prospective white buyer. Even a seemingly small aspect of the slave's presentation—such as an inappropriate emotional response, a bored expression, or a weak gesture—could call into question the slave's soundness or able-bodiedness. As ex-slave John Brown remarked, "the price a slave fetches depends, in a great measure, upon the general appearance he or she presents to the intending buyer. A man or a woman may be well made, and physically faultless in every respect, yet their value be impaired by a sour look, or a dull, vacant stare, or a general dullness of demeanour [*sic*]."[60] Some slaves for sale were more forthcoming in their undesirable behavior; one man named Blaney, sold in South Carolina in 1824, was "rude, agitated, and threaten[ing] vengeance against [a prospective buyer] for bidding."[61]

Traders understood the importance of making slaves appealing to buyers, and attempted to conceal defects with a variety of different techniques. They made slaves seem healthier by feeding them more food prior to sale and making them exercise; some coached bondspeople to lie about their true ages or instructed them to smile and look "smart" and "spry" for buyers.[62] According to John Brown, traders emphasized the appearance of happiness, and told slaves that, "when spoken to, they must reply quickly, with a smile on their lips, though agony is in their heart, and the tear trembling in their eye."[63] Traders also attempted to minimize signs of old age in some slaves—William Wells Brown, who had been enslaved by a "soul driver" named Mr. Walker, described shaving old men's beards and plucking out or blacking gray hairs on older slaves in preparation for sale—while others received new clothes, and had their skin greased to cover shiny keloid scars.[64] To discipline and coerce slaves for sale, traders also utilized small rewards, threats, and corporal punishments designed to leave no traces of disfigurement on the slaves' bodies. John Brown recalled the "flogging room" at a New Orleans market, in which traders and their employees anchored recalcitrant slaves to the floor and beat them with a wide leather strap for half an hour "for various offences [*sic*], especially the unpardonable one of "not speaking up and looking bright and smart" when the buyers were choosing."[65] However, there were significant limits to the power that traders had over their human wares. For instance, traders who utilized corporal punishment always ran the risk of damaging the bodies they hoped to sell. Furthermore, coaching or coercing slaves to present themselves as *too* attractive could invite the suspicions of prospective buyers, particularly since many slave traders had reputations for dishonesty.[66] This is evident in the 1852 narrative of fugitive Richard Hildreth, the son of a light-skinned slave and a patrician Virginia planter, who described his experience of being sold as punishment for insubordination. Although the auctioneer had hyped Hildreth as an obedient, healthy slave,

> a suspicion seemed to spread itself that my master had some reasons for selling me, which he did not think to avow. One [prospective buyer] suggested I might be consumptive; another thought it likely that I was subject to fits; while a third expressed the opinion that I was an unruly fellow and "mighty hard to manage." The scars on my back tended to confirm these suspicions, and I was knocked off, at last, at a very low price.[67]

These realities of the slave auction indicate that, ultimately, traders could not control the presentation of slaves in sales encounters,[68] and slaves—aware of their own power to influence sales—could utilize their roles in the auction to their advantage. While several historians have argued that slaves did not define themselves in the same terms of soundness that masters and traders used, they certainly understood the qualities that were desirable in the slave trade and actively participated in the market transactions at the stage of inspection, deliberately presenting themselves as sound or unsound to prospective buyers. Since many auctions were local affairs, we can speculate that many slaves and buyers were acquainted, at least by reputation, so it is likely that slaves had information about the desirability of prospective masters even before the bidding began. As Walter Johnson has noted, "by knowing what slaveholders were looking for, slaves could turn their own commodification against their enslavement," using their bodies to act out the market language of soundness.[69] There were certainly a variety of motives for exaggerating or downplaying soundness on the auction block; some bondspeople may have concluded that their new masters would have more incentive to care for them if they sold for a higher price, while others may have been concerned about inflating a prospective buyer's expectations if they seemed too fit. Some slaves, taking cues from prospective buyers, could perform "likely" able-bodiedness and conceal defects to make themselves more attractive, particularly if it would allow their families to stay together.[70] For instance, in his account of the Butler's 1859 estate sale in Savannah, Mortimer Thompson described the practice of parents highlighting the qualities of their children, and children "excusing and mitigating the age and inability of [their] parents," to secure a kind buyer who would purchase them as an entire family.[71] One man, Elisha, pitched himself as a "prime rice planter" and "not a bit old yet" and pleaded with prospective buyers to also buy his family, inviting buyers to inspect his wife's arms and teeth and proudly displayed his children.[72] In this example, Elisha demonstrates his understanding of desirable qualities in slaves, as well as the market terms commonly used to denote those qualities; by presenting himself and his family as "prime" and able-bodied, Elisha used their bodies to participate in the dialogue of the sale.

Conversely, slaves had significant power to highlight or feign disability to discourage their purchase, since evidence of a disability—even an obviously counterfeit one—could lower their prospective values and even terminate dealings with prospective buyers.[73] John Boggs, a field hand from Maryland, described being sold for $1,000 to a cotton planter in Georgia, "but he wouldn't take me because I had been disfigured by poison-oak, and the loss of a finger; so my master had to put in two other young fellows instead of me. I would have been in a cotton-field forty years ago if it hadn't been for that."[74] Boggs's condition was a genuine unsoundness that prevented him from being sold to an undesirable location and master, and he identified his disability as good fortune in that circumstance, an opinion that other slaves at market shared. The awareness that slaves could feign or exaggerate disability on the auction block was a major concern, and source of frustration, for slaveholders and traders. Some prospective buyers suspected slaves of feigning conditions and refused to allow any possible sham to influence their prices. Mary, another slave from the Butler estate auctioned in 1859, "insisted that she was lame in her left foot, and perversely would walk lame" during her presale inspection, but the auctioneer and a physician he had hired to examine her disbelieved her claim. Although Mary's supposed ruse of disability did not succeed in precluding her sale, Thompson noted that her attempt, if she was indeed feigning her condition, was certainly worthwhile:

> Whether she really was lame or not, no one knows but herself, but it must be remembered that to a slave a lameness, or anything that decreases his market value, is a thing to be rejoiced over. A man in the prime of life, worth $1,600 or thereabouts, can have little hope of ever being able, by any little savings of his own, to purchase his liberty. But let him have a rupture, or lose a limb, or sustain any other injury that renders him of much less service than his owner, and reduces his value to $300 or $400, and he may hope to accumulate that sum, and eventually to purchase his liberty. Freedom without health is infinitely sweeter than health without freedom.[75]

These examples indicate that slaves, like their masters, understood their role as agents the dialogue about slave soundness and value. Furthermore, some slaves had a significant incentive to use the language of slave soundness for their own benefit, highlighting their able-bodiedness to attractive prospective masters and presenting or counterfeiting disability to undesirable purchasers.

The nebulous language of guarantee was a major project for antebellum Southern courts as well. Buyers suing sellers for breach of warranty after the purchase of "defective" human chattel made up the bulk of litigation in some Southern jurisdictions; indeed, as Ariela J. Gross points out, "contests over whether a slave was 'sound in body and mind' at the time of sale or hire were the most common cases involving slaves . . . throughout the South, at the trial as well as the appellate level."[76] In many of these cases, assessments of disability (visible or invisible) seemed to hinge on the simple question of whether or not a slave was able to perform the labor expected of them.[77] However, all conditions that might affect a slave's soundness—including character, vice, health, emotional state, and body—were brought to bear in court, and the language of the slave market was judged and reconsidered.[78] Richard Tansey, in his study of Bernard Kendig, claimed that "the laws governing slaves offered customers little protection," and that it was difficult for plaintiffs to demonstrate that slaves were disabled at the time of sale.[79] However, as more recent scholars have argued, the sheer number of breach-of-warranty cases in the early-nineteenth-century South indicates that some slaveholders and traders knowingly sold defective slaves whom they claimed were sound, and while the burden of proof still fell to the purchaser, Southern states had a number of different laws designed to protect buyers from fraudulent sales guarantees.[80] In Louisiana, where fraud cases involving slaves were particularly common, the transfer of slave property was highly regulated, and redhibition laws—which allowed for the cancellation of slave or livestock sales up to one year later if hidden defects were discovered—provided a good deal of protection to buyers.[81] The state civil code specified a number of "relative" vices of slaves' character, such as theft or a propensity to run away, and three "absolute vices" of their bodies—madness, leprosy, and epilepsy—that could provide legal ground to rescind a sale or demand a price reduction.[82] Other Southern states, while employing some regulations to protect purchasers, relied more heavily on the principle of *caveat emptor* in soundness warranty cases. In South Carolina, for instance, a "sound price" rule—based on market calculations—dictated that a purchaser who paid the full value for a slave with no obvious or observable defect at the time of the sale could presume to receive an "implied warranty" that the slave was physically sound; a buyer who paid less than full value needed to produce an express guarantee to make a claim for a fraudulent sale.[83] A similar practice existed in other states as well. For instance, in the Alabama case of *Clopton v. Martin* (1847), the seller of a boy with a long history of "spasms or fits" had disclosed the slave's condition and negotiated a discounted price, but accidentally issued a warranty of soundness in the bill of sale, finalized three days after the transaction. The state Supreme Court decreed that the purchaser had no right to sue for breach of warranty because the seller had issued the guarantee by mistake, and that the seller had been aware of the slave's unsoundness at the time of the transaction.[84] Similarly, in the Texas case of *Williams v. Ingram* (1858), the state Supreme Court affirmed that general soundness warranties did not cover slaves if buyers "traded with their eyes open" and were aware of "a particular unsoundness" at the time of sale.[85] The fact that buyers could sue for breach of warranty if slaves they had purchased turned out to be unsound, usually due to a hidden defect, might also provide a motive for slave malingering. Such hidden defects in redhibitory cases included any number of conditions, including peritonitis, scrofula, venereal diseases, leg ailments as well as epileptic fits and insanity.[86] As Judith K. Schafer and Ariela J. Gross have noted, it is likely that many slaves were aware disease or disability could legally negate sales and may have feigned or exaggerated hidden defects to reverse an undesirable sale.[87]

In states where the rule of *caveat emptor* prevailed, courts took the precise language of warranties into account in their determinations of slave soundness. In *Harrell v. Norvill* (1857), the North Carolina Supreme Court determined that Kennedy, a slave with impaired motor skill because the little fingers on both hands were permanently contracted, was not "sound," but his observed defect was not covered under the warranty in his sale, which only guaranteed him to be "sound in mind and health." Thus, because his physical state was otherwise unmentioned in the bill of sale, Kennedy's purchaser could not sue for breach of warranty.[88] In one Georgia case, *Nelson v. Biggers* (1849), the court ruled that a warrant for a woman named Betty containing the word "healthy," rather than "sound," only extended to the body of the slave. Although the jury originally found that "that the said negro Betty, from imbecility of mind, was, as a slave, incapable of performing the ordinary work and labor," the state Supreme Court overturned the decision, noting that "we do not say a person has a healthy mind, when we wish to convey the idea of a sound intellect, nor do we say a person has an unhealthy mind, when we wish to convey the idea of a weak intellect."[89] These cases indicate important distinctions between health and able-bodiedness in the nineteenth century; the presence of "disease," which was often read as acute or curable, did not necessarily render the body "unsound." Conversely, the presence of a psychological condition like insanity, or a developmental impairment like "idiocy" or "imbecility," did not make a person "unhealthy." Such distinctions of language were an important element of slave sales, and the legal consequences of breach of warranty, but they also illustrate the fluid nature of such distinctive terms in assessing slave disability in sales situations.

Mortimer Neal Thompson's ironically blunt assessment of the Butler estate sale raises a significant point about the languages of slave sales, and the way that able-bodiedness and disability in human property were negotiated in terms of value and price. All parties involved in slave sales—masters, traders, prospective buyers, and slaves on the block—communicated about the fitness of slaves based on a variety of factors, including labor and productivity, compliance, physical appearance and attractiveness, potential for investment return, and sources of unsoundness or defect. A close examination of slave prices, discrepancies in advertisements describing slaves for sale, the physical inspection and presentation of slaves on the auction block, and customs for providing warranties of slave bodies indicates that any number of factors could contribute to a slave's being deemed unsound and devalued at sale. The languages of price, description, presentation, and guarantee thus enabled participants at the slave market to engage in dialogues about slave value, but the concept of value itself remained highly subjective and negotiable; as a result, there were many instances of disputes between slaveholders, traders, buyers, and slaves about meanings and assumptions of slave disability.

Part III

Power

6 Disability, Mastery, and Power Dynamics in the Antebellum South

James L. Smith, disabled by a disjointed knee as a child, remembered that his master deliberately chose not to seek treatment for the injury. According to Smith, "he said he had niggers enough without me; I was not worth much any how [*sic*], and he did not care if I did die. He positively declared that he should not employ a physician for me." As a result, Smith's knee gradually grew worse, until he began to lose range of motion and the knee could not be reset.[1] Later in his life Smith was assigned to scaring crows in a corn field every day of the week, and recalled an attempt to use malingering to "break up, or put an end to [his] Sunday employment." At first, Smith considered feigning a stomachache, but was worried that Mr. and Mrs. Mitchell, his masters, would administer "something that would physic me to death";[2] thus, he devised to pretend to refracture his disabled leg. Mr. Mitchell threatened Smith with the lash if he did not get back to his duties, injured or not, but Smith, "groaning and crying with every step," did not make it back to the field before Mitchell relented. After eating some breakfast, Smith went to his bedroom to lie on the floor, and "pretended that I was in so much pain that I could not raise myself." Mrs. Mitchell found him there, and after bathing his seemingly injured leg with camphor liniment and binding him up, she "rebuked her husband by telling him he had no business to send me out in the field . . . for I was not able to be there." Smith remained in his room for two weeks, until he received news that the crows had moved on from the cornfield; "after hearing this joyful news I began to grow better very fast . . . when Saturday came I could walk quite a distance to see my mother, who lived some ten miles off."[3]

This anecdote provides an interesting perspective on the role that disability plays in power dynamics in the antebellum South. Although he could not be certain of their masters' reactions and risked severe punishment, Smith ultimately was able to capitalize on existing impairments to negotiate the terms of his bondage, exaggerating his disability to mitigate forced labor, but proudly described his ability to walk ten miles to visit his mother, an arduous physical task of his own choosing. Later, Smith would go on to make several physically arduous escape attempts as well.

Such negotiations, undertaken with the presence of a physical limitation, were a significant challenge to the authority of his masters. Viewing African

"I Made a Desperate Effort."—*Page* 44.

Figure 6.1 "I Made a Desperate Effort." From James L. Smith, *Autobiography of James L. Smith, Including, Also, Reminiscences of Slave Life, Recollections of the War, Education of Freedmen, Causes of the Exodus, etc.* (Norwich, CT: The Bulletin, 1881), courtesy of the Carolina Digital Library & Archives, www.docsouth.unc.edu.

American slavery through a lens of disability history identifies power structures that were more fluid and contested than contemporaries would have admitted. Ideas about mastery and control over human property, cornerstones of white slaveholding supremacy in the South, were very much influenced by ideas about slave disability or "soundness," and expectations for slaves' bodies, but in somewhat surprising ways. Questions of who actually had power to regulate slavery overlapped with questions of who had the power to define soundness and dictate the treatment of slaves with unsound or disabling qualities. These questions were raised repeatedly in a variety of sites in antebellum slave society, including interactions between slaves and their masters or overseers, medical encounters, and courtrooms. Ultimately, it is clear that a variety of individuals—including physicians, slaveholders, and slaves themselves—participated in ongoing discourses about the meanings of slave disability, and how those meanings affected the treatment of unsound human property.[4]

The South's economy was intimately linked with the health and productivity of its enslaved labor force, and the medical care of slaves was an important concern for many slaveholders.[5] Southern doctors, perceiving themselves to be isolated from centers of medical learning in the North and Europe, claimed that, due to a distinct climate, social structure, agricultural system, diet and materia medica, their regional medical knowledge was vital for treating the unique medical issues of the South.[6] This concept of medical distinctiveness supposedly was particularly important for the treatment of slaves; according to physician Samuel Cartwright, "it is only the country and village practitioners of the Southern States . . . who appear to know any thing at all about the peculiar nature of negroes—having derived their knowledge, not from books or schools, but in the field of experience."[7] In Cartwright's view, slaveholders should only hire Southern physicians to treat their bondspeople, a situation that was mutually beneficial for planters and doctors.[8]

Indeed, enslaved African Americans—particularly those with chronic or disabling conditions—were a large part of some Southern doctors' patient bases. Masters hired doctors to tend to all medical needs of their human chattel, and the fact that some doctors offered reduced rates for treating slaves indicates that there was enough of a patient volume to compensate for the discount.[9] In some cases, slaveholders hired the same doctors that treated their own families to attend their slaves.[10] Some doctors located near large plantations even contracted "retainer" agreements with planters to provide all necessary medical attention for their bondspeople for a set period of time, guaranteeing the physicians not only a stable source of income but also a working relationship with an elite patron who could improve a doctor's social standing.[11] However, medical authority of Southern physicians went far beyond care for slaves on individual plantations. Physicians also were intimately involved in most aspects of the slave economy, including assessments of slaves arriving on ships, offering their opinions about a slaves' soundness in markets and courts, and conducting medical examinations of bondspeople for life insurance companies.[12] In 1858 Juriah Harriss noted the widespread demand for medical opinions regarding the soundness of slaves:

> Physicians in the South are daily called upon to give medical evidence in court, in cases of prosecution for sale of an unsound negro, or by a citizen to pronounce upon the soundness of a negro slave, whom he proposes purchasing, or finally as a medical examiner for insurance companies, to determine the condition of negroes as regards health.[13]

As Harriss indicates, physicians' depositions were a necessary piece of evidence in legal trials concerning the sale of potentially unsound slaves; in the first half of the nineteenth century, Southern courts increasingly focused on aspects of slave soundness—including character and vice—as medicalized conditions, and employed doctors as medicolegal authorities.[14] One early example of this is the certificate of Louisiana physician Samuel Robinson, who deposed on 6 July 1809 that a "negro woman" belonging to a Mr. C. Stuart was "much diseas'd" and "intirely [*sic*] unfit for any kind of labour."[15] Five decades later, in the Arkansas case of *Thompson v. Bertrand*, the court upheld that only medical professionals have the authority to determine the causes and prognoses of "unsound" conditions in slaves.[16]

The importance of physician's judgments of slave soundness is also apparent in the correspondence between South Carolina slave traders Z. B. Oakes and A. J. McElveen in 1853. McElveen, traveling to collect slaves to sell at Ryan's Mart in Charleston, describes several slaves with potentially disabling conditions to Oakes, and notes the necessity of having them "Examind by a Doctor you approve off."[17] In the case of a young man with a "Soar leg" that seemed like it might be curable, McElveen notes that "I had him Examined by Dr Ingram [and] he advises his owner Mr Mcleod to warrant him Sound."[18] Significantly, the doctors that McElveen hired had the authority to assess the marketability of slaves with potential physical problems as well as to vouch for the soundness of a slave with a known sore leg, which was widely accepted as an unsound condition. These examples indicate that physicians, even in a nontherapeutic role, had authority to judge slaves' soundness and disability.

The summoning of a physician for advice or treatment in any arena almost always came from a white authority figure, not from slaves themselves. As mentioned above, masters normally discounted slaves' accounts of their own physical conditions, particularly those concerning chronic problems or debilities; this mistrust may have stemmed in part from abundant evidence that slaves did not trust white doctors and preferred to consult their own healers.[19] In many cases, suffering slaves simply avoided their masters and overseers while they sought treatment, concealing their symptoms and continuing their regular routines as well as they could. This phenomenon is apparent in the following entry, dated 3 March 1840, of planter Bennet H. Barrow's journal: "Luces childs foot verry [sic] badly burnt—never said a word about it for 8 days—nearly mortified &c."[20] Slave healers utilized a number of herbal and "superstitious" remedies to treat chronic conditions. Rheumatism, for example, might be treated with buckeyes,[21] or as one physician observed, "a ligature around each thigh, drawn so tight as nearly to impede altogether the circulation." In this case, the slave suffering from rheumatism believed "one of his fellow servants had bewitched him, and placed in his legs a number of crawfish, which he was endeavoring to prevent from getting into his belly."[22] Such examples indicate that slaves often diagnosed and treated their medical issues on their own, rather than relying on the white "regular" physicians supplied by slaveholders. However, slaves generally were not given a choice of practitioners or therapeutic interventions, and, ultimately, most slaveholders requested physicians to make decisions for the diagnosis and care of slaves with chronic or potentially disabling medical conditions.

Given the volume of services that physicians provided for slaveholders, it is unsurprising that the treatment of slaves was a very lucrative practice in the antebellum South.[23] This was particularly true for physicians who treated slaves with chronic ailments or injuries that could render them useless as laborers. Such conditions often required multiple visits to patients as well as costly surgical interventions, like amputation. It is difficult to make generalizations about the cost of treating disabling conditions in slaves because prices for consultations and interventions varied widely; however, according to many physicians' records, the most expensive procedures for slaves were for those that treated chronic conditions and disabling injuries, which were often four or five times more expensive than charges for visits and routine prescriptions for acute illnesses.[24] Indeed, there was a lot of money to be made in treating or attempting to cure the disabling conditions of bondsmen. As physician Richard D. Arnold noted in 1836,

> it is amongst the slave population that I consider the greatest field to lie . . . The interest, if no other motive, causes the Master to obtain medical aid for his slave, & instead of looking to the laborer for his renumeration [*sic*], the Physician looks to the Employer. This is the true reason why physicians get into practice more readily at the South than at the North, and that here he stands some chance of making his bread while he has teeth to chew it.[25]

One of the reasons that plantation practice could be so lucrative for physicians was the duration of therapy for slaves' chronic conditions. Most doctors made home visits, but treatment of many disabling conditions— particularly those involving surgery—could require very long and intense regimens. In fact, many slaveholders with debilitated slaves chose to lodge their bondspeople with doctors for the duration of their treatment. Long treatment regimens for disabled or infirm slaves at the expense of their owners were common in Southern medical practice, not because masters necessarily were primarily benevolent but because they wanted to protect their economic investment in their slaves' bodies.[26] In some cases, it seems to have been less expensive to send an ailing, burdensome slave to live at a hospital, or in the home of a physician for a long period of time. In 1845, for instance, J. Marion Sims boarded a man named Sam while he performed a jaw resection to treat Sam's advanced syphilis; as historian Walter Fisher observed, "[Sam] was sent from rural Alabama to Montgomery, which suggests the owner's desperation over the constant expenditure for the care of an infirm chattel."[27] South Carolina rice planter Robert F. W. Allston suggested leaving Sary, a slave he described as "worse than useless on the plantation," at "the hospital of some Physician in town till she gets well."[28] Similarly, in an 1825 letter to Fredericksburg, Virginia, doctors James and Edward Carmichael, slaveholder George M. Cooke described a man, belonging to Cooke's sister, who required surgery to treat "a Fistula on his posterior" and requested that the doctors provide care for the slave in their house:

> If so it will require the attention of an operator perhaps for some time and thus be of so much expense as would attend visits to him at Home would be more than they could conveniently bare [*sic*] and have

requested me to enquire of you if you would be so obliging as to take him in house and provide for him what might be necessary.[29]

However, there is also evidence that boarding slaves with physicians or hospitals for long periods of time was still very costly. Prominent South Carolina planter Langdon Cheves noted this in his reactions to bills for the board and care of several slaves in 1852 and 1853; according to his records, Cheves paid Drs. Wildman and Ganahl $116 "To Board & Attention of Billy," who may have been "infirm" or "liable to sore leg," and $223 "to board & attendance" for Abram, Jessee, Caroline, and Solomon. In a letter to his son on 12 April 1853, Cheves stated "the charges are enormous, made up almost altogether with the charge for boarding . . . I was shocked by the charges."[30] Cheves' example indicates that, while it may have been more convenient to lodge a disabled slave with physicians for treatment, their care and boarding could still be extremely expensive. Some physicians may have also purchased slaves needing treatment with the intent of reselling them at a profit after their treatment, but this was likely not the case for slaves with seemingly chronic or disabling ailments.[31]

To be sure, evidence of this distinct kind of medical authority over slaves usually appeared in published medical articles by well-known Southern physicians who had a financial and professional incentive to make such a claim. Furthermore, health-care providers and patients of all races and social classes utilized a variety of different, overlapping treatments for chronic or seemingly incurable conditions, and medicine in the antebellum South is better characterized as a dual system in which slaves and their masters borrowed from one another's healing traditions.[32] However, many Southern physicians noted the necessity of applying different treatments to black and white patients.[33] In identifying unsound or disabled slaves, some physicians discussed diagnoses that were unique to African Americans. Some of these examples, most notably Cartwright's definitions of *drapetomania* (a disease that compelled slaves to run away repeatedly) and *dysaesthesia Ethiopica* (a more general laziness or insensibility) medicalized vicious character traits that masters observed in their human chattel.[34] Although it is difficult to ascertain how influential Cartwright's racialist theories were in everyday southern medical practice, legal historian Ariela J. Gross has argued that many Southerners discussed slave vice in terms of "negro diseases."[35] Furthermore, many physicians and slaveholders argued that physicians treating slaves needed to have a keen eye to detect malingering, since many believed slaves were especially prone to feigning illness and debility to avoid work.[36] Suspicions of invented illness, or "possuming," in slaves were particularly strong among Southern masters, traders, and physicians; Cartwright even argued that malingering was an inherent trait among African Americans.[37] Evidence from plantation records and medical discourse suggests that, while some slaveholders certainly were concerned about their slaves' well-being, masters often doubted the authenticity of health complaints and physical weakness among their bondspeople. Slave-holders faced the prospect of wasted capital and productivity by allowing feigned illnesses to go unnoticed or unpunished, and white doctors—who built their reputations on their ability to expose malingering as well as on their healing skills—risked losing their lucrative practices if they were deceived by black patients. Thus, many members of white slaveholding society often assumed that ailing slaves feigned their conditions, and con-ducted rigorous investigations to ensure that slave health problems were genuine before seeking or administering treatment.[38] This pervasive dis-course of slave malingering focused on maintaining control over enslaved bodies as well as on definitions of *sick* and *well*.[39]

Of course, not all slaveholders opted to hire physicians to treat their seemingly injured or disabled bondspeople. Medical literature and case reports also include many examples of masters who neglected to provide treatment for potentially disabling conditions in their slaves for months, and even years.[40] One influential factor was the economic value of the slave who needed treatment; as a recent study of Touro Hospital records in New Orleans between 1855 and 1860 indicates, prime, male workers or those with "higher prices" were more likely to be admitted for medical treatment, and far more of those were treated for acute illnesses than for chronic or dis-abling conditions.[41] However, it is clear from primary evidence that, despite the cost and inconvenience, it was very common for slaveholders to employ doctors in the care of slaves with disabilities, or those who were at risk of being permanently disabled from chronic illness or injury.

The privileged position that white Southern physicians had in the slave South gave them, it seemed, nearly free reign to assess, treat, and study debilitating conditions in enslaved African Americans. However, there were significant limits to physicians' decision-making power, particularly when their medical roles threatened the proprietary roles of slaveholders. In an honor-bound society, Southern doctors often had to negotiate meanings of illness and disability, not to mention therapeutic interventions, based on the complicated motives and desires of masters with potentially unsound slaves. The lucrative practices and social standing that many Southern physicians enjoyed could be threatened as doctors attempted to "cure" incurable cases and provide care for patients while weighing the considerations of their masters; as a result, the reality of medical care for disabled slaves was often not as good as slaveholders and doctors claimed.

Given the cost of medical treatment for African American slaves, it is unsurprising that many slaveholders expected their hired physicians to "cure" bondspeople of a variety of chronic afflictions. Just as physicians and slaveholders defined able-bodiedness and disability in slaves based on their controllability and economic value as chattel, they often defined "cures" for potentially disabling conditions based on the doctors' ability to bring afflicted slaves under control and make them more productive. Epilepsy, for example, was considered an unpredictable, incurable disability in the mid-nineteenth century, but some Southern physicians proudly reported successful cures of slaves suffering epileptic fits if no fits followed immediately after their treatment. In October 1842, South Carolina physician John Douglass attempted to treat a blacksmith who suffered convulsions for two years after a blow to his head, noting that "for some time before I operated, he was . . . unable to labor." Following Douglass's operation, the patient "has remained free from convulsions, and has fine health ever since, being a constant and valuable hand in the shop."[42] The primary concern for Douglass, and presumably the blacksmith's owner, was that the slave could again be a reliable, "controlled" source of labor, which the threat of unpredictable epileptic fits had prevented. Physicians certainly had an incentive to claim they could cure disorders that rendered slaves useless for labor or resale; according to some observers, certain health conditions in the mid-nineteenth century, such as fistula, only produced unsoundness in a slave if they were left untreated.[43] Dialogues between physicians and masters about disability in their slaves and the possibility of curing those disabilities usually said more about the comfort and desires of the masters than of the afflicted African Americans. As discussed earlier in this dissertation, definitions of slave disability often involved underlying fears of unpredictable physical conditions that negated slaves' economic value as laborers or market commodities. These concerns are apparent in the reasons that slaveholders offered for seeking doctors' advice. For example, J. Marion Sims recounted a conversation he had with the owner of Anarcha, his first vesicovaginal fistula patient, in June 1845. Sims informed Anarcha's owner that she had "an affection that unfits her for all the duties required of a servant. She will not die, but will never get well, and all you have to do is take good care of her so long as she lives"; fortunately for Anarcha, the "kind-hearted man" agreed.[44] In this case, Sims identified Anarcha's fistula foremost as a condition that unfitted her for servitude, rather than a state that was intensely uncomfortable for the patient herself. Similarly, letters to James and Edward Carmichael reflect masters' motives for seeking treatment for chronic or disabling conditions. For example, in February 1823 William Jackson, Jr. wrote to the Carmichaels that "one of My Small Negroes has a very bad eye . . . I am afraid it will burst, it matters very Much & he is entirely blind in it as he can not open it . . . If you think it can be saved you will please Send the necessary Medicine."[45] The phrase "if you think it can be saved" indicates that Jackson's primary concern is that his slave retain his sight; he says nothing to the doctors about the boy's pain and suffering, implying that, if his slave's eye could not be saved, he would not pursue further attention from a physician. The obsession that doctors and slaveholders had with "cures" for chronic ailments in their slaves indicates that control was paramount in the culture of mastery; in this sense, controllability was probably an even greater concern than the overall integrity or comfort of the slave's body.

The failure of physicians to affect an expected cure for disabilities in slaves could arouse distrust. Due to the uncertain nature of chronic ailments, the skepticism of slaveholders certainly would have been a frequent issue for southern doctors. As medical student Moses McLoud noted, it was imperative for a physician to hone their diagnostic skills when treating slaves because "sooner or later his judgement [*sic*] will be disputed, and his fair prospects blighted, if he prescribes without fully ascertaining the true nature of cases offered to him."[46] Occasionally, masters even blamed physicians for overestimating their authority to treat and causing or aggravating debilitating conditions in the slaves they treated and sued for damages for the loss of a slave's productivity.[47] Some claimed that physicians caused infections, hernias, and secondary infertility in their attendance of pregnant slave women[48] while others criticized doctors for their hesitation to perform surgery on their bondspeople. For example, J. Anton Freemon, a Georgia medical student who owned a female slave with a debilitating fourteen-year-old growth on her thigh, disparaged the doctors who had attended her previously for their reluctance to remove the tumor "for want of the proper knowledge of surgical anatomy and pathology, and a capability to make a correct diagnosis."[49] In a subsequent article, Dr. F.W.B. Hemming, one of the operating physicians, noted "the reader must make some allowance for the strictures of Mr. Freemon, as he is the owner of the negress who was the subject of the operation, and naturally feels some resentment in having been unnecessarily deprived of her services for so many years."[50] These examples indicate that slaveholders had some clear expectations for the successful medical treatment of slaves with disabling conditions and occasionally faulted physicians for their suspected roles in prolonging a slave's impairment.

Another factor that complicated southern medical practice was the issue that circumstances of slavery itself could endanger health and able-bodiedness, a fact that physicians could rarely discuss in public. Some slaveholders warned that labor could cause disabilities in slaves; however, unlike abolitionists, they only discussed certain aspects of slavery as dangerous, not the institution itself. For example, Thomas Affleck of Washington, Mississippi, a self-described "unprofessional gentleman of fine talents and extensive experience,"[51] printed a series of responses to slave management questions in an 1851 issue of *Southern Medical Reports*, noting that several, very specific aspects of cotton cultivation were injurious to slaves. According to Affleck, working after dark and carrying heavy baskets of cotton on the head were among the most dangerous practices in cotton cultivation—"a load of 100 to 150 pounds pressing upon the skull, neck and back-bone, when the muscles are relaxed by fatigue, cannot but be injurious"[52]—but he does not take issue with cotton cultivation itself, or the inherent potential for abuse in a slave labor system. Physicians involved in the care of slaves had a difficult time ignoring the debilitating effects of slaves' forced lifestyles and mistreatment. For example, in the 1843 case of a young Virginia woman who developed epileptic fits in a slave trader's jail following an appealed arson conviction, physician G. G. Minor wrote to the governor that the girl's fits were "likely to be incurable while she is confined in a jail" and recommended her removal from the facility.[53] Minor seemed to believe that the experience of being in a slave-jail was sufficiently traumatic to aggravate Virginia's epilepsy, which suggests he was aware that abuse, confinement, or extreme conditions could lead to more serious medical problems, including epilepsy, in slaves.

However, physicians like Minor could not overtly link physical impairment with the institution of slavery itself if they desired professional acceptance in Southern society. Although medical historian Richard Shryock pointed out that physicians treating slaves were usually supporters of slavery and thus could not be accused of an antislavery bias,[54] doctors treating bondspeople could not question publicly the honor of masters by faulting them for the impairments of their human chattel or make medical recommendations that appeared to conflict with basic prerogatives of ownership.[55] As historian Steven Stowe pointed out in his discussion of medical student thesis topics in the South, "common threats to slaves' health that might easily have been highlighted in theses—how best to treat the wounds worked by the lash, for example, or the medical problems of rape or abuse—went unmentioned in obvious deference to slave owners."[56] Some writing about slave health issues placed the blame for debility on the slaves themselves, not the masters. For example, many medical reports of nervous ailments among slaves mention trauma or abuse only in the context of suspected slave malingering, disavowing abuse as a cause for "actual" pain or disability.[57] In his 1850 thesis for the Medical College of South Carolina, Moses McLoud reported a case of an enslaved carriage driver who, after being hit on the head with a whip-butt for sleeping on the carriage, experienced a stupor that McLoud discredited because there was no swelling or change to the pupils. McLoud uses this example to make a more general claim that slaves were prone, "through anger and malevolence," to feigning concussions, epileptic fits and other brain injuries "when they are beaten for their negligence," and even suggests that whipping could be a useful technique for catching a slave in the throes of a feigned fit.[58] For the most part, physicians negotiated with masters to define what constituted a "medical" problem for slaves, which resulted in some causes of chronic ill health or disability—most notably corporal punishment and abuse—rarely being mentioned.

The one disability issue that physicians and slaveholders did link explicitly with mistreatment was female reproductive problems, including infertility and miscarriage.[59] The connection between women's reproductive capacity and the institution of slavery may be due to the fact that planters often measured the health of their chattel population by their fertility, as opposed to their morbidity, particularly after the international slave trade closed in 1808; therefore, protecting the fertility of female slaves was paramount.[60] To be sure, doctors and slaveholders blamed reproductive dysfunctions on a variety of factors; for instance, there were many criticisms of midwives and inept medical attendants for their treatment of reproductive disorders in enslaved women. As Robert C. Carroll, resident physician at Jackson Street

Hospital in Augusta, Georgia, noted, "the exposure to which negro women are liable . . . and their disposition, in some localities, to treat themselves or to submit to ignorant or improper medication, in all affections involving their sexual organs, render them more liable than white patients, to prolonged cases of menstrual disease."[61] Another physician complained that "an ignorant midwife" had damaged "a valuable negress" of his by forcibly extracting the placenta after childbirth.[62] Some scholars claim that feigned disability was more common among female slaves because their soundness was often linked so closely with their reproductive health. Brenda Stevenson, Jenny Bourne Wahl, Deborah Gray White and Sharla M. Fett have remarked that malingering occurred more frequently among black women than men because reproductive problems were easier to simulate, and although such ailments were difficult to authenticate, white masters eager to protect the fecundity of their female chattel were more likely to heed their bondswomen's complaints.[63] Occasionally, enslaved women pretended to be pregnant to obtain more food rations as well as a decreased workload, but such a deception was difficult to maintain; more frequently, female slaves simulated or exaggerated chronic disorders like menstrual pain, amenorrhea, or repeated miscarriages to mitigate their work.[64] There is evidence that such malingering could be successful; for instance, on 2 April 1857, South Carolina slaveholder James Abney purchased three slaves—one woman and two children—at a discounted rate because "they were diseased, and were sold as unsound." The nature of the woman's supposed defect seems to have been her barrenness, but after Emancipation she bore three children, which prompted the administration of the seller's estate to sue for compensation in 1868.[65] However, others clearly placed responsibility for fertility problems on the mistreatment of female slaves. For example, instructions to overseers at Haller Nutt's Araby plantation in Louisiana include the claim that miscarriage "should never be the case in a well organized plantation . . . when women miscarry there is something wrong—she has been badly managed—worked improperly."[66] Writing in 1860, Tennessee physician John H. Morgan noted that abuse was a common cause of spontaneous abortion, citing his colleague Dr. Avent as saying "'I am satisfied that if negro women were kindly treated, and with proper regard to their catamenial periods, we should hear of but few cases of abortion among them.'"[67] The example of female reproductive dysfunction, however, is an exception in the medical discourse on causes of slave debility, and physicians who made a more explicit connection between the institution of slavery and the condition of slaves' bodies ran the risk of questioning the honor of slaveholders and the authority they held over their bondspeople.

As a result, physicians—acting more in the interests of slaveholders rather than their enslaved patients—often did not treat slaves with disabilities as well as they claimed. Planters were far more concerned with the loss of labor than the comfort of their human chattel, a fact evinced by plantation records that focus more on the time lost to illness and injury than descriptions of specific health conditions among slaves.[68] Medical decisions were often weighted by the relative economic and esthetic worth of the slave in question, thus favored (and able-bodied) slaves usually received better treatment. For example, T. P. Bailey's 1859 report of surgical cases discussed an enslaved patient named Hector, whose leg was crushed in a mill. Bailey elected to save Hector's knee joint not only because the rest of his leg seemed healthy but also because "the negro was very valuable to his owners"; unfortunately, Hector developed gangrene after the operation, and had to have a second amputation above the knee joint.[69] Furthermore, masters certainly considered the cost of surgical interventions and treatments for chronic ailments in their bondspeople; if the cost of treatment exceeded the value of the afflicted slave, there was a good chance the slave would not be treated. Juriah Harriss noted this in discussing the marketability of slaves with congenital deformities, such as an imperforate anus; the condition easily could be remedied with surgery but would create permanent unsoundness in the slave, and "the vendee cannot reasonably be supposed to purchase a slave, and an expense of a surgical operation."[70] Thus, Southern physicians treating disabled slaves based their medical decisions on a variety of factors, including slaveholders' economic interests and other motives, and disabled slaves did not always receive the high standard of care of which physicians and planters boasted.

The sheer volume of documentary evidence from physicians and slaveholders in the antebellum South indicates that allopathic doctors held considerable authority to judge the soundness and, conversely, unsoundness of African American slaves. In a society where the medical opinions of slaves themselves were largely ignored or silenced, white physicians relied on their self-proclaimed expertise on the health issues of bondspeople to assess the ability and debility of slaves as well as to make significant, even life-altering decisions for their treatment. However, there were significant limits to physicians' power in Southern society. In return for their costly fees, physicians were often obligated to affect "cures" in slaves with purportedly incurable conditions and were guarded against making medical recommendations that threatened to question masters' honor, authority, or the proprietary rules of the institution of slavery itself. In this respect, the "best" course of treatment held multiple layers of meaning where bondspeople with disabilities were concerned. The most obvious question to be asked of this evidence is, for whom would the doctor's advice be considered best: the patient, the slaveholder and financier of the treatment, or the doctor, whose social standing and livelihood could be threatened by making the wrong decision in the encounter? Slaveholders and physicians may have had very different ideas about what the best course of action would be, based on a complicated variety of motives, interests, and social obligations.

In addition, the law played a significant role in negotiating tensions and contradictions of slavery, mastery, and power.[71] Issues of slave disability entered Southern courtrooms in a variety of ways, and slaves with disabilities—most frequently as unsound chattel sold to unwitting buyers but also as damaged property, victims of unlawful physical abuse, or potential public burdens—presented significant challenges to antebellum law. As South Carolina Judge Abraham Nott noted in 1821, there were no universal legal definitions of slave "vice" or unsoundness.[72] Legal discourse on slave disability relied on many different perspectives, including local juridical culture, medical testimony, attitudes and expertise of slaveholders, and widespread assumptions about race and gender, to establish boundaries between able-bodiedness and disability in human chattel, but those boundaries were a constant source of conflict.[73] As James L. Petigru complained to planter Robert F. W. Allston in an 1837 letter,

> that opens the door to the whole contest, as to what does or does not constitute unsoundness. As regards horseflesh there is a vast contrariety of opinions, some judges holding that every sickness or defect almost is ground to rescind a sale, others that nothing short of some constitutional, radical infirmity will answer the purpose. Then again if Judges would agree Juries cannot and the whole subject is one of the greatest uncertainty.[74]

Many legal histories of slavery have noted such legal "uncertainty" in constructing and reconstructing meanings of race and bondage in the antebellum South. In a 1997 review essay, Walter Johnson emphasizes how everyday practices and contradictions were reflected in the law, which served to constantly define and redefine slavery. These legal "transformations," Johnson argues, were negotiated by a variety of historical actors and continued to be contested even after cases were resolved; indeed, in Johnson's view, "the most prominent feature of the law of slavery was complete confusion."[75] Andrew Fede and Jenny Bourne Wahl have argued for the significance of common law in southern legal history, have noted that state courts—hearing cases regarding slave sales, hiring practices, and abuse from a variety of individuals—"strengthened the shackles of slavery" in many ways.[76] It is therefore unsurprising that, as Judith K. Schafer has noted in her study of slave law in Louisiana, legal protection was woefully inadequate for slaves who were treated inhumanely.[77] Thomas Morris built on that point to argue that issues concerning race—including the soundness and innate inferiority of African American slaves, definitions of property, and arguments about legal protection of slaves—were a predominant factor in slave society law.[78] Furthermore, although slaves were rarely present in Southern courtrooms, historians have identified their agency in legal proceedings, and "the slippery slope" of determining whether slaves counted as "persons" in the eyes of the court. As Ariela J. Gross has noted in her analysis of how court cases arbitrated meanings of slave "character," redhibitory cases "reveal . . . the *indirect* influence of slaves on legal proceedings: both as a result of the white participants' fears of slaves' manipulations, and as a by-product of slaves' efforts to resist their masters in other domains."[79] In this respect, slave-holders, traders, lawyers, judges, and slaves alike participated in ongoing discourses about power and disability in slaveholding society.

One particular concern for antebellum courts was liability in cases of slaves who were injured, or otherwise acquired disabling conditions, while working under overseers or outside employers. As a number of legal scholars have noted, African American slaves were exempt from the "fellow-servant rule," which dominated industrial accident cases in the United States and Britain from around 1840 until the adoption of workman's compensation laws in the early twentieth century. According to the rule, injured workers could not sue their employers for damages if a coworker was responsible for the injury.[80] However, as industrialization increased in the South and more African American slaves entered the industrial workforce,[81] it became apparent to Southern jurists that the fellow-servant rule could not apply to bondspeople, primarily since slaves themselves could not be sued, so the burden of liability would be shifted to slaveholders. Instead, courts considered injuries to slave laborers under bailment law, as "rented property" that needed to be returned in the same condition. In this respect, employers of slaves could be held liable for disabling or fatal industrial accidents, an interpretation of the law that reflected the cultural priority of slaveholding interests in Southern society.[82] At the same time, the exemption also illuminates how Southern courts considered social and racial inferiority of slaves in their consideration of liability. Slaves could not be expected to provide "mutual notice"—to reprimand or correct white coworkers or each other if they worked under white supervision—or to leave service if they chose, but courts also explicated that no one could presume African American slaves would have the intelligence or capability for self-governance to make their own decisions.[83] Thus, ideas about the inherent social disability and mental inferiority of slaves, as well as considerations of the worthlessness of slaves who incurred disabling injuries, influenced decisions in liability cases.

As the Kentucky case of *Redding v. Hall* (1809) noted, an employer who hired another person's slave was required to attend to protect the health of their employee; otherwise, "'he can have no incentive to treat the slave humanely.'"[84] Indeed, there are many examples of slaveholders who sued hirers for damages if slaves acquired a disabling condition under their supervision, particularly if the hired-out slaves were assigned to a task not expressly agreed upon by the slave owner. This occurred more frequently in the years leading up to the Civil War, as more slaveholders hired out their bondspeople for dangerous work, such as mining and road construction, a trend that is also reflected in the increased number of life insurance policies purchased for slaves.[85] For instance, in *Mullen v. Ensley* (1847), the Tennessee Supreme Court awarded the slave owners damages after their hired-out slave, Jordan, "was blown up" while blasting rock for a new turnpike, losing an eye and the use of one hand.[86] Similarly, in 1856 the Louisville & Nashville Railroad Company was found liable when a slave, hired to connect cars and attend brakes, fell off of a cow-catcher and needed to have part of his leg amputated.[87] Judgments in negligence cases, which often held hirers liable for disabling injuries and deaths of slaves,[88] emphasized that African American laborers were not subject to the same conventions as free white laborers in dangerous industries. As *Scudder v. Woodbridge* (1846) indicates, individuals occupied in steamboat and railroad operations were required to be responsible for each other and to see that every other laborer performed his duties; a slave, however, could risk being accused of impertinence by calling out a white coworker, and would be subjected to strictures and punishments that white workers were not.[89] Other cases pointed out that slaves were inherently less intelligent than free workers and required more supervision and protection when engaged in dangerous labor. As the Supreme Court of Georgia opined in the appellate case of *Council of Columbus v. Howard* (1849), which involved a slave named Braden who had been killed while working on a city sewer, "the want of discretion in our slave population is notorious. They need a higher degree of intelligence than their own, not only to direct their labor, but likewise to protect them from the consequences of their own improvidence."[90] In the Louisville & Nashville Railroad Company case, the Kentucky Supreme Court overturned the verdict, because the original jury had been given erroneous instructions, but affirmed that the Louisville & Nashville Railroad Company was liable for the slave's crippling injury, even if it resulted from his own carelessness, because "'slaves, to be sure, are rational beings, but without the power of obeying, at pleasure, the dictates of their reason and judgment.'" According to Kentucky law, the railroad company was more liable for the slave's injury than they would be if it worker had been "an ordinary careful man," which can be read to mean free and white. The railroad company's defense focused on its objection to this "false principle of humanity," arguing that slaveholders, as well as slaves themselves, were at least as responsible as the railroad for injuries that occurred during dangerous labor.[91] Despite their reversal of the original verdict, the Kentucky court deliberately accepted a double standard of liability as it applied to employers of slaves.

In other cases, slave owners sought damages from other white authority figures—including overseers, hirers, and even sheriffs—for abusive treatment of slaves that led to physical impairment or death.[92] For instance, in *Dabney v. Taliaferro* (1826), the Supreme Court of Virginia upheld the conviction of a sheriff who had refused an incarcerated slave food, clothing, and heat during the winter; consequently, "the slave became diseased, frost-bitten, crippled and maimed to the extent that he was useless as a slave."[93] The ruling in *Jones v. Glass* (1852) held a hirer responsible for an overseer who had paralyzed Willie, a slave hired to work in a mine, by hitting him on the head with a large piece of wood. The overseer, a man named Massey, had claimed that the blow was intended to be disciplinary, and although the North Carolina court affirmed his right to correct slaves in his charge, ruled Massey's action "an unreasonable and dangerous blow" that disabled Willie's body and "permanently impaired" his value.[94] It is significant that the court describes Willie's body and economic value in similar terms; indeed, many cases involving slaves who were disabled by other parties determined damages based on the value of the slave. In one famous example, the Louisiana case of *Jourdan v. Patton* (1818), a slave named James was blinded by another slave, Mangé, who belonged to the defendant. James' owner sued for damages because the injury rendered James "worthless" and "a burden," receiving $1,200—estimated to be James' "full" value before the injury—in addition to payment for a physician's bill, and funds to sustain James. However, on appeal, the State Supreme Court determined that the defendant could either pay James' value as a blind, disabled slave, or pay the plaintiff the "full" price of James before the injury, but then claim ownership of the plaintiff's property. As the court opined, "the principle of humanity, which would lead us to suppose that the mistress . . . would treat her miserable, blind slave with more kindness than the defendant, to whom the judgment ought to transfer him, cannot be taken into consideration." James' owner agreed to take $1,200 from the defendant, and confer James' title.[95] Antislavery writers like Harriet Beecher Stowe, Theodore Dwight Weld, and William Goodell described this case to deplore the lack of consideration of disabled slaves' well-being in legal cases designed to protect slaveholders, and the "calm legal explicitness" of such decisions. As William Goodell pointed out, "the disabled slave is 'transferred' from perhaps a kind master . . . and turned over to the tender mercies of his persecutor, rendered the more bitter against him for the losses sustained in the transaction, and the prospect of receiving no valuable service from him!"[96] In these cases, slaves who had been disabled from injury appeared in court records as damaged property, and the extent of the damage was determined by the decreased value of the slave. Thus, judges who awarded damages to slaveholders utilized market prices and assumptions about future labor capacity to define disability in their bondspeople, a standard of practice that was applied in slave cases alone.

In a much smaller number of cases, Southern courts also provided a degree of specific protection for elderly or impaired slaves. For instance, emancipation laws in many Southern states were designed to punish slaveholders who refused to support elderly and infirm slaves by freeing them to "go at large" and fend for themselves or become wards of the county. Instead, state courts retained "full power to demand bond and sufficient security of the emancipator . . . for the maintenance of any slave or slaves that may be *aged or infirm* either of body or mind."[97] In some cases, that provision was supposed to come from fellow slaves; one 1818 Virginia estate emancipated all slaves but charged seven of them "to pay for some person appointed by the Overseers of the Poor for the support of Milly a lunatick ten dollars per year, and her mother Tener"; if the former slaves could not provide the annual fund, the overseers were at liberty to "hire them to some person."[98] One Louisiana provision also dictated that elderly and disabled parents offered for public sale should not be sold without their children on whom they depended, even though masters were permitted to sell the children away from their parents.[99] While such examples seem to acknowledge the "personhood" of slaves with disabilities, we can speculate that the spirit of the law was less concerned with the protection of slaves than with community and market interests. In emancipation cases, provisions for elderly or infirm slaves who were incapable of labor were designed to prevent freed bondspeople with disabilities from becoming public burdens; the fact that slaveholders were always at liberty to decide for themselves how to provide for their unemancipated slaves indicates that the care of elderly or infirm slaves was not the major issue. Furthermore, the Louisiana law regarding the sale of disabled parents away from their children seems to have been motivated by slave market interests rather than compassion. The children of elderly or impaired slaves often took responsibility for their care, providing their parents with food, water, and other means of subsistence and social interaction. Slaveholders who opted to sell the children away from disabled parents, however, chose to assume the care for their disabled chattel rather than attempt to pass off the burden of disabled slaves to buyers in the slave market where a surplus of "unsound" commodities could drive down prices or stimulate more redhibitory litigation. Thus, such laws more likely relied on assumptions about the "uselessness" and burden of slaves with disabilities and sought to protect the interests of slaveholders with elderly or impaired bondspeople rather than the dignity or bodies of slaves themselves, but the existence of these laws suggests potential conflict with the prerogatives of individual slaveholders and the possibility of challenge to mastery.

Furthermore, courts could indict white authorities—even masters themselves—for unlawfully maiming or killing their slaves. While disciplinary measures such as whipping with permitted instruments, confinement, and leg irons were considered appropriate and perfectly legal, by the 1830s all Southern states except North Carolina had passed fines and/or jail time for the abusive treatment of bondspeople. The imposed fines for mistreatment were not necessarily inconsequential; for instance, Louisiana's "Black Codes" charged up to $500 for the maiming or killing of slaves.[100] Some states specified acts that were considered unlawful—including castration, cutting out the tongue or eyes, scalding or cutting off "any limb or member," and "tearing with dogs"—while others, like Alabama, enacted more general codes that barred owners from cruel punishments and dictated humane treatment for slaves.[101] In one such case, Tennessee slaveholder Gabriel Worley was convicted of punishing his twenty-one-year-old slave, Josiah, by castrating him with a razor and leaving him "maimed and disabled." Worley appealed the case, and although witnesses claimed "that Josiah was turbulent, insolent, and ungovernable . . . lewd and incontinent," and that Worley "was remarkable for his kindness and humanity towards his slaves," the state supreme court upheld the decision. In his opinion, Justice Totten affirmed that Worley's action was a direct violation of an 1829 law prohibiting "cutting . . . or disabl[ing] the organs of generation of another," be they white or black, but also stated that Worley's deliberate and malicious disabling of his slave was immoral; in Totten's words, "we utterly repudiate the idea of any such power and dominion of the master over the slave, as would authorise [*sic*] him thus to maim his slave for the purpose of his moral reform. Such doctrine would violate the moral sense and humanity of the present age."[102] Although Worley's conviction was exceptional, the existence of these laws indicate that southern jurists had a sense of what disabilities were considered the most damaging for slaves, and enacted laws to prevent others, even masters, from creating certain impairments in bondspeople.

However—as a number of abolitionist writers argued—laws against the mistreatment or assault of slaves were applied inconsistently and contained significant loopholes that favored slaveholding defendants; as George M. Stroud phrased it in 1856, "where the *life* of the slave is . . . feebly protected, his *limbs*, as might be expected, share no better fate."[103] For one thing, although Eugene Genovese has noted that physical evidence of abuse could suffice for conviction in some cases,[104] disabling mistreatment was nearly impossible to prove since African American slaves were barred from giving testimony against white people in court. In her *Appeal in Favor of that Class of Americans Called Africans*, Lydia Maria Child argued that, since cases of neglect needed to be brought "by a white man upon oath" who would incur expenses if the court did not find sufficient evidence for a ruling, aged or disabled slaves with no means of subsistence rarely found their way to the legal system; in her estimation, few white men were "so desperately enamored of justice, as to take all this trouble, and incur all this risk, for a starving slave."[105] Furthermore, in cases of abusive treatment that resulted in disability or death, Southern laws often contained enough "gray area" to allow white authorities to clear their names. In Georgia, for instance, it was illegal to "maliciously dismember or deprive a slave of life" unless the slave in question was committing an insurrection, or the injury or death was an accidental result of "moderate correction"; as William Craft lamented in his narrative, "I have known slaves to be beaten to death, but as they died under 'moderate correction,' it was quite lawful; and of course the murderers were not interfered with."[106] Given that a white slaveholder could clear himself of indictment "by his own oath"[107] indicates that the burden of proof would have been effectively impossible in cases of slave assault. As abolitionist author William Goodell claimed, such cases involved questions of whether a slave should be considered a person, deserving of legal protection in case of injury or disability.[108] Throughout the South, courts debated this significant issue, returning again and again to the same conclusion; ultimately, legal protection in cases of slave disability extended to slaveholders whose property had been damaged rather than to the damaged slaves themselves. Even fine structures in slave law reflected the trend; Theodore Dwight Weld noted that the maximum penalty for cruelly mistreating a slave in Louisiana was only half of the maximum fine for cutting a chain to free another person's slave, a trespass that also carried up to two years' imprisonment. Weld cited this example to demonstrate "that the 'public opinion' of the slave states far more effectually protects the property of the master than the person of the slave."[109]

The most famous example of this issue is the 1829 case of *State v. Mann*, in which the North Carolina Supreme Court explicated the authority of masters over the bodies of their bondspeople. Lydia, an enslaved woman belonging to Elizabeth Jones, suffered a disabling gunshot wound at the hands of John Mann, her hired master for one year, who shot her while she attempted to escape punishment for "some small offence." In the original indictment, the jury found Mann guilty of "cruel and unwarrantable" punishment of another individual's property. Mann appealed the verdict, impelling the Court not only to reverse the decision but also to make a strong declaration of the meaning of mastery in North Carolina. Justice Thomas Ruffin freely admitted his reluctance to consider this case; in his words, "the struggle . . . in the Judge's own breast between the feelings of man, and the duty of the magistrate is a severe one." However, his opinion in the case clearly states that masters (owners and hirers alike) must have absolute control over the discipline of slaves for the institution to function, even in cases of disabling assault:

> That there may be particular instances of cruelty and deliberate barbarity, where, in conscience the law might properly interfere, is most probable. The difficulty is to determine, where a Court may properly begin. Merely in the abstract it may well be asked, which power of the master accords with right. The answer will probably sweep away all of them. But we cannot look at the matter in that light. The truth is, that we are for-bidden to enter upon a train of general reasoning on the subject. We cannot allow the right of the master to be brought into discussion in the Courts of Justice.[110]

In Ruffin's view, such a proclamation was certainly harsh, but he offered several rationalizations for the court's position; he claimed that the humane treatment of enslaved property was more effectively policed by public opinion as well as masters' benevolence and economic incentives to maintain the able-bodiedness of their human chattel. He also intimated that he would welcome legislative changes to the system that would accord more protection and respect to African American enslaved bodies but concluded unequivocally that, unless the law specifically forbade a particular cruelty, it was "the imperative duty" of courts "to recognize the full dominion of the owner over the slave"[111] in cases of assault. By making this precedent, the North Carolina court determined that laws indicting masters for disabling their slaves were largely ineffective. *State v. Mann* therefore exemplifies the saddest double standard of all: by protecting the power of slaveholders and viewing abused slaves as damaged property rather than victims, the court established a separate benchmark for indictable assault and mistreatment if the victim was a slave.

Finally, slaves themselves—certainly aware of prevalent negative ideas about disability in nineteenth-century society—could, and often did, use disability (real or feigned) to negotiate their bondage. From a slave's perspective, there were certainly a number of benefits to being considered ill or disabled, although there were significant differences between feigning an acute illness and a chronic impairment. Several scholars have indicated that the primary motive for slave malingering was to avoid labor; a short-term illness could provide a temporary respite from work, but a long-term ailment or disability—including vague presentations like paralysis, rheumatism, or loss of limb function—could allow a slave to obtain lighter work assignments permanently or even be retired.[112] Some slaves may also have exaggerated their age to be excused from hard labor, as well as to garner respect within the plantation community; although Deborah Gray White has argued that feeble enslaved men experienced decreased status on plantations because of their loss of strength and able-bodiedness, elderly slaves were often revered by masters and fellow slaves alike.[113] In his discussion of factors influencing the collection of slaves' vital statistics, Samuel Forry noted the phenomenon of slaves lying about their real age "from the circumstance that it flatters [their] self-love, enhances [their] dignity, and excuses [them] from labor . . . dignity and ease depend on [their] years."[114] In other cases, evidence of a disability could provide a slave with special allowances that others did not receive. For example, in his romanticized memoir of growing up on a South Carolina plantation, John G. Clinkscales described a disabled slave named Richard Harris who lived with his family. Although it was illegal to teach slaves to read in the state of South Carolina, "somehow not a member of the family regarded Dick as a slave," and Clinkscales's sisters agreed to instruct him "when the helpless cripple asked for assistance."[115] As a result, Harris learned to read, a skill that he likely would not have acquired had he been able-bodied and working in the family's fields. Evidence from ex-slave narratives indicates that many slaves were aware that illness or disability could be a blessing in market situations, since evidence of a disability—even an obviously counterfeit one—could lower their prospective values, and even terminate dealings with prospective buyers.[116]

Historians since the 1970s have debated the prevalence of slave malingering. In their statistical study *Time on the Cross*, Robert Fogel and Stanley Engerman claimed that feigned illness was rare among slaves on the plantations they analyzed, and white observers did not always assume that ill slaves were malingerers; instead, they argued, planters "were generally more concerned about losing slaves or impairing their health through the neglect of real illness."[117] However, many other historians—including Herbert Gutman, Kenneth Stampp, Eugene Genovese, Todd Savitt, and Sharla Fett—have argued against this view, claiming that malingering was a pervasive and effective tool of day-to-day resistance and was a prominent concern for slaveholders and the doctors they employed to care for their slaves.[118] These authors discuss the discourse of slave malingering in the antebellum South—many white observers assumed that feigned illness and impairment was widespread among African American bondspeople, and there were numerous admissions of the practice in ex-slave narratives—but pay little attention to the underlying mechanisms of malingering. I argue that it is constructive to consider how antebellum understandings of disability in slaves enabled malingering to be an effective means of resistance. As Heidi M. Hackford points out in her 2004 dissertation on malingering, feigned illness requires conformity to a shared set of ideas about health and bodies; feigned disability provided, in a sense, a "contested space" for masters and slaves to negotiate authority over enslaved bodies. Evidence from trickster tales indicates that techniques of feigning illness or disability were common knowledge among slaves but were also considered risky, and were a matter of debate among slaves as well.[119] However, Hackford's argument that slave malingering was largely a domestic concern[120] overlooks the reality that slaves who feigned disability often did so publicly, at many different sites in antebellum slave society.

There is strong evidence that slaves attempted to feign or exaggerate disabling conditions to avoid working, if not always successfully. In 1844, Louisiana planter Bennet H. Barrow suspected a man named Demps of exaggerating a vision problem to get out of working; on 12 June, Barrow complained in his journal that "Demps has been doing nothing since Last November[;] Dr King tending him for Loss of his Eye sight, gave him up— to appearance seemed as well as ever gave him 25 cuts yesterday morning & ordered him to work Blind or not. to show the scoundrel." After that punishment, Demps absconded, causing Barrow to vow that he "will make him see sights as Long as I live."[121] This journal entry indicates that Demps was able to utilize his blindness—which he made prominent enough to earn the attention of a physician—to absent himself from work for more than six months, much to the frustration of his master. Demps's conspicuous blindness failed to provide him with a longer absence from work, however, and Barrow eventually turned the tables on him by ordering him to work in full view of others despite his blindness and the disfiguring injury of "25 cuts." Demps responded by physically removing himself from the plantation, which confirmed his malingering in Barrow's mind. Thus, Demps relied on assumptions about blindness to compel his master and overseer to "obscure" his disability by absenting him from work; when that ultimately did not work, Demps absented himself by running away.

In some cases, slaves intentionally disabled themselves as a form of sabotage. Historians Kenneth Stampp and Leslie Howard Owens have cited several examples of self-mutilation, including a woman in Kentucky who repeatedly stuck her hand into a beehive to aggravate a disabling "swelling in her arms" and a male "prime hand" who chopped off several of his toes to prevent a sale away from his wife and family. In Arkansas, one slave discovered that he could "throw his left shoulder out of place" and thereby avoid "an hour's work," and a man named Yellow Jacob, after receiving a kick from a mule, deliberately kept his bruises from healing to avoid going back to work.[122] In *This Species of Property*, Owens argues that these mutilations were examples of slaves, frustrated by their oppression, striking out against their own bodies as a form of aggression;[123] this conclusion, however, overlooks the possibility that slaves could benefit from creating disability in themselves, particularly if they did so publicly, or if their self-inflicted defects were highly visible. In antislavery publications and ex-slave narratives there are several accounts of slaves attempting to negate sales agreements by sabotaging their own bodies.[124] Abolitionist James Redpath described an encounter with a young woman offered for auction in a Richmond market, whose "right hand was entirely useless—'dead,' as she aptly called it":

> One finger had been cut off by a doctor, and the auctioneer stated that she herself chopped off the other finger—her forefinger—because it hurt her, and she thought that to cut it off would cure it. This remark raised a laugh among the crowd . . .
>
> "Didn't you cut your finger off," asked a man, " 'kase you was mad?"
> She looked at him quietly, but with a glance of contempt, and said:
> "No, you see it was sort o' sore, and I thought it would be better to cut it off than be plagued with it."
> Several persons around me expressed the opinion that she had done it willfully, 'to spite her master or mistress, or to keep her from being sold down South.'
> I do not doubt it.[125]

Similarly, *Domestic Manners of the Americans*, Frances Trollope's popular travel memoir and account of life in the United States, contains an example of a Virginia man who was to be sold further South. According to Trollope, "within an hour after it was made known to him, he sharpened the hatchet with which he had been felling timber, and with his right hand severed his left from the wrist,"[126] presumably to decrease his value as a field laborer. Fugitive slave Milton Clarke, writing with his brother Lewis in 1846, described a Lexington carpenter named Ennis, whose master, General Leslie Coombs, negotiated to sell him "down the river" to work on a cotton plantation. Clarke notes "Ennis was determined not to go. He took a broadaxe and cut one hand off; then contrived to lift the axe, with his arm pressing it to his body, and let it fall upon the other, cutting off the ends of the fingers"; Ennis was sold anyway, albeit "for a nominal price," to a Louisiana planter.[127] In all of these examples, slaves about to be sold intentionally disabled their bodies with very visible and disfiguring injuries. While it is likely that they chose to chop off fingers, hands, and toes because it was expedient—slaves had easy access to sharp tools and could quickly complete the task without interference—it is also remarkable that such injuries were impossible to ignore at auction. Hands and feet were important elements of a prospective buyer's inspection, and slave traders could not afford to conceal such defects as missing digits or extremities. Furthermore, the fact that these slaves sabotaged their bodies publicly—by committing the act in front of others or admitting to their actions after the fact—is a significant element in the masquerade. Marking their own bodies as disabled allowed slaves to claim an element of control over themselves but also tempted observers to read other kinds of "unsoundness" into their bodies. For example, the woman who claimed to cut off her own finger because it was "sore" invited prospective buyers to question her mental state; those who laughed at her claim and asked her if she was "mad" read her deliberate injury as a sign of possible stupidity or insanity. Thus, slaves who employed self-sabotage relied on conspicuous signs of disability to manipulate observers' reactions, and thereby gained a measure of power over their own bodies.

A number of participants—including masters, traders, judges, physicians, employers, and slaves themselves—participated in a complicated discourse on the nature of slave soundness as well as the responsibilities and prerogatives inherent in controlling "unsound" slaves. Doctors had powerful roles as experts on slave health and soundness, and engaged in a lucrative practice of attending to slaves with chronic and disabling conditions, but there were significant limits of doctors' authority, including the pressure to "cure" disabling conditions in valuable bondspeople and slaveholders' accusations that medical treatment actually aggravated or caused infirmities in slave patients. Furthermore, although Southern states enacted laws that seemed to protect elderly and impaired slaves from neglect, or from the disabling abuse of white authority figures, such laws were selectively applied and mainly enforced to serve the interests of the slaveholding community, rather than the slaves themselves. For many slaves, though, there were significant advantages to being considered "disabled," and malingering—feigning, exaggerating, or intentionally creating a disability in their bodies—was an important way for slaves to negotiate control over the bodies and resist the authority of their masters.[128] Almost paradoxically, performing disability—a condition normally associated with dependence and powerlessness—could allow slaves to achieve a degree of power in many different situations

A close reading of these examples indicates important conversations about the nature of disability in general, and its impact on power dynamics in the slave South. Medical and legal practice in the South was influential in regulating the institution of slavery but had to walk a delicate line to avoid interfering with the prerogatives of mastery; where issues of slave disability were concerned, however, ideas about mastery could be called into question. Medical treatment and legal protection of disabled or "unsound" slaves, in some instances, mitigated the absolute control that many slaveholders expected to hold over their human property. Thus, slaves with disabilities presented an important challenge to power structures in the slaveholding South. Just as James L. Smith was aware that his disabled body could afford him a degree of power, other slaves realized the importance of disability, genuine or feigned, as a tool of negotiation. The volume of evidence that slaves could, and did, utilize disability as a tool of power negotiation indicates that there were significant advantages for slaves to be considered disabled, and that malingering was a pervasive concern among the master class in the American South. Slaves' ability to deceive their masters was an important means of resistance; as historian Ira Berlin has noted, "even when their power was reduced to a mere trifle, slaves still had enough to threaten their owners—a last card, which, as their owners well understood, could be played at any time."[129] These conversations belied a deeper concern about the nature of able-bodiedness and disability in general, and suggest that southern doctors, courts, slaveholders and slaves discussing the unique fitness of slaves were also establishing a discourse about the "soundness" of all.

7 Epilogue and Conclusion
Seeing "Moses"

At the South Carolina Historical Society in Charleston, a city that proudly preserves and celebrates its antebellum heritage, are kept three leather-bound scrapbooks of memorabilia from the family of rice planter and lawyer Louis Manigault. These books contain transcriptions of family documents and reminiscences, neatly and lovingly recorded with a steady hand in the 1870s, of the Manigault family's French Huguenot origins, estates, and genealogical ties, as well as several photographs and portraits. Towards the end of the second volume is a photograph of "Moses," described as "the last African belonging to our family."[1] The family's records note that Moses had been a "prime," fifty-five-year-old worker on the Manigault rice plantations at Gowrie and Hermitage in 1848;[2] the photograph, taken nine years later, depicts an elderly man with a blinding cataract in his right eye, dressed in a suit with a clean white vest and cravat. Before "he died of an apoplectic fit" in 1863, Moses had worked as a gardener, and the description of him fondly proclaims that "he worked to the last."[3]

This photograph and account of a favored family servant, recorded more than a decade after his death, seems to have been meant as a loving tribute not only to Moses but also to the family whom he served. The implication of his description, as well his picture—in which he appears visibly disabled but well-dressed and seemingly healthy—is that the benevolence of the Manigaults and the strong bond they had with Moses enabled him to reach old age, and continue to work despite his impairments up until the day he died. In this sense, "Moses" appears in the scrapbook not so much as an individual, but as a romantic symbol of antebellum plantation life the Manigaults wanted to remember. The family was certainly not alone in using the image of a slave to create a memory of the prewar South; depictions of elderly and debilitated freedpeople were an intriguing part of collective cultural projects of "forgetting" in the later decades of the nineteenth century.

The imagining of a benevolent Southern plantation past was not the only cultural project of forgetting realities of bondage and its effect on African American bodies. During the war and early years of Reconstruction, emancipationist images of African Americans had promoted the image of slaves released from crippling bondage, overcoming impairments to participate in

"Moses": the last African belonging to our family. This likeness was taken February 1857. He died of an apoplectic fit in Charleston So. Ca. 16th July 1863. He worked to the la.. his occupation being to keep the yard clean, and garden from weeds. ———

Figure 7.1 "Moses" Manigault, 1857. From Louis Manigault Family Record, 1756–1887, used with permission of the South Carolina Historical Society, Charleston.

free society. According to this ableist myth of freedom, physical disabilities represented the social disability of slavery. As early as 1862, William Davis, "a fine, intelligent-looking mulatto," told a meeting of the American Missionary Society about an old man he had known prior to the war who "had to recline upon a staff. One day news came that this man was free. He dropped his staff, and stretched and stretched himself until he got quite straight, and went and earned his own living . . . it is all nonsense to say that niggers won't work and support themselves. They will."[4] Similarly, oral narratives of former slaves describe elderly slaves tossing away their walking sticks and paralyzed slaves standing up to praise God when they were emancipated.[5] As Jim Downs has pointed out, Reconstruction images of African Americans expressed an excitement about the political and social opportunities of emancipation, and created illustrations of freedpeople as free laborers, soldiers, and voters, strong, independent, and above all, able.

"THE FIRST VOTE."—Drawn by A. R. Waud.—[See next Page.]

Figure 7.2 Alfred R. Waud, "The First Vote," *Harper's Weekly* (16 November 1857), used with permission of the Picture Collection, New York Public Library, Astor, Lenox and Tilden Foundations.

In Alfred R. Waud's illustration "The First Vote," which appeared in *Harper's Weekly* in 1867, three clearly able-bodied African American men stand confidently in line at a polling station. Although the first man in the line is elderly—he has a head of white hair and a white beard—he appears strong, and the mallet and chisel visible in his pocket indicate he is a skilled and able worker.[6] The illustration propagated the abolitionist ideal of race and servitude that had circulated since the 1830s, indicating that the institution

Figure 7.3 J. J. Cade, "Fleeing from the Land of Bondage: on the Mississippi River in 1863" (New York: A. D. Worthington, 1887), used with permission of the Picture Collection, New York Public Library, Astor, Lenox and Tilden Foundations.

of slavery alone had "disabled" African Americans, and freedom removed the impairment. Their erect statures and straightforward gazes are a significant departure from illustrations of slaves in bondage, who are often shown hunched over or limping. This is certainly evident in an 1887 engraving, based on an older work by Felix Carr Darley, entitled "Fleeing from the Land of Bondage: On the Mississippi River in 1863." Under the watchful gaze of a Union soldier, a family of freed slaves board a steamship, including "old men and women, gray, nearly blind, some of them bent almost double." Conveniently sidestepping the real disabling effects of slavery, as well as questions of who would be responsible for them in free society, illustrations of able-bodied freedpeople and images of former slaves tossing away their canes reified the mythical ableism of freedom in the years immediately following the Civil War.

However, as historian David Blight has demonstrated, the devastation of the war and the political necessity of reconciliation overwhelmed emancipationist visions of Reconstruction in the decades following the Civil War. In order to find meaning in the war's unprecedented scale of morbidity and mortality, many white Northerners and Southerners emphasized brotherhood and healing, and collectively overlooked the racial implications of emancipation. The nation established a cultural propaganda of the "Old

South" that embraced romanticized, pastoral remembrances of slavery and, ultimately, resubjugated African Americans to an inferior and socially disabled role as faithful and docile servants.[7] In this sense, the image of freedpeople as able-bodied citizens was overrun with innocent depictions of elderly and disabled slaves, serving both Old South sentimentalism and the collective "forgetting" of the war and its social aftermath. Reminiscences of faithful old family slaves—particularly loyal bondsmen like Moses Manigault and black "mammies"—were very common in the South well into the twentieth century and emphasized the love and support that slaveholding families provided to their bondspeople, particularly those who were old or impaired. The United Daughters of the Confederacy even campaigned for the erection of stone monuments to old "mammies" in former slaveholding states; as one Tennessee member claimed in 1905, these monuments would "prove that the people of the South who owned slaves valued and respected their good qualities as no one else ever did or will do."[8] Such memorials to beloved old slaves used the age and impairments of bondspeople as visual proof of the gracious plantation past they sought to create, implying that the benevolence of slavery allowed faithful bondspeople to reach old age, and cared for them when they became too feeble or impaired to be "valued and respected." In this sense, the visual cues of disability were neutralized, and elderly or debilitated individuals were objectified as representations of a bygone era, not as reminders of the cruelty of slavery. Around the same time, blackface minstrelsy continued to rise in popularity, providing a cheerful, if not genteel, image of plantation life as well as stereotypes of African Americans that would linger in popular culture for decades. Blackface performers portrayed slaves as mentally stunted yet devilishly clever, childlike yet grotesque, telling stories of bondage that served the emotional needs of white audience members to both remember the antebellum South with nostalgia but also to place themselves at a considerable distance from the past as well as from the newly emerging caste of freedpeople. The carnivalesque "Other" of black minstrel characters also carried implications of dangerous derangement, which fed into the myth of the "Negro rapist" that was portrayed in films like *Birth of a Nation*, and inspired many lynchings in the Jim Crow era.[9] All of these romanticized images of former slaves—able-bodied freedpeople, sentimental and debilitated reminders of a benevolent Old South, deranged and threatening minstrels—entered American culture, and as they interacted and overtook one another in postbellum decades, the racial and status implications of disability, as well as realities of life for disabled slaves in bondage, were largely forgotten in popular culture and the historical canon.

The goal of this book has been to revisit the history of African American slavery with a focus on disability to identify some of the patterns and interactions that have been largely overlooked in cultural assumptions as well as scholarship, and the endeavor has led me to a number of significant conclusions. Most important has been the discovery of the sheer volume of evidence in the primary record that addresses issues and constructions of slave disability. Slave "soundness," as other historians have noted, was a central element of discourse in the South, but assumptions about disability, as well as its associations with race and social status, were also featured prominently on both sides of the slavery debate that raged in both the North and South in the antebellum decades. Proslavery advocates claimed that Africans' "natural" mental inferiority and peculiar physical traits suited them to bondage under white masters in the southern climate, while abolitionists argued that the institution of slavery was inherently disabling, while freedom would confer able-bodiedness upon even the most wretched bondspeople. However, these two positions were not as polarized as they might seem; both sides of the debate relied on similar assumptions about disability as dependence and weakness, and promoted a stigmatizing view of impairment.

Furthermore, this research has uncovered intriguing contradictions and double standards in how white authority figures assessed disability in African American bondspeople in labor schemes, slave markets, Southern courts, and medical practice. The planters who categorized their impaired servants as "useless," even as they described the jobs those servants performed, exposed a more complicated set of assumptions and expectations for slaves with that seemingly small inconsistency. At slave auctions, traders, buyers and masters (not to mention slaves themselves) employed a complicated variety of languages to establish a calculus of slave worth that was both arbitrary and highly individualized, indicating a very complex set of economic, social, cultural, and esthetic desires that influenced how the market valued the "soundness" of enslaved bodies. Interestingly, by reading different kinds of evidence against each other—such as two different versions of an estate inventory of slaves for auction—we can see glimpses of those desires, and how they interacted. In addition, Southern jurists and physicians applied a number of double standards in their determinations of slave disability, creating sets of expectations for able-bodiedness and impairment that were racially and socially unique to slaves, with awareness of the prerogatives of mastery. These findings illuminate webs of meaning and assumptions about slave disability that go far beyond individual physical or mental conditions, highlighting the complex social construction of disability in nineteenth-century American society. Finally, evidence of slave perspectives on disability has illuminated a number of interesting conclusions. Although many African American bondspeople expressed similar assumptions about impairment, particularly the association of disability with weakness, it is clear that many slaves also recognized the utility of disability as a resistance strategy. There could be significant advantages for slaves to be considered "unsound," and primary evidence indicates that slaves used visual signs of disability—whether inborn or acquired, self-inflicted, exaggerated, or feigned—to negotiate the terms of their bondage in labor, slave markets, and escape attempts. In this respect, disability was an important element of slave agency and resistance in antebellum America, thus illuminating a new dimension in studies of power dynamics in slaveholding states.

My attempt to reconstitute a disability history of African American slavery raises significant questions about constructs of disability in other aspects of American society and points toward a number of intriguing possibilities for future research. One potentially fruitful avenue for scholarship would be a comparison between disability experiences of slaves and the free black population, which increased rapidly in the first half of the nineteenth century,[10] as well as between immigrant groups and the white working class in the United States. The examples of slave perspectives on able-bodiedness and disability also indicate the potential for more analysis of disability constructs in slave folklore and ex-slave narratives, both pre- and postwar, and the few instances of disability discourse in other slaveholding colonies—particularly the West Indies—raise the possibility of a transatlantic study of race and disability. Furthermore, as Jim Downs has already indicated, the experiences of African American freedpeople in the aftermath of the Civil War and into the Jim Crow era indicate that disability was a significant, and largely overlooked, aspect of black identity and experience. The histories of slave disability I have uncovered for this book, therefore, represent a mere fraction of the wealth of possibilities for American disability history more generally, and it is my hope that this evidence will provide us with new interpretations of disability as a viable category of analysis. More importantly, I hope that examining the experiences of slaves and disability will help us to find new ways of seeing slaves like Moses Manigault, staring blindly from the pages of an ancient leather scrapbook in a historical society, without repeating the meanings and metaphors the scrapbook creators attributed to their visions of the past.

Notes

NOTES TO CHAPTER 1

1. John W. Blassingame, ed., [Interview of Tom Wilson], in *Slave Testimony*: *Two Centuries of Letters, Speeches, Interviews, and Autobiographies* (Baton Rouge: Louisiana State University Press, 1977), 338–39. Originally published in the *Liverpool Albion*, 20 February 1858.
2. Ibid., 338.
3. Elizabeth B. Clark, "'The Sacred Rights of the Weak': Pain, Sympathy, and the Culture of Individual Rights in Antebellum America," *Journal of American History* 82 (September 1995): 463–67, 481, 484; John Stauffer, *The Black Hearts of Men*: *Radical Abolitionists and the Transformation of Race* (Cambridge, MA: Harvard University Press, 2002), 50, 56; Phillip Lapsansky, "Graphic Discord: Abolitionist and Antiabolitionist Images," in *The Abolitionist Sisterhood*: *Women's Political Culture in Antebellum America,* eds. Jean Fagin Yellin and John C. Van Horne (Ithaca, NY: Cornell University Press, in cooperation with the Library Company of Philadelphia, 1994), 207; Jeannine DeLombard, "'Eye-Witness to the Cruelty': Southern Violence and Northern Testimony in Frederick Douglass' 1845 *Narrative*," *American Literature* 73 (June 2001): 248; John Sekora, "Black Message/White Envelope: Genre, Authenticity, and Authority in the Antebellum Slave Narrative," *Callaloo* 32 (Summer 1987): 496, 501; Mary Klages, *Woeful Afflictions*: *Disability and Sentimentality in Victorian America* (Philadelphia: University of Pennsylvania Press, 1999), 2; James Brewer Stewart, *Holy Warriors*: *The Abolitionists and American Slavery* (New York: Hill & Wang, 1976), 138–39; Saidiya Hartman, *Scenes of Subjection*: *Terror, Slavery, and Self-Making in Nineteenth-Century America* (New York: Oxford University Press, 1997), 3; Ann Fabian, *The Unvarnished Truth*: *Personal Narratives in Nineteenth-Century America* (Berkeley: University of California Press, 2000), 102.
4. See Jonathan Prude, "To Look Upon the 'Lower Sort': Runaway Ads and the Appearance of Unfree Laborers in America, 1750–1800," *Journal of American History* 78 (June 1991): 133.
5. Douglas C. Baynton, "Disability and the Justification of Inequality in American History," in *The New Disability History*: *American Perspectives*, eds. Paul K. Longmore and Lauri Umansky (New York: New York University Press, 2001), 52.
6. See Paul K. Longmore and Lauri Umansky, "Introduction. Disability History: From the Margins to the Mainstream," in *The New Disability History*: *American Perspectives*, eds. Paul K. Longmore and Lauri Umansky (New York: New York University Press, 2001), 2–7; Simi Linton, *Claiming*

Disability: Knowledge and Identity (New York: New York University Press, 1998), 132–33; Catherine J. Kudlick, "Disability History: Why We Need Another 'Other,'" *American Historical Review* 108 (June 2003): 767.

7. Daniel Wickberg, "Heterosexual White Male: Some Recent Inversions in American Cultural History," *Journal of American History* 92 (June 2005), http://www.historycooperative.org.proxy.lib.umich.edu/journals/jah/92.1/wickberg.html, paragraphs 8, 10, 37; Kenneth S. Greenberg, *Honor and Slavery: Lies, Duels, Noses, Masks, Dressing as a Woman, Gifts, Strangers, Death, Humanitarianism, Slave Rebellions, the Proslavery Argument, Baseball, Hunting and Gambling in the Old South* (Princeton, NJ: Princeton University Press, 1996), xi.

8. Ulrich Bonnell Phillips, *American Negro Slavery: A Survey of the Supply, Employment and Control of Negro Labor as Determined by the Plantation Régime* (New York: D. Appleton, 1918; repr., Gloucester, MA: Peter Smith, 1959), vii, 261–90, 296, 306, 309, 329.

9. Stanley M. Elkins, *Slavery: A Problem in American Institutional and Intellectual Life*, 3rd ed. rev. (Chicago: University of Chicago Press, 1976), 6–7, 9–20, 82–89, 98–102.

10. Ann J. Lane, Introduction to *The Debate Over Slavery: Stanley Elkins and His Critics*, ed. Ann J. Lane (Urbana: University of Illinois Press, 1971), 10–11, 18.

11. Ira Berlin, *Generations of Captivity: A History of African-American Slaves* (Cambridge, MA: Harvard University Press; London: Belknap Press, 2003), 4. See also Eugene D. Genovese, *Roll, Jordan, Roll: The World the Slaves Made* (New York: Vintage, 1976); Kenneth M. Stampp, *The Peculiar Institution: Slavery in the Ante-Bellum South* (New York: Knopf, 1956); Herbert G. Gutman, *Slavery and the Numbers Game: A Critique of* Time on the Cross (Urbana: University of Illinois Press, 2003); John W. Blassingame, *The Slave Community: Plantation Life in the Antebellum South*, rev. ed. (Oxford: Oxford University Press, 1979); David Brion Davis, *Inhuman Bondage: The Rise and Fall of Slavery in the New World* (New York: Oxford University Press, 2006); Stanley Feldstein, *Once a Slave: The Slave's View of Slavery* (New York: Morrow, 1971); Charles Joyner, *Down by the Riverside: A South Carolina Slave Community* (Urbana: University of Illinois Press, 1984); Leslie Howard Owens, *This Species of Property: Slave Life and Culture in the Old South* (New York: Oxford University Press, 1976).

12. Ira Berlin, *Many Thousands Gone: The First Two Centuries of Slavery in North America* (Cambridge, MA: Harvard University Press, 1998); Steven M. Stowe, *Intimacy and Power in the Old South: Rituals in the Lives of the Planters* (Baltimore, MD: Johns Hopkins University Press, 1987); Drew Gilpin Faust, "Culture, Conflict, and Community: The Meaning of Power on an Ante-Bellum Plantation," *Journal of Social History* 14 (Autumn 1980): 84; Brenda E. Stevenson, *Life in Black & White: Family and Community in the Slave South* (New York: Oxford University Press, 1996), especially 179–83; Ariela Gross, *Double Character: Slavery and Mastery in the Antebellum Courtroom* (Princeton, NJ: Princeton University Press, 2000); Judith K. Schafer, "'Guaranteed Against the Vices and Maladies Prescribed by Law': Consumer Protection, the Law of Slave Sales, and the Supreme Court in Antebellum Louisiana," *American Journal of Legal History* 31 (October 1987): 306–21; Judith K. Schafer, *Slavery, the Civil Law, and the Supreme Court of Louisiana* (Baton Rouge: Louisiana State University Press, 1994); Michael Tadman, *Speculators and Slaves: Masters, Traders, and Slaves in the Old South* (Madison: University of Wisconsin Press, 1989); James W. Cook, *The Arts of Deception: Playing with Fraud in the Age of Barnum*

(Cambridge, MA: Harvard University Press, 2001), 1–12, 119–62; Benjamin Reiss, *The Showman and the Slave: Race, Death, and Memory in Barnum's America* (Cambridge, MA: Harvard University Press, 2001); Greenberg, *Honor and Slavery*; Stauffer, *Black Hearts of Men*.

13. Stephanie M. H. Camp and Edward E. Baptist, "Introduction: A History of the History of Slavery in the Americas," in New *Studies in the History of Slavery*, eds. Edward E. Baptist and Stephanie M. H. Camp (Athens: University of Georgia Press, 2006), 2.

14. Blassingame, *Slave Community*, 300–303.

15. Nell Irvin Painter, *Southern History across the Color Line* (Chapel Hill: University of North Carolina Press, 2002), 6, 21 (quote on 21).

16. For more general studies of nineteenth-century medicine and disease constructs, see Joan Burbick, *Healing the Republic: The Language of Health and the Culture of Nationalism in Nineteenth-Century America* (Cambridge: Cambridge University Press, 1994); Charles E. Rosenberg, "Framing Disease: Illness, Society, and History," in *Framing Disease: Studies in Cultural History*, eds. Charles E. Rosenberg and Janet Golden (New Brunswick, NJ: Rutgers University Press, 1992), xiii–xxvi; John Harley Warner, "The Idea of Southern Medical Distinctiveness: Medical Knowledge and Practice in the Old South," in *Science and Medicine in the Old South*, eds. Ronald L. Numbers and Todd L. Savitt (Baton Rouge: Louisiana State University Press, 1989), 179–205; Gerald N. Grob, *Edward Jarvis and the Medical World of Nineteenth-Century America* (Knoxville: University of Tennessee Press, 1978); Peter McCandless, *Moonlight, Magnolias, and Madness: Insanity in South Carolina from the Colonial Period to the Progressive Era* (Chapel Hill: University of North Carolina Press, 1996); Conevery Bolton Valencius, *The Health of the Country: How American Settlers Understood Themselves and their Land* (New York: Basic Books, 2002); Steven M. Stowe, "Seeing Themselves at Work: Physicians and the Case Narrative in the Mid-Nineteenth-Century American South," *American Historical Review* 101 (February 1996): 41–79. For histories of African American health, illness, and medical practices, see Eugene D. Genovese, "The Medical and Insurance Costs of Slaveholding in the Cotton Belt," *Journal of Negro History* 45 (July 1960): 141–55; Margaret Humphreys, *Intensely Human: The Health of the Black Soldier in the American Civil War* (Baltimore, MD: Johns Hopkins University Press, 2008); Katherine Bankole, *Slavery and Medicine: Enslavement and Medical Practices in Antebellum Louisiana* (New York: Garland, 1998); David McBride, "'Slavery as It Is': Medicine and Slaves of the Plantation South," *Magazine of History* 19 (1 September 2005): 36–39, http://www.proquest.com; William Dosite Postell, *The Health of Slaves on Southern Plantations* (Baton Rouge: Louisiana State University Press, 1951); William Dosite Postell, "Mental Health among the Slave Population on Southern Plantations," *American Journal of Psychiatry* 110 (July 1953): 52–54; Todd L. Savitt, "Slave Health and Southern Distinctiveness," in *Disease and Distinctiveness in the American South*, eds. Todd L. Savitt and James Harvey Young (Knoxville: University of Tennessee Press, 1988), 120–53; Steven M. Stowe, *Doctoring the South: Southern Physicians and Everyday Medicine in the Mid-Nineteenth Century* (Chapel Hill: University of North Carolina Press, 2004), 103–7, 208–18.

17. Felice Swados, "Negro Health on the Ante Bellum Plantations," *Bulletin of the History of Medicine* 10 (1941): 460, 472 (quote on 472); Richard H. Shryock, "Medical Practice in the Old South," *South Atlantic Quarterly* 29 (April 1930): 160–78; Richard H. Shryock, "Medical Sources and the Social Historian," *American Historical Review* 41 (April 1936): 458–73.

18. See Genovese, "Medical and Insurance Costs," 148–49; Tadman, *Speculators and Slaves*, 28–29, 237–38; Stowe, *Doctoring the South*, 103–7, 114–19; Kenneth F. Kiple and Virginia Himmelsteib King, *Another Dimension to the Black Diaspora: Diet, Disease, and Racism* (Cambridge: Cambridge University Press, 1981), xii, 76–77, 105–6, 117–18.

19. Todd L. Savitt, *Medicine and Slavery: The Diseases and Health Care of Blacks in Antebellum Virginia* (Urbana: University of Illinois Press, 1978), 3, 8, 47, 150; Todd L. Savitt, "The Use of Blacks for Medical Experimentation and Demonstration in the Old South," *Journal of Southern History* 48 (August 1982): 332, 334. More recently, Harriet A. Washington's *Medical Apartheid* illuminates the assessment of slave debility and the use of disabled slaves as experimental patients and clinical "specimens" in antebellum America. Washington devotes several chapters of her history of medical experimentation on African Americans to slaves, discussing physicians who made careers of guaranteeing slave "soundness," famous examples of experimentation conducted using enslaved subjects (particularly Thomas Hamilton's intentional induction of heat stroke and J. Marion Sims' surgical treatment for vesico-vaginal fistula), the use of black bodies (living and deceased) as clinical material for Southern medical students, and the popular display of disabled slave bodies in circuses. Although Washington calls attention to interesting and significant examples of slaves with disabilities and their treatment at the hands of white physicians, she draws problematic conclusions that are removed from historical context and attributes all of her findings to a monolithic concept of pseudoscientific racism, which Washington takes for granted as the standard of southern medical practice. Furthermore, the author neglects to analyze fully the concepts of disability that she presents, assuming a more essentialist, medicalized definition of disability when her focus shifts from assessments of "soundness" to atrocities perpetrated on debilitated black bodies. Harriet A. Washington, *Medical Apartheid: The Dark History of Medical Experimentation on Black Americans from Colonial Times to the Present* (New York: Doubleday, 2006), 26, 43, 52–74, 103–14.

20. See Savitt, *Medicine and Slavery*, 83, 247–79.

21. Sharla M. Fett, *Working Cures: Healing, Health, and Power on Southern Slave Plantations* (Chapel Hill: University of North Carolina Press, 2002), 2.

22. Ibid., 16.

23. Ibid., 20.

24. Ibid., 16, 21.

25. Walter Johnson, *Soul by Soul: Life inside the Antebellum Slave Market* (Cambridge, MA: Harvard University Press, 1999), 20, 134; see also 58, 119, 150, 157.

26. Ibid., 13–14, 19–20.

27. Gale Whiteneck, "Conceptual Models of Disability: Past, Present, and Future," in *Workshop on Disability in America: A New Look*, eds. Marilyn J. Field, Alan M. Jette, and Linda Martin (Washington, DC: National Academies Press, 2006), 56. See also Kudlick, "Disability History," 767; Lisa I. Iezzoni and Vicki A. Freedman, "Turning the Disability Tide: The Importance of Definitions," *Journal of the American Medical Association* 299 (23 January 2008): 332.

28. David T. Mitchell and Sharon L. Snyder, *Narrative Prosthesis: Disability and the Dependencies of Discourse* (Ann Arbor: University of Michigan Press, 2000), xiii; Lennard J. Davis, *Enforcing Normalcy: Disability, Deafness, and the Body* (London: Verso, 1995), xii–xiii; Linton, *Claiming Disability*, 6; Tobin Siebers, "Disability as Masquerade," *Literature and Medicine* 23 (Spring 2004): 4. See also Alan Gartner and Tom Joe, Introduction to *Images of the Disabled, Disabling Images* (New York: Praeger, 1987), 1.

29. Longmore and Umansky, "Introduction," 3, see also 2, 7.
30. Ibid., 7, 8. See also Kudlick, "Disability History," 765; Iezzoni and Freedman, "Turning the Disability Tide," 332–33; Julie Anderson, "Review Essay: Voices in the Darkness: Representations of Disability in Historical Research," *Journal of Contemporary History* 44, no. 1 (January 2009): 108.
31. See Kudlick, "Disability History"; Anderson, "Review Essay"; Baynton, "Disability and the Justification of Inequality"; Douglas C. Baynton, "Disability in History," *Disability Studies Quarterly* 28, no. 3 (Summer 2008), http://www.dsq-sds.org/article/view/108/108; Rosemarie Garland Thomson, *Extraordinary Bodies: Figuring Physical Disability in American Culture and Literature* (New York: Columbia University Press, 1997); Benjamin Reiss, *Theaters of Madness: Insane Asylums and Nineteenth-Century American Culture* (Chicago: University of Chicago Press, 2008); Kim E. Nielsen, "Historical Thinking and Disability History," *Disability Studies Quarterly* 28, no. 3 (Summer 2008), http://www.dsq-sds.org/article/view/107/107; Jerrold Hirsch and Karen Hirsch, "Disability in the Family? New Questions about the Southern Mill Village," *Journal of Social History* 35 (Summer 2002): 919–33; Diane Price Herndl, *Invalid Women: Figuring Feminine Illness in American Fiction and Culture, 1840–1940* (Chapel Hill: University of North Carolina Press, 1993), 5; Klages, *Woeful Afflictions*, 2–5.
32. See Hartman, *Scenes of Subjection*, 22.
33. Kudlick, "Disability History," 767, 773, 776, 782. See also Whiteneck, "Conceptual Models of Disability," 52; Audra Jennings, "Introduction: Disability and History," *Disability Studies Quarterly* 28, no. 3 (Summer 2008), http://www.dsq-sds.org/article/view/108/108.
34. Barbara J. Fields, "Ideology and Race in American History," in *Region, Race, and Reconstruction: Essays in Honor of C. Vann Woodward*, eds. J. Morgan Kousser and James M. McPherson (New York: Oxford University Press, 1982), 144.
35. See L. J. Davis, *Enforcing Normalcy*, xv, 2; Mitchell and Snyder, *Narrative Prosthesis*, 33; Baynton, "Disability and the Justification of Inequality," 37–41; Linton, *Claiming Disability*, 48; Andrew M. Fearnley, "Primitive Madness: Re-Writing the History of Mental Illness and Race," *Journal of the History of Medicine and Allied Sciences* 63 (April 2008): 246; Cynthia Wu, "'The Mystery of their Union': Cross-Cultural Legacies of the Original Siamese Twins" (PhD dissertation, University of Michigan, 2004), 12, 19–20; Ron Amundson, "Disability, Ideology, and Quality of Life: A Bias in Biomedical Ethics," in *Quality of Life and Human Difference: Genetic Testing, Healthcare, and Disability*, eds. David Wasserman, Jerome Bickerbach, and Robert Wachbroit (Cambridge: Cambridge University Press, 2005), 111–12.
36. Leonard Kriegel, "Uncle Tom and Tiny Tim: Some Reflections on the Cripple as Negro," *American Scholar* 38 (Summer 1969): 414, 416, 421.
37. David Mitchell and Sharon Snyder, "The Eugenic Atlantic: Race, Disability, and the Making of an International Eugenic Science, 1800–1945," *Disability & Society* 18 (December 2003): 843–45, 851 (quote on 851).
38. Klages, *Woeful Afflictions*, 147–53. See also Barbara Baumgartner, "The Body as Evidence: Resistance, Collaboration, and Appropriation in 'The History of Mary Prince,'" *Callaloo* 24 (Winter 2001): 261.
39. Jerrold Hirsch and Karen Hirsch have conducted research on representations of disability in WPA ex-slave narratives collected in the 1930s. See Jerrold Hirsch and Karen Hirsch, "Disability and Ex-Slave Narratives," H-Civwar Post (30 June 1994), http://www.h-net.org/~civwar/logs/archives/log9406/0100.html. More recently, Jenifer Barclay completed a PhD dissertation entitled "'Cripples All! Or, the Mark of Slavery': Disability and Race

in Antebellum America, 1820–1860" (Michigan State University, 2011), and Daina Ramey Berry and Deleso A. Alford, eds., *Enslaved Women in America: An Encyclopedia* (Westport, CT: ABC-CLIO/Greenwood, 2012) contains entries that address issues of disability. In 2001 poet, lecturer, and disability rights advocate Leroy Moore published an appeal for more research that combine disability studies and African American history. Leroy Moore, "Buried Alive Not Dead," *Poor Magazine Online* (5 March 2001), http://www.poormagazine.org/index.cfm?L1 = news&story = 2.

40. Jim Downs, "The Continuation of Slavery: The Experience of Disabled Slaves during Emancipation," *Disability Studies Quarterly* 28 no. 3 (Summer 2008), http://www.dsq-sds.org/article/view/112/112.

41. Anderson, "Review Essay," 108.

42. See Savitt, *Medicine and Slavery*, 104.

43. Berlin, *Generations of Captivity*, 168–69.

44. Paul Gilroy, *The Black Atlantic: Modernity and Double Consciousness* (Cambridge, MA: Harvard University Press, 1993), 4, 7, 13–17; Berlin, *Generations of Captivity*, 17, 188; Camp and Baptist, "Introduction," 9–10, 12. In her study of Nancy Prince's narrative, Sandra Gunning agrees with this perspective but warns that an overemphasis on the cultural identity of a "black diaspora" could ignore important intraracial differences based on skin color, gender, status, and region. Sandra Gunning, "Nancy Prince and the Politics of Mobility, Home and Diasporic (Mis)identification," *American Quarterly* 53 (March 2001): 33.

45. Gilroy, *Black Atlantic*, 13, 16–17; Berlin, *Generations of Captivity*, 188; Clark, "'Sacred Rights of the Weak,'" 468.

46. D. B. Davis, *Inhuman Bondage*, 183; Berlin, *Generations of Captivity*, 16.

47. According to Richard H. Steckel's statistical study of trends in the African American population in the United States, 97.7% of slaves in 1790 lived in Delaware, Maryland, Washington, DC, Virginia, Georgia, and the Carolinas. That percentage had declined to 45% by the eve of the Civil War, and the remaining 55% had been relocated to the "New South" states of Kentucky, Tennessee, Missouri, Florida, Alabama, Mississippi, Arkansas, Louisiana, and Texas. Richard H. Steckel, "The African American Population of the United States, 1790–1920," in *A Population History of North America*, eds. Michael R. Haines and Richard H. Steckel (New York: Cambridge University Press, 2000), 433–82, cited in Laird W. Bergad, *The Comparative Histories of Slavery in Brazil, Cuba, and the United States* (New York: Cambridge University Press, 2007), 117.

48. Berlin, *Generations of Captivity*, 214; Edward E. Baptist, "'Stol' and Fetched Here': Enslaved Migration, Ex-slave Narratives, and Vernacular History," in *New Studies in the History of Slavery*, eds. Edward E. Baptist and Stephanie M. H. Camp (Athens: University of Georgia Press, 2006), 244; Leslie J. Pollard, *Complaint to the Lord: Historical Perspectives on the African American Elderly* (Selinsgrove: Susquehanna University Press; London: Associated University Presses, 1996), 32; Savitt, *Medicine and Slavery*, 201.

49. Berlin, *Generations of Captivity*, 18; D. B. Davis, *Inhuman Bondage*, 128, 175. Davis makes a distinction between "societies with slaves" and "slave societies," arguing that colonial North America fell into the former category whereas colonies in the West Indies fell into the latter, but agrees with Berlin that the United States had become a "slave society" by the nineteenth century.

50. Wickberg, "Heterosexual White Male," paragraph 33.

51. Beginning in the late 1830s, abolitionists began to take advantage of new forms of visual culture, and antislavery images—most popularly the kneeling supplicant—began to appear in books, pamphlets, etchings, broadsheets,

periodicals and almanacs, candy wrappers, envelope stickers, song sheets, stationery, and china patterns. See Lapsansky, "Graphic Discord," 202, 206.

52. Clark, "'Sacred Rights of the Weak,'" 480–81; Prude, "To Look Upon the 'Lower Sort,'" 137. For examples, see "Slavery a System of Inherent Cruelty," in *Five Hundred Thousand Strokes for Freedom*, Leeds Anti-Slavery Series, no. 7 (Miami, FL: Mnemosyne, 1969. Originally published London: W. & F. Cash; William Tweedie, 1853), 6; Theodore Dwight Weld, *American Slavery as It Is: Testimony of a Thousand Witnesses* (New York: American Anti-Slavery Society, 1839), 55, 82.

53. Fabian, *Unvarnished Truth*, 2; Gilbert Osofsky, "Introduction. Puttin' on Ole Massa: The Significance of Slave Narratives," in *Puttin' on Ole Massa: The Slave Narratives of Henry Bibb, William Wells Brown, and Solomon Northup* (New York: Harper & Row, 1969), 11. Most antebellum ex-slave narratives were written by male slaves who had escaped from the Upper South. John Blassingame notes although the demographic of ex-slave authors was certainly not representative of the entire enslaved population in the United States, their perspective should not be dismissed, because most biographers in United States literary history have been exceptional. See John W. Blassingame, Introduction to *Slave Testimony: Two Centuries of Letters, Speeches, Interviews, and Autobiographies*, ed. John W. Blassingame (Baton Rouge: Louisiana State University Press, 1977), xvii–lxv.

54. Sterling Lecater Bland Jr., *Voices of the Fugitives: Runaway Slave Stories and Their Fictions of Self-Creation* (Westport, CT: Greenwood Press, 2000), 3–4.

55. John W. Blassingame, "Using the Testimony of Ex-slaves: Approaches and Problems," *Journal of Southern History* 41 (November 1975): 474; Blassingame, "Introduction," xviii. See also Osofsky, "Introduction," 12–13.

56. Baumgartner, "The Body as Evidence," 254, 261, 267; Arna Bontemps, "The Slave Narrative: An American Genre," in *Great Slave Narratives*, ed. Arna Bontemps (Boston: Beacon Press, 1969), xv–xviii; Blassingame, "Using Testimony," 478.

57. See Sekora, "Black Message/White Envelope," 509; Blassingame, "Introduction," xli.

58. See Harriet Newby to [Dangerfield Newby], Brentville (16 August 1859), in Blassingame, *Slave Testimony*, 116–18; Cyfax Brown to [St George Tucker], Prince Edward (15 May 1822), in Blassingame, *Slave Testimony*, 9–10; Samuel Robertson to [Louisa Lord], Charleston (16 April 1857), Louisa Lord Papers, 1850–1862, Correspondence 1856–1858, South Carolina Historical Society, Charleston.

59. Blassingame, "Introduction," lxiii–lxiv.

60. See Baptist, "'Stol' and Fetched Here,'" 245–48.

61. Blassingame, "Using Testimony," 484; Blassingame, "Introduction," xlii–xlviii. See also Joyner, *Down by the Riverside*, xv–xvi; Valencius, *Health of the Country*, 8; Stowe, *Doctoring the South*, 118; Baptist, "'Stol' and Fetched Here,'" 246; Hirsch and Hirsch, "Disability in the Family?" 919; Hirsch and Hirsch, "Disability and Ex-slave Narratives."

NOTES TO CHAPTER 2

1. *The Life of Joice Heth, the Nurse of Gen. George Washington, (the Father of Our Country,) Now Living at the Astonishing Age of 161 Years, and Weighs Only 46 Pounds* (New York, 1835), 7.

2. P. T. Barnum, *The Life of P. T. Barnum, Written by Himself* (London: Sampson Low, Son & Co., 1855), 148–49. See also Reiss, *The Showman and the Slave*, 19–20, 134–35, 139; Cook, *The Arts of Deception*, 5, 8.

3. D. Tilden Brown, "Theatrical Performances at the New York State Lunatic Asylum," *Medical Examiner* 3 (April 1847): 260, cited in Reiss, *Theaters of Madness*, 60. This aim was reflected in reactions noted in the patient newsletter, which had significant editorial input from administrators: a review of the November 1854 performance noted "more merry and jocund laughter we have never heard, and the happy effect it produced upon our children speaks volumes in favor of these exhibitions, both as a remedial agent and promoter of happiness and contentment here." "Negro Melodies," *The Opal* (December 1854), http://www.disabilitymuseum.org/lib/docs/1318.htm?page = 1. For more discussion of interpreting patient voices in *The Opal*, see Benjamin Reiss, "Letters from Asylumia: The *Opal* and the Cultural Work of the Lunatic Asylum, 1851–1860," *American Literary History* 16 (2004): 1–28.
4. "Negro Melodies."
5. Hartman, *Scenes of Subjection*, 26, 87. See also Klages, *Woeful Afflictions*, 12–13; Reiss, *Showman and Slave*, 6, 9; Cook, *Arts of Deception*, 121.
6. One prevalent tale of blackface minstrelsy's origins is that T. D. Rice developed the first American routine in the 1840s after observing a disabled slave, but English literature scholar W. T. Lhamon Jr. presents compelling evidence that minstrelsy actually had been an early-nineteenth-century display among black and white workers alike in upstate New York before becoming a popular middle-class, "white" form of entertainment in the 1840s. W. T. Lhamon Jr., *Raising Cain: Blackface Performance from Jim Crow to Hip Hop* (Cambridge, MA: Harvard University Press, 1998), 1–7, 22, 35–40. See also Reiss, *Theaters of Madness*, 52, 60.
7. A. P. Merrill, "An Essay on Some of the Distinctive Peculiarities of the Negro Race," *Memphis Medical Recorder* 4 (July 1855): 4; John S. Haller Jr., "The Negro and the Southern Physician: A Study of Medical and Racial Attitudes 1800–1860," *Medical History* 16 (July 1972): 252; Ariela J. Gross, "Pandora's Box: Slave Character on Trial in the Antebellum Deep South," *Yale Journal of Law and the Humanities* 7 (1995): 281–83, 288; Mitchell and Snyder, "The Eugenic Atlantic," 848–50.
8. Baynton, "Disability and the Justification of Inequality," 35; E. B. Clark, "'The Sacred Rights of the Weak,'" 471–72.
9. L. J. Davis, *Enforcing Normalcy*, 24; Martin S. Pernick, "Defining Disability: The History and Implications of Pre-ADA Controversies," paper presented at *The Americans with Disabilities Act: Directions for Reform* symposium, sponsored by The University of Michigan Journal of Law Reform (Ann Arbor, Michigan, 4 November 2000), 5.
10. Burbick, *Healing the Republic*, 2, 7.
11. Cindy LaCom, "'It Is More than Lame': Female Disability, Sexuality, and the Maternal in the Nineteenth-Century Novel," in *The Body and Physical Difference: Discourses of Disability*, eds. David T. Mitchell and Sharon L. Snyder (Ann Arbor: University of Michigan Press, 1997), 190.
12. Greenberg, *Honor and Slavery*, 15.
13. Erving Goffman, *Stigma: Notes on the Management of Spoiled Identity* (Englewood Cliffs, NJ: Prentice Hall, [1963]), 2–4.
14. See Jennifer L. Morgan, "'Some Could Suckle over Their Shoulder': Male Travelers, Female Bodies, and the Gendering of Racial Ideology," in *New Studies in the History of Slavery*, eds. Edward E. Baptist and Stephanie M. H. Camp (Athens: University of Georgia Press, 2006), 23; Carla L. Peterson, *"Doers of the Word": African-American Women Speakers and Writers in the North (1830–1880)* (New York: Oxford University Press, 1995), 21; Anderson, "Review Essay," 109.

15. Baynton, "Disability and Justification of Inequality," 33–34, 39 (quote on 39). See also Mitchell and Snyder, "Eugenic Atlantic," 852.
16. Samuel A. Cartwright, "Philosophy of the Negro Constitution," *New Orleans Medical & Surgical Journal* 9 (1853): 195.
17. Ibid., 199–202; Samuel A. Cartwright, "Slavery in the Light of Ethnology," in *Cotton is King, and Proslavery Arguments*, ed. E. N. Elliott (Augusta, GA: Pritchard, Abbott & Loomis, 1860), 695–99.
18. Thomas Jefferson, *Jefferson's Notes on the State of Virginia; with the Appendixes—Complete* (Baltimore: W. Pechin, 1800), 143.
19. Merrill, "Essay on Some . . . Distinctive Peculiarities," 3.
20. Susan J. Matt, "You Can't Go Home Again: Homesickness and Nostalgia in U.S. History," *Journal of American History* 94 (September 2007): 477. See also Lindon Barrett, "Hand-Writing: Legibility and the White Body in *Running a Thousand Miles for Freedom*," *American Literature* 69 (June 1997): 318, 332.
21. Gilroy, *The Black Atlantic*, 8; W. Michael Byrd and Linda A. Clayton, *An American Health Dilemma: A Medical History of African Americans and the Problem of Race, Beginnings to 1900* (New York: Routledge, 2000), 1:296–99; R. Dunglison, *Human Physiology with Three Hundred and Sixty-Eight Illustrations*, 2 vols., 6th ed. (Philadelphia: Lea and Blanchard, 1846), 631, cited in Byrd and Clayton, *American Health Dilemma*, 301; H. A. Ramsay, "The Pulse, Cranial Dimensions, &c., of the Southern Negro Child, with some Remarks upon Infantile Therapeutics," *Boston Medical & Surgical Journal* 48 (1853): 396–97; Stowe, *Doctoring the South*, 216; Mitchell and Snyder, "Eugenic Atlantic," 847–48. David Brion Davis has argued that the Biblical "Curse of Ham" argument, which disagreed with the notion of polygenesis, was a more prominent element of proslavery arguments in the South. D. B. Davis, *Inhuman Bondage*, 187, 189.
22. Richard D. Arnold to A. P. Merrill (23 May 1854), in Shryock, *Letters of Richard D. Arnold*, 66–67.
23. See Deborah Gray White, *Ar'n't I a Woman? Female Slaves in the Plantation South*, rev. ed. (New York: Norton, 1999), 43; Martin S. Pernick, *a Calculus of Suffering: Pain, Professionalism, and Anesthesia in Nineteenth-Century America* (New York: Columbia University Press, 1985), 156–57.
24. Josiah C. Nott, "The Mulatto a Hybrid—Probable Extermination of the Two Races if the Whites and Blacks Are Allowed to Intermarry," *American Journal of the Medical Sciences* 6 (July 1843): 253–54 (quote on 253).
25. Ibid., 253; also quoted in Samuel Forry, "Vital Statistics Furnished by the Sixth Census of the United States, Bearing upon the Question of the Unity of the Human Race," *New York Journal of Medicine, and the Collateral Sciences* 1 (September 1843): 158. See also Peterson, "*Doers of the Word*," 158.
26. Forry, "Vital Statistics," 159–61.
27. H. A. Ramsay, "The Southern Negro, etc.," *Philadelphia Medical & Surgical Journal* 1 (1852–53): 295. The disease construct of erethism indicated a morbid excitability that was linked with emotional and sexual volatility, a condition that would have had severe behavioral and disciplinary implications in southern slave society.
28. Merrill, "Essay on Some . . . Distinctive Peculiarities," 70–71 (quote on 71).
29. John H. Van Evrie, *White Supremacy and Negro Subordination, or Negroes a Subordinate Race* (New York: Van Evrie, Horton), 1868. See also Davis, *Inhuman Bondage*, 188–89; Haller, "Negro and Southern Physician," 253; Baynton, "Disability and Justification of Inequality," 38.
30. Josiah C. Nott, "Statistics of Southern Slave Population, with Especial Reference to Life Insurance," *DeBow's Review* 4 (November 1847): 288.

31. Josiah C. Nott, *Two Lectures, on the Natural History of the Caucasian and Negro Races* (Mobile, AL: Dade & Thompson, 1844), 19.
32. Nott, *Two Lectures*, 29–30; exclamation points are included in the original.
33. See Harriet Beecher Stowe, *A Key to Uncle Tom's Cabin: Presenting the Original Facts and Documents upon Which the Story is Founded* (London: T. Bosworth, 1853), 258–59; Samuel Forry, "On the Relative Proportion of Centenarians, of Deaf and Dumb, of Blind, and of Insane, in the Races of European and African Origin, as Shown by the Census of the United States," *New York Journal of Medicine and the Collateral Sciences* 2 (May 1844): 312; Forry, "Vital Statistics," 167; Benjamin Pasamanick, "Myths Regarding Prevalence of Mental Disease in the American Negro," *Journal of the National Medical Association* 56 (January 1964): 6–8; Herbert W. Morais, *The History of the Negro in Medicine* (New York: Publishers Co. Inc. for the Association for the Study of Negro Life and History, 1967), 208–9.
34. Baynton, "Disability and Justification of Inequality," 39. See also Forry, "On Relative Proportion of Centenarians," 314; Forry, "Vital Statistics," 155.
35. Thornton Stringfellow, *Scriptural and Statistical Views in Favor of Slavery*, 4th ed. (Richmond, VA: J. W. Randolph, 1856), 128.
36. A Citizen of Mississippi, "The Negro," *DeBow's Review* 3 (May 1847): 419.
37. A Professional Planter [Dr. Collins], *Practical Rules for the Management and Medical Treatment of Negro Slaves, in the Sugar Colonies* (London: printed by J. Barfield for Vernor, Hood and Sharp; Hatchard, 1811. repr. Freeport, NY: Books for Libraries Press, 1971), 31. See also 29–30.
38. William L. McCaa, "Observations on the Manner of Living and Diseases of the Slaves of the Wateree River" (M.D. Thesis, University of Pennsylvania, 1822), 2. See also Kiple and Himmelsteib King, *Another Dimension to the Black Diaspora*, xii.
39. Cartwright, "Slavery in Light of Ethnology," 692–93.
40. Berlin, *Generations of Captivity*, 214; Savitt, *Medicine and Slavery*, 201; Baptist, "'Stol' and 'Fetched Here'", 244; Pollard, *Complaint to the Lord*, 32.
41. McCaa, "Observations," 3. Forry also noted that the number black slaves who reached "extreme" old age was higher than whites, although he suggested that this may have been due to slaves exaggerating their real age rather than an innate biological difference between the races. Forry, "On Relative Proportion of Centenarians," 314, 320.
42. See Reiss, *Showman and Slave*, 42–44.
43. F. Perry Pope, "A Dissertation on the Professional Management of Negro Slaves" (M.D. Thesis, Medical College of the State of South Carolina, 1837), Waring Historical Library, Medical University of South Carolina, Charleston, 6; McCaa, "Observations," 6.
44. Merrill, "Essay on Some . . . Distinctive Peculiarities," 16. See also Pernick, *Calculus of Suffering*, 154–60. Some abolitionists argued against assertions that African Americans were less sensitive to pain, while others, notably Lydia Maria Child, argued that insensitivity to pain was an adaptation to the cruel conditions of slavery. See Savitt, "The Use of Blacks for Medical Experimentation," 341; Clark, "'Sacred Rights of the Weak,'" 473–74.
45. Cartwright, "Philosophy of the Negro Constitution," 197.
46. Samuel A. Cartwright, "The Diseases and Physical Peculiarities of the Negro Race," *Southern Medical Reports* 2 (1850): 427; Charles S. Johnson and Horace M. Bond, "The Investigation of Racial Differences Prior to 1910," *Journal of Negro Education* 3 (July 1934): 334.
47. Samuel A. Cartwright, "Dr. Cartwright on the Caucasians and the Africans," *DeBow's Review* 25 (July 1858): 47.

48. Cartwright, "Philosophy of the Negro Constitution," 203–4.
49. For background on intellectual foundations of the abolitionist movement and the role of sentimentality and suffering in antislavery propaganda, see Bergad, *The Comparative Histories* , 257, 260–62; D. B. Davis, *Inhuman Bondage*, 16, 260; Pernick, *Calculus of Suffering*, 78–79, 117; E. B. Clark, "'Sacred Rights of the Weak,'" 463.
50. John G. Fee, *Autobiography of John G. Fee, Berea, Kentucky* (Chicago: National Christian Association, 1891), 16.
51. William L. Andrews, *To Tell a Free Story: The First Century of Afro-American Autobiography, 1760–1865* (Urbana: University of Illinois Press, 1986), 11.
52. See George M. Fredrickson, *The Black Image in the White Mind: The Debate on Afro-American Character and Destiny, 1817–1914* (New York: Harper & Row, 1971), 38; D. B. Davis, *Inhuman Bondage*, 253, 260.
53. See Baynton, "Disability and Justification of Inequality," 36; Burbick, *Healing the Republic*, 3–4.
54. Baynton, "Disability and Justification of Inequality," 36.
55. Patrick Rael, *Black Identity and Black Protest in the Antebellum North* (Chapel Hill: University of North Carolina Press, 2002), 172–73.
56. Klages, *Woeful Afflictions*, 11.
57. Ellen Samuels, "'A Complication of Complaints': Untangling Disability, Race, and Gender in William Craft's *Running a Thousand Miles to Freedom*," *MELUS* 31 (Fall 2006): 518.
58. James Redpath, *The Roving Editor: Or, Talks with Slaves in the Southern States* (New York: A. B. Burdick, 1859, repr. New York: Negro Universities Press, 1968), 263.
59. *Eighth Annual Report of the Board of Managers of the Mass. Anti-Slavery Society* (22 January 1840), xviii. Samuel J. May Anti-Slavery Collection, Division of Rare and Manuscript Collections, Cornell University Library, http://digital.library.cornell.edu:80/m/mayantislavery.
60. Jermain Wesley Loguen, *The Rev. J. W. Loguen, as a Slave and as a Freeman: A Narrative of Real Life* (Syracuse: J.G.K. Truair & Co., 1859), 122.
61. John Thompson, *The Life of John Thompson, a Fugitive Slave: Containing His History of 25 Years in Bondage, and His Providential Escape* (Worcester: John Thompson, 1856), 38.
62. [Interview with Reverend Nelson Hammock, b. 1842] in *Weevils in the Wheat: Interviews with Virginia Ex-Slaves*, eds. Charles L. Perdue Jr., Thomas E. Barden, and Robert K. Phillips (Bloomington: Indiana University Press, 1976), 127; Norman Yetman, *Life under the "Peculiar Institution": Selections from the Slave Narrative Collection* (New York: Hold, Rinehart and Winston, 1970), 14.
63. Baynton, "Disability and Justification of Inequality," 41; Leonard Kriegel, "The Cripple in Literature," in *Images of the Disabled, Disabling Images*, eds. Alan Gartner and Tom Joe (New York: Praeger, 1987), 32; DeLombard, "'Eye-Witness to the Cruelty,'" 249, 256.
64. Frederick Douglass, *Narrative of the Life of Frederick Douglass, an American Slave* (New York: Viking Penguin, 1986. Originally published Boston: Anti-Slavery Office, 1845), 55–56; see also Frederick Douglass, *Life and Times of Frederick Douglass, Written By Himself . . .*, rev. ed., 137–38 (Boston: De Wolfe & Fiske Co., 1892).
65. *Anti-slavery Songs: A Selection from the Best Anti-slavery Authors.* (Salem, OH: Trescott, 1849), 14. The song also appears in William Wells Brown, *Clotel; or, The President's Daughter: A Narrative of Slave Life in the United States* (London: Partridge & Oakey, 1853). Another example of a disabled boy separated from a maternal figure (in this case, an older sister) is found

in Martha Griffith Browne, *Autobiography of a Female Slave* (New York: Redfield, 1857), 177.

66. President Hitchcock, "The Blind Slave of the Mines," *North Star* (24 November 1848).

67. Stephanie M. H. Camp, "The Pleasures of Resistance: Enslaved Women and Body Politics in the Plantation South, 1830–1861," in *New Studies in the History of Slavery*, eds. Edward E. Baptist and Stephanie M. H. Camp (Athens: University of Georgia Press, 2006), 90. See also Fett, *Working Cures*, 16.

68. Lawrence W. Levine, *Black Culture and Black Consciousness: Afro-American Folk Thought from Slavery to Freedom* (Oxford: Oxford University Press, 1977), 103. See also Joyner, *Down by the Riverside*, 174.

69. See Levine, *Black Culture and Black Consciousness*, 97; D. B. Davis, *Inhuman Bondage*, 195.

70. Elsie Clews Parsons, *Folk-Lore of the Sea Islands, South Carolina* (Cambridge, MA: American Folk-Lore Society, 1923), 117, cited in Norrece T. Jones Jr., *Born a Child of Freedom, Yet a Slave: Mechanisms of Control and Strategies of Resistance in Antebellum South Carolina* (Hanover: Wesleyan University Press; London: University Press of New England, 1990), 134.

71. See Fett, *Working Cures*, 58; Marie Jenkins Schwartz, *Birthing a Slave: Motherhood and Medicine in the Antebellum South* (Cambridge, MA: Harvard University Press, 2006), 12; Pollard, *Complaint to the Lord*, 51. For the primary role of religion in slave culture and worldviews, see Blassingame, *The Slave Community*; Vincent Brown, "Spiritual Terror and Sacred Authority: The Power of the Supernatural in Jamaican Slave Society," in *New Studies in the History of Slavery*, eds. Edward E. Baptist and Stephanie M. H. Camp (Athens: University of Georgia Press, 2006), 179–210; Margaret Washington Creel, "*A Peculiar People*": *Slave Religion and Community-Culture among the Gullahs* (New York: New York University Press, 1988); Elliott J. Gorn, "Black Magic: Folk Beliefs of the Slave Community," in *Science and Medicine in the Old South*, eds. Ronald L. Numbers and Todd L. Savitt (Baton Rouge: Louisiana State University Press, 1989), 295–326; Levine, *Black Culture and Black Consciousness*.

72. *A Sketch in the Life of Thomas Greene Bethune (Blind Tom)* (Philadelphia: Ledger Book and Job Printing Establishment, 1865), 7.

73. Wilson Armistead, *A Tribute for the Negro: Being a Vindication of the Moral, Intellectual, and Religious Capabilities of the Coloured Portion of Mankind* (Manchester: William Irwin; New York: William Harned, Anti-Slavery Office, 1848), 356.

74. Ibid., 547–48.

75. [Charlotte] Forten, "Life on the Sea Islands, Part II," *Atlantic Monthly* 80 (June 1864): 672; see also Creel, "*A Peculiar People*," 265.

76. Rael, *Black Identity and Black Protest*, 5. See also Mia Bay, "See Your Declaration Americans!!! Abolitionism, Americanism, and the Revolutionary Tradition in Free Black Politics," in *Americanism: New Perspectives on the History of an Ideal*, eds. Michael Kazin and Joseph A. McCartin (Chapel Hill: University of North Carolina Press, 2006), 39.

77. Elaine Scarry, *The Body in Pain: The Making and Unmaking of the World* (New York: Oxford University Press, 1985), 170; L. J. Davis, *Enforcing Normalcy*, 92.

78. Peterson, "*Doers of the Word*," 21.

79. See Pollard, *Complaint to the Lord*, 52.

80. D. B. Davis, *Inhuman Bondage*, 196.

81. [James Curry], "Narrative of James Curry," in *Slave Testimony: Two Centuries of Letters, Speeches, Interviews, and Autobiographies*, ed. John W. Blassingame (Baton Rouge: Louisiana State University Press, 1977), 134.

82. James L. Smith, *Autobiography of James L. Smith, Including, Also, Reminiscences of Slave Life, Recollections of the War, Education of Freedmen, Causes of the Exodus, Etc.* (Norwich: Press of the Bulletin Company, 1881), 2–3, 98 (quote on 98).

83. F. Douglass, *Life and Times*, 140.

84. [Harriet Jacobs], *Incidents in the Life of a Slave Girl: Written by Herself*, ed. Lydia Maria Child (Boston, 1861), 150.

85. [Interview with Harriet Tubman], *Freedmen's Record* 1 (March 1865), 34–38, cited in Blassingame, *Slave Testimony*, 461. In 1857 Tubman did help her parents escape using a wagon because "they were too feeble to walk," but noted that it "added greatly to the perils of the journey" (459).

86. Charles Ball, *Fifty Years in Chains; or, the Life of an American Slave* (New York: H. Dayton; Indianapolis, IN: Asher & Company, 1859), 355–56.

87. Smith, *Autobiography*, 43.

88. John Hope Franklin and Loren Schweininger, *Runaway Slaves: Rebels on the Plantation* (New York: Oxford University Press, 1999), 233.

89. *Richmond Enquirer* (30 August 1808), cited in Daniel Meaders, ed., *Advertisements for Runaway Slaves in Virginia, 1801–1820* (New York: Garland, 1997), 107.

90. *Milledgeville Recorder* (6 November 1838), cited in T. D. Weld, *American Slavery as It Is*, 168.

91. *New Orleans Picayune* (16 May 1840) and *New Orleans Bee* (27 June 1829, 29 October 1829), cited in Franklin and Schweininger, *Runaway Slaves*, 39.

92. Smith, *Autobiography*, 7, 11–12.

93. Lydia Maria Child [and Lewis Clarke], "Leaves from a Slave's Journal of Life," in *The Anti-Slavery Standard* (27 October 1842), cited in Blassingame, *Slave Testimony*, 163.

NOTES TO CHAPTER 3

1. "Plantatino [*sic*] Journal of Coffee Bluf for the year 1838 Beginning the Fifth of February" (14), George J. Kollock Plantation Journals, Southern Historical Collection, University of North Carolina, Chapel Hill, Subseries 1.1, Box 1, Folder 2 (5 February–28 November 1838), Southern Historical Collection, University of North Carolina, Chapel Hill.

2. George J. Kollock Plantation Book (4), George J. Kollock Plantation Journals, Subseries 1.3, Box 1, Folder 7 (1849), Southern Historical Collection, University of North Carolina, Chapel Hill.

3. Plantation Book, Ossabaw Island, 1850 (36–38), George J. Kollock Plantation Journals, Subseries 1.3, Box 1, Folder 12 (1855). The mention of "1 Blind" slave appears again on 1 November (94).

4. Fett, *Working Cures*, 18–20.

5. Juriah Harriss, "What Constitutes Unsoundness in the Negro?" *Savannah Journal of Medicine* 1 (September 1858): 147 (italics in original).

6. Ibid., 151.

7. Harriss, "What Constitutes Unsoundness in the Negro?," 11.

8. Cartwright, "Diseases and Physical Peculiarities," 427. See also Valencius, *The Health of the Country*, 244.

9. T. D. Weld, *American Slavery as It Is*, 135–36.

10. Postell, *The Health of Slaves*, 159–63.
11. See Prude, "To Look Upon the 'Lower Sort,'" 143.
12. McCaa, "Observations on the Manner of Living," 5.
13. Gorn, "Black Magic," 303. See also Herbert J. Gutman, *The Black Family in Slavery and Freedom, 1750–1925* (New York: Pantheon, 1976), 278; Owens, *This Species of Property*, 42; Albert J. Raboteau, *Slave Religion: The "Invisible Institution" in the Antebellum South* (New York: Oxford University Press, 1978), 14, 33, 82, 276; Creel, "*A Peculiar People*," 56, 58, 315; Joyner, *Down by the Riverside*, 146.
14. F. Douglass, *Life and Times of Frederick Douglass*, 46–47.
15. William Wells Brown, *My Southern Home: Or, the South and Its People* (Boston: A. G. Brown, 1880), 70.
16. Gorn, "Black Magic," 317. See also D. B. Davis, *Inhuman Bondage*, 203; Owens, *This Species of Property*, 35; Fett, *Working Cures*, 84–108.
17. Henry Clay Bruce, *The New Man: Twenty-Nine Years a Slave. Twenty-Nine Years a Free Man* (York, PA: P. Anstadt & Sons, 1895), 53; Cartwright, "Dr. Cartwright on the Caucasians and the Africans," 52; "Serpent Worship Among the Negroes," *DeBow's Review* 31 (July 1861): 98; Owens, *This Species of Property*, 43; Gorn, "Black Magic," 317; Fett, *Working Cures*, 93.
18. "Recollections of a Runaway Slave," *The Emancipator* (11 October 1838). See also Savitt, *Medicine and Slavery*, 83, 104, 106; Theodore Rosengarten, *Tombee: Portrait of a Cotton Planter* (New York: William Morrow, 1986), 156; Swados, "Negro Health on the Ante Bellum Plantations," 471; Stampp, *The Peculiar Institution*, 185–86, 303.
19. The modern medical construct of pica—which is sometimes linked with cultural practices as well as with iron deficiency—is more complex and controversial than nineteenth-century constructs of dirt-eating in Africans. Kiple and King, *Another Dimension to the Black Diaspora*, 119–22.
20. Phillip D. Morgan, "The Poor: Slaves in Early America," in *Slavery in the Development of the Americas*, eds. David Eltis, Frank D. Lewis, and Kenneth L. Sokoloff (Cambridge: Cambridge University Press, 2004), 304; Richard H. Shryock, "Medical Practice in the Old South," *South Atlantic Quarterly* 29 (April 1930): 160–61; Tadman, *Speculators and Slaves*, 185; Postell, *Health of Slaves*, 85; Owens, *This Species of Property*, 52, 57–61.
21. Meaders, *Advertisements*, 22, 42, 50, 90, 129, 141, 142, 146, 159–61, 163, 173, 197, 206, 220, 232, 243, 261, 289, 321, 324. See also Kiple and King, *Another Dimension to the Black Diaspora*, 105–6.
22. Richard D. Arnold to Heber Chase (13 October 1836), in Shryock, *Letters of Richard D. Arnold*, 13; Richard D. Arnold to Samuel C. Sheppard (3 September 1838) in Shryock, *Letters of Richard D. Arnold*, 19; Stampp, *Peculiar Institution*, 306; A Professional Planter [Dr. Collins], 370–71, 432–34.
23. See Edwin Adams Davis, ed., *Plantation Life in the Florida Parishes of Louisiana, 1836–1846, as Reflected in the Diary of Bennet H. Barrow* (New York: Columbia University Press, 1943), 79; Frederic Bancroft, *Slave Trading in the Old South* (Baltimore: J. H. Furst, 1931), Southern Classics Series, ed. John G. Sproat (Columbia: University of South Carolina Press, 1996), 179; Savitt, *Medicine and Slavery*, 135.
24. Harriss, "What Constitutes Unsoundness in the Negro?" (May 1859), 12; John Nevitt Record Book, 15 December 1828 (170), Box 1, Folder 5 (typescript of Volume, 131–200, 10 May 1828—13 May 1829), Southern Historical Collection, University of North Carolina, Chapel Hill; Postell, *Health of Slaves*, 88. For examples of runaways with swelling or "sore" legs, see *Richmond Enquirer* (5 July 1815), cited in Meaders, *Advertise-*

ments, 253; *Alexandria Gazette and Daily Advertiser* (3 June 1817), cited in Meaders, *Advertisements*, 300; *Richmond Enquirer* (15 May 1807), cited in Franklin and Schweininger, *Runaway Slaves*, 216n16.

25. T. P. Bailey, "Surgical Cases," *Charleston Medical Journal and Review* 14 (November 1859): 740. For examples of slaves described as having "sore leg," see Henry Ravenel Day Book 1816–1834 (7 April 1818; 18 December 1824 entries), Thomas P. Ravenel Collection, 12-313-7, South Carolina Historical Society, Charleston; Langdon Cheves to [Son], Columbia (12 April 1853), Langdon Cheves Papers, Correspondence January–May 1855, 12-49-1, South Carolina Historical Society, Charleston; *For Sale by Shingler Brothers/7 Broad Street, /Charleston, S. C./A Remarkably Prime Gang of 235 Negroes, Belonging to the Estate of the Late General James Gadsden* (1 November 1859), Slave Ads, 1859, Hutson Lee Papers, 11-260-2; *A Prime Gang of 158 Negroes: By Louis B. DeSaussure: On Tuesday, the 13th March, 1860, at 11 o'clock, A.M., will be sold in Charleston, S.C., at the Mart in Chalmers St. By order of the Executors of the late T. Bennett Lucas* . . . Hutson Lee Papers, Slave Ads, 1860, 11-260-5.

26. Thomas W. Peyre Journal, 1834–c.1850 (12, 157), 34–466, South Carolina Historical Society, Charleston.

27. Harriss, "What Constitutes Unsoundness in the Negro?" (January 1859): 289–90.

28. Moses Grandy, *Narrative of the Life of Moses Grandy; Late a Slave in the United States of America* (London: C. Gilpin, 1843), 29.

29. John Douglass, "Surgical Cases," *Charleston Medical Journal and Review* 4 (May 1849): 298, 300–301 (quote on 298). See also Harriss, "What Constitutes Unsoundness in the Negro?" (January 1859): 291; Jemima Fretwell to Charles Brown (27 September [1815 or 1816]), Charles Brown Papers, Folder 2, in *Records of the Ante-Bellum Southern Plantations from the Revolution through the Civil War* (microfilm), ed. Kenneth M. Stampp, Series L, Part 4, Reel 35.

30. *Winyah Observer* (23 June–29 December 1852), cited in Joyner, *Down by the Riverside*, 27.

31. *Alexandria Daily Gazette, Commercial and Political* (11 October 1811), cited in Meaders, *Advertisements*, 156.

32. J. Douglass, "Surgical Cases," 299; Swados, "Negro Health," 470; Stampp, *Peculiar Institution*, 306–7.

33. Smith, *Autobiography*, 2–3.

34. Ibid.

35. *Richmond Enquirer* (31 May 1815), cited in Meaders, *Advertisements*, 250.

36. See "List of the Gordon Gang," Edmund Ravenel Plantation Papers 1835–1866, Ford-Ravenel Collection, 11-132-11, South Carolina Historical Society, Charleston; T. D. Weld, *American Slavery as It Is*, 77–84; Franklin and Schweininger, *Runaway Slaves*, 216.

37. *A Prime Gang of 27 Orderly Country-Raised Negroes, Accustomed to the Culture of Rice, Cotton, and Provisions: By Wilbur & Son*, Hutson Lee Papers, Slave Ads, 1860, 11-260-3.

38. "List of the Gordon Gang," South Carolina Historical Society, Charleston.

39. Professional Planter, *Practical Rules*, 287; Byrd and Clayton, *An American Health Dilemma*, 226; Kenneth F. Kiple, *The Caribbean Slave: A Biological History* (Cambridge: Cambridge University Press, 1984), 90.

40. Professional Planter, *Practical Rules*, 289–90; Owens, *This Species of Property*, 59.

41. *A Sketch in the Life*, 4, 6–7; Bancroft, *Slave Trading in the Old South*, 156.

42. Forry, "On the Relative Proportion," 311.

43. E. A. Davis, *Plantation Life*, 314–15, 318. Barrow also had a slave identified as "one-eyed Sam" in his journals from the mid-1830s to the mid-1840s (46, 98).
44. *A Prime Gang of 158 Negroes*, Hutson Lee Papers, Slave Ads, 1860, 11-260-5.
45. Stevenson, *Life in Black and White*, 101; Rosengarten, *Tombee*, 180.
46. Professional Planter, *Practical Rules*, 371–72 (quote on 372).
47. F. Perry Pope, "A Dissertation on the Professional Management of Negro Slaves" (M.D. thesis, Medical College of the State of South Carolina, 1837), Waring Historical Library, Medical University of South Carolina, Charleston, 10.
48. Harriss, "What Constitutes Unsoundness in the Negro?" (January 1859): 292. See also Jones, *Born a Child of Freedom*, 61; Byrd and Clayton, *American Health Dilemma*, 229; Tadman, *Speculators and Slaves*, 128. In an estate auction in Charleston in 1859, four female slaves between the ages of 20 and 35 were identified as having uterine prolapse. *For Sale by Shingler Brothers/7 Broad Street, /Charleston, S.C./A Remarkably Prime Gang of 235 Negroes, Belonging to the Estate of the Late General James Gadsden. November 1, 1859.* Slave Ads, 1859, Hutson Lee Papers, 11-260-2.
49. "Negro List of Southfield, Jany 17, 1860," Langdon Cheves Papers, Correspondence, January 17–31, 1860, 12-49-22; *A Prime Gang of 158 Negroes . . .* Hutson Lee Papers, Slave Ads, 1860, 11-260-5.
50. J. L. Morgan, "'Some Could Suckle over Their Shoulder,'" 23. See also Dorothy Roberts, *Killing the Black Body: Race, Reproduction, and the Meaning of Liberty* (New York: Pantheon Books, 1997), 24–25; Sharla M. Fett, "Consciousness and Calling: African American Midwives at Work in the Antebellum South," in *New Studies in the History of Slavery*, eds. Edward E. Baptist and Stephanie M. H. Camp (Athens: University of Georgia Press, 2006), 68.
51. Bankole, *Slavery and Medicine*, 64–65. See also White, *Ar'n't I a Woman?*, 83; Swados, "Negro Health," 468; Stampp, *Peculiar Institution*, 306; Savitt, *Medicine and Slavery*, 41, 120; Byrd and Clayton, *American Health Dilemma*, 229; Stevenson, *Life in Black and White*, 246.
52. Professional Planter, *Practical Rules*, 384–85 (quote on 385). See also John H. Morgan, "An Essay on the Causes of the Production of Abortion among Our Negro Population," *Nashville Journal of Medicine & Surgery* 19 (1860): 117.
53. McCaa, "Observations," 4–5; Merrill, "An Essay on Some of the Distinctive Peculiarities of the Negro Race," 69. John M. Galt, superintendent of the Eastern Lunatic Asylum in Virginia, argued that not only were African Americans less likely to become insane, they were also more easily cured of it—Samuel B. Thielman, "Southern Madness: The Shape of Mental Health Care in the Old South," in *Science and Medicine in the Old South*, eds. Ronald L. Numbers and Todd L. Savitt (Baton Rouge: Louisiana State University Press, 1989), 274.
54. See Blassingame, *The Slave Community*, 298–99; Stampp, *Peculiar Institution*, 305.
55. Postell, "Mental Health among the Slave Population on Southern Plantations," 53–54. See also Postell, *Health of Slaves*, 87.
56. Savitt, *Medicine and Slavery*, 247–52 (quote on 252). See also Thielman, "Southern Madness," 261, 273; Stampp, *Peculiar Institution*, 305.
57. Harriss, "What Constitutes Unsoundness in the Negro?" (September 1858), 149.
58. H. P. DeWees, "On Paralytic and Convulsive Diseases of the Cerebro-Spinal System, Including Epilepsy, Its Physiology, Pathology, and Treatment," *The American Medical Monthly and New York Review* 15 (April 1861): 262.

See also Savitt, *Medicine and Slavery*, 250; Dea H. Boster, "An 'Epeleptick' Bondswoman: Fits, Slavery, and Power in the Antebellum South," *Bulletin of the History of Medicine* 83, no. 2 (Summer 2009): 276.

59. Guion Griffis Johnson, *Ante-Bellum North Carolina: A Social History* (Chapel Hill: University of North Carolina Press, 1937), 528. See also "List of the Gordon Gang," South Carolina Historical Society, Charleston.

60. Genovese, *Roll, Jordan, Roll*, 520.

61. "Ages of Negroes for Direct [Fasc?], April 1815," Ball Family Papers, Slave Lists 1815–1818, 11-515-11C, South Carolina Historical Society, Charleston. See also Pollard, *Complaint to the Lord*, 33.

62. E. A. Davis, *Plantation Life*, 429.

63. Pollard, *Complaint to the Lord*, 35.

64. Ibid., 44.

65. See Stevenson, *Life in Black and White*, 183.

66. J. Douglass, "Surgical Cases," 298–301.

67. J. Anton Freemon, "Removal of a Large Tumor from the Thigh of a Negro Woman, Aged 30 Years, by Professors H. L. Byrd and F. W. B. Hemming, of Oglethorpe Medical College, Assisted by Dr. W. L. Davis," *Oglethorpe Medical and Surgical Journal* 1 (March 1860): 400–404, quote on 401.

68. F.W.B. Hemming, "Notes on the Surgical Pathology and Character of the above Tumor, Removed by Drs. H. L. Byrd and F.W.B. Hemming," *Oglethorpe Medical and Surgical Journal* 1 (March 1860): 407.

69. Harriss, "What Constitutes Unsoundness in the Negro?" (January 1859), 295.

70. Bailey, "Surgical Cases," 742.

71. Journal of Araby Plantation, Parish of Madison, Louisiana [1843–1850] (22–23), Haller Nutt Papers, FF-3224.

72. Richard Jarrot, "Amputation for Gangrene of the Foot, Successfully Performed on a Negro, at the Advanced Age of One Hundred and Two Years," *Charleston Medical Journal and Review* 4 (May 1849): 302.

73. Senex, "On Surgical Operations," *Virginia Medical Journal* 6 (February 1856): 109.

74. W. H. Robert, "Surgical Cases Occurring in the Practice of L. A. Dugas, M.D. Professor in the Medical College of Georgia," *Southern Medical & Surgical Journal* 3 (February 1839): 290–91.

75. Ibid., 292–93.

76. Ibid., 293. See also Fett, *Working Cures*, 28–29.

77. Thomas S. Powell, "Reports of the Case Book of Thos. S. Powell, M.D., Sparta, Georgia," *Atlanta Medical & Surgical Journal* 1 (May 1856): 516–17; cited also in Walter Fisher, "Physicians and Slavery in the Antebellum Southern Medical Journal," *Journal of the History of Medicine and Allied Sciences* 23 (January 1968): 42.

78. Robert, "Surgical Cases," 293.

79. Thornton Stringfellow, *Scriptural and Statistical Views in Favor of Slavery*, 4th ed. (Richmond, VA: J. W. Randolph, 1856), 128–29.

80. "Statistics of a Rice Plantation—with 100 Negroes, made in answer to a request from the Executive Department of the State of So Carolina," Robert F. W. Allston papers, Slave Papers 1851–1854, South Carolina Historical Society, Charleston.

81. "Deposition of Daniel Colman in Case of *Mary Hill & other et al. vs. Memerable W. Creagh & Alexd. M. Creagh*," [n.d.], Dick Brown (collector), Slave Records Collection, 1844–1864/n.d. Folder, Rare Book, Manuscript, and Special Collections Library, Duke University, Durham, North Carolina.

82. See Prude, "To Look Upon the 'Lower Sort,'" 128, 137.

83. Weld, *American Slavery as It Is*, 77–82; Stampp, *Peculiar Institution*, 187.

84. Greenberg, *Honor and Slavery*, 48.
85. See Weld, *American Slavery as It Is*, 77, 83; Tadman, *Speculators and Slaves*, 187; Greenberg, *Honor and Slavery*, 3; Gross, *Double Character*, 125, 130.
86. Genovese, *Roll, Jordan, Roll*, 65–67.
87. Stevenson, *Life in Black and White*, 194.
88. John Brown, *Slave Life in Georgia: A Narrative of the Life, Sufferings, and Escape of John Brown, a Fugitive Slave, Now in England*, ed. L. A. Chamerovzow (London: [W. M. Watts], 1855), 130–31.
89. See Savitt, *Medicine and Slavery*, 112, 114; Stevenson, *Life in Black and White*, 195; Rosengarten, *Tombee*, 185.
90. Grandy, *Narrative*, 10.
91. See Jones, *Born a Child of Freedom*, 171.
92. "Slave-Branding," in *Five Hundred Thousand Strokes for Freedom*, Leeds Anti-Slavery Series, no. 23, (London: W. & F. Cash; William Tweedie, 1853, repr., Miami, FL: Mnemosyne Publishing Co., 1969), 3.
93. Cited in Weld, *American Slavery as It Is*, 77.
94. Henry Bibb, [Interview of James Smith], orig. pub. *Voice of the Fugitive* (1852), cited in *Slave Testimony: Two Centuries of Letters, Speeches, Interviews, and* Autobiographies, ed. John W. Blassingame (Baton Rouge: Louisiana State University Press, 1977), 280.
95. Josiah Henson, *The Life of Josiah Henson, Formerly a Slave, Now an Inhabitant of Canada, as Narrated by Himself* (Boston: Arthur D. Phelps, 1849), 17–18.
96. [Interview of Tom Wilson], orig. pub. *Liverpool Albion* (20 February 1858), cited in Blassingame, ed., *Slave Testimony*, 339.
97. Professional Planter, *Practical Rules*, 178.
98. For example, see descriptions of slave Maria in 29 April 1827 entry (41), John Nevitt Record Book, Box 1, Folder 3 (typescript of Volume, 1–60, 1 January 1826–26 July 1827) and 9 November 1827 (84), John Nevitt Record Book, Box 1, Folder 4 (typescript of Volume, 61–130, 26 July 1827–10 May 1828).
99. Israel Campbell, *An Autobiography: Bond and Free: Or, Yearnings for Freedom, from My Green Brier House: Being the Story of My Life in Bondage, and My Life in Freedom* (Philadelphia: C.E.P. Brinckloe & Co., 1861), 50.
100. Samuel G. Howe, [Interview with Robert Smalls], cited in Blassingame, *Slave Testimony*, 378.
101. Weld, *American Slavery as It Is*, 77 (italics in original).
102. A. E. Davis, *Plantation Life*, 239.

NOTES TO CHAPTER 4

Portions of this chapter were previously published in Dea H. Boster, "'Useless': Disability, Slave Labor, and Contradiction on Antebellum Southern Plantations," *Review of Disability Studies* 7 (December 2011): 26–33, www.rds.hawaii.edu. Included with permission.

1. "List of Negroes" (n.d.), Estate Books, Samuel G. Barker Papers, 34-336-3, South Carolina Historical Society, Charleston.
2. [Untitled list of slaves, n.d.], Business & Plantation Correspondence, Negroes, 1825, Ford-Ravenel Papers, 11-131-3.
3. T. D. Weld, *American Slavery as It Is*, 132–33.
4. James Oakes, *The Ruling Race: A History of American Slaveholders* (London: Norton, 1998), 51–52, 153.
5. Bankole, *Slavery and Medicine*, 56; Joyner, *Down by the Riverside*, 60–63; D. B. Davis, *Inhuman Bondage*, 199.

6. Oakes, *Ruling Race*, 154–58.
7. Genovese, *Roll, Jordan, Roll*, 330–31.
8. Richard D. Arnold to Jacob McCall (29 August 1849), in Shryock, *Letters of Richard D. Arnold*, 33.
9. Oakes, *Ruling Race*, 153.
10. Ball, *Fifty Years in Chains*, 117.
11. P. D. Morgan, "The Poor," 317.
12. Pollard, *Complaint to the Lord*, 41.
13. D. B. Davis, *Inhuman Bondage*, 199; Genovese, *Roll, Jordan, Roll*, 292, 303.
14. Jones, *Born a Child of Freedom*, 32, 40–41.
15. "Negroes to Work on the High Roads" (18 November 1811 and [1812]), Slave Lists, 1810–1814, Ball Family Papers, 11-515-11B. See also Jones, *Born a Child of Freedom*, 107; Joyner, *Down by the Riverside*, 64, 67.
16. "List of Negroes," Barker Papers.
17. Rockingham Plantation Journal, 1828–1829, Section A (1), Rare Book, Manuscript, and Special Collections Library, Duke University, Durham, North Carolina.
18. J. G. Clinkscales, *On the Old Plantation: Reminiscences of His Childhood* (Spartanburg, SC: Band & White, 1916), 41–42. See also Pollard, *Complaint to the Lord*, 40–41.
19. See Postell, "Mental Health," 52.
20. Journal of Araby Plantation, Parish of Madison, Louisiana [1843–1850] (5), Haller Nutt Papers, FF-3323.
21. Emily Burke, *Pleasure and Pain: Reminiscences of Georgia in the 1840's* (Savannah, GA: Beehive Press, 1991), 41.
22. Ibid., 91.
23. "Male Slaves at Limerick Liable to Work on the Roads, 1807," Slave Lists 1804–1810, Ball Family Papers, 11-515-11A.
24. *Estate Sale! By Order of Executor. By Louis B. DeSaussure. On Wednesday, 19th Inst. at 11 O'Clock, A.M. will be Sold in Charleston, S. Carolina, at Messrs. Ryan & Son's Mart, in Chalmers Street . . .* , Hutson Lee Papers, Slave Ads, n.d., 11-260-6.
25. "Negroes Brt 15 Feby 1849 for McAlphins Place adjoining Gowrie . . ." Louis Manigault Papers, Box 2, Papers 1847–1849, Rare Book, Manuscript, and Special Collections Library, Duke University, Durham, North Carolina. Moses is also described as "prime" two months later, when he was listed as a slave at Manigault's Hermitage plantation. This may be the same "Moses" described in the Epilogue and Conclusion "Negroes at Gowrie, 3rd Decr 1848/Negroes at the Hermitage April 1849," Louis Manigault Papers, Box 2, Papers 1847–1849.
26. Ball, *Fifty Years in Chains*, 120; "List of the Gordon Gang," South Carolina Historical Society, Charleston.
27. Anderson F. Henderson to [Mr. and Mrs. Archibald Henderson], Wilmington (14 June 1857), John S. Henderson Papers, Series 1.1, Box 2, Folder 23 (1857), Southern Historical Collection, University of North Carolina, Chapel Hill.
28. Nancy Venture Woods to Master [John Haywood?], Newbern [NC] (5 February 1825), cited in Robert S. Starobin, ed., *Blacks in Bondage: Letters of American Slaves* (New York: New Viewpoints, 1974), 87.
29. Smith, *Autobiography*, 13, 24 (quote on 24).
30. Inventory, George J. Kollock Plantation Journals, Southern Historical Collection, University of North Carolina, Chapel Hill, accessed 12 November 2009, http://www.lib.unc.edu/mss/inv/k/Kollock,George_J.html.
31. Plantation Book, Ossabaw Island, 1855 (4), Subseries 1.3, Box 1, Folder 12 (1855), George J. Kollock Plantation Journals, Southern Historical Collection,

University of North Carolina, Chapel Hill. On other plantations, the descriptor "old" was often used to differentiate older and younger slaves with the same first name; however, Kollock's slave community did not seem to have many slaves with the same first names in 1855.

32. Ibid., 4, 100.
33. Plantation Book for the Plantation on the South end of Ossabaw, 1850 (3, 66–68), Subseries 1.3, Box 1, Folder 8 (21 January 1850—4 March 1852), George J. Kollock Plantation Journals, Southern Historical Collection, University of North Carolina, Chapel Hill; Plantation Book for the Plantation on the South end of Ossabaw, 1851 (3), Subseries 1.3, Box 1, Folder 9 (1 January 1851—21 January 1852), George J. Kollock Plantation Journals, Southern Historical Collection, University of North Carolina, Chapel Hill.
34. Plantation Book, Ossabaw Island, 1855 (12, 52), Subseries 1.3, Box 1, Folder 12 (1855), George J. Kollock Plantation Journals, Southern Historical Collection, University of North Carolina, Chapel Hill.
35. Plantation Book, Ossabaw Island, 1858 (2), Subseries 1.3, Box 2, Folder 15 (1858), George J. Kollock Plantation Journals, Southern Historical Collection, University of North Carolina, Chapel Hill.
36. [H. Jarrel to Mr. Kollock, 1859] in back of Plantation Book, Ossabaw Island (1858), George J. Kollock Plantation Journals, Southern Historical Collection, University of North Carolina, Chapel Hill.
37. Plantation Book, Ossabaw Island, 1855 (36–38), Subseries 1.3, Box 1, Folder 12 (1855), George J. Kollock Plantation Journals, Southern Historical Collection, University of North Carolina, Chapel Hill.
38. Postell, "Mental Health," 52.
39. Fett, *Working Cures*, 25–26.
40. Franklin and Schweininger, *Runaway Slaves*, 17.
41. "Inventory and Appraisement of Real and Personal Property of the Est. D. L. McDonald Dec'd, Camden Wilcox County Ala May 15, 1854," Slave Records Collection, 1844–1864/n.d., Dick Brown (collector).
42. E. A. Davis, *Plantation Life*, 394–97.
43. Todd L. Savitt, "Slave Life Insurance in Virginia and North Carolina," *Journal of Southern History* 43 (November 1977): 583–84; Fett, *Working Cures*, 23–24. See also Jenny Bourne Wahl, *The Bondsman's Burden: An Economic Analysis of the Common Law of Southern Slavery* (Cambridge: Cambridge University Press, 1998), 214n79.
44. Savitt, "Slave Life Insurance," 594.
45. Nott, "Statistics of Southern Slave Population," 286–87 (quote on 286). See also Owens, *This Species of Property*, 25–26; Savitt, "Slave Life Insurance," 586; Genovese, *Roll, Jordan, Roll*, 520.
46. [Life Insurance Policy for Slave Mary, Beneficiary Bertha Byck, 19 May 1860 (typescript)], African American Miscellany File, Slavery Division: 1757–1867, n.d., Rare Book, Manuscript, and Special Collections Library, Duke University, Durham, North Carolina.
47. See *Life Insurance: Its Principles, Operations and Benefits, as Presented by the N.C. Mutual Life Insur. Co.* (Raleigh, NC: Seaton Gales, 1849), 12, 17; Savitt, "Slave Life Insurance," 587, 597; Pollard, *Complaint to the Lord*, 34–35.
48. *Life Insurance*, 17.
49. [Life Insurance Policy for Slave Mary], African American Miscellany File.
50. Savitt, "Slave Life Insurance," 587. See also 592–93.
51. Savitt, *Medicine and Slavery*, 203–4, 206; Fett, *Working Cures*, 26; Jones, *Born a Child of Freedom*, 26–27; Pollard, *Complaint to the Lord*, 36.
52. Phillis to [Mr. and Mrs. St George Tucker] [1824?], cited in John W. Blassingame, ed., *Slave Testimony: Two Centuries of Letters, Speeches, Interviews,*

and Autobiographies (Baton Rouge: Louisiana State University Press, 1977), 10. Evidence suggests that her request was granted; Phillis's family lived with Beverley Tucker, and her name also appears in his inventory from 1845.

53. Samuel Robertson (cobbler) to [Louisa Lord], Charleston (16 April 1857), Louisa Lord Papers 1850–1862: Correspondence, 1856, 1858, 11-271-4.

54. See "Ingraham's Travels in the South-West," in H. B. Stowe, *A Key to Uncle Tom's Cabin*, 11–12. Itinerant South Carolina minister Alexander Glennie noted in his journal that he would travel to some plantations to administer communion to elderly slaves. Alexander Glennie Journal (Commonplace Book) 1831–1859, South Carolina Historical Society, Charleston.

55. William [Irvin] to Vardry McBee, Greenville Co., SC (16 March 1850), Vardry McBee Letters, 1818–1857/n.d., Rare Book, Manuscript, and Special Collections Library, Duke University, Durham, North Carolina.

56. Francis Cope Yarnall, *Letters on Slavery* (1853), 2–3. Diary Folder, Francis Cope Yarnall Papers, Rare Book, Manuscript, and Special Collections Library, Duke University, Durham, North Carolina.

57. [Unknown] to My Dear Daughter (8 October 1858), Galt Family Papers (Personal, Reel 9), Colonial Williamsburg Inc. Research Library, cited in Savitt, *Medicine and Slavery*, 207.

58. "Ex-Slave Story, Ottawa, Kansas," Kansas Narratives6:9, *Born in Slavery: Slave Narratives from the Federal Writers' Project, 1936–1938*, accessed 16 March 2006 and 12 September 2008, Library of Congress. http://memory. loc.gov/ammem/snhtml/snhome.html. Also cited in Yetman, *Life Under the "Peculiar Institution*, 275.

59. See Genovese, *Roll, Jordan, Roll*, 298.

60. T. D. Weld, *American Slavery as It Is*, 103.

61. F. Douglass, *Narrative of the Life of Frederick Douglass*, 61.

62. See Genovese, *Roll, Jordan, Roll*, 520–21; Pollard, *Complaint to the Lord*, 37.

63. [Jacobs], *Incidents in the Life*, 142.

64. White, *Ar'n't I a Woman?*, 117. See also Pollard, *Complaint to the Lord*, 38; Owens, *This Species of Property*, 47.

65. See William Craft, *Running a Thousand Miles for Freedom; or, The Escape of William and Ellen Craft from Slavery* (London: William Tweedie, 1860), 9–10.

66. H[enry] Bibb to Albert G. Sibley (4 November 1852), cited in Blassingame, ed., *Slave Testimony*, 54–55.

67. F. Douglass, *Life and Times*, 137–38; F. Douglass, *Narrative*, 55–56.

68. Burke, *Pleasure and Pain*, 24–25.

69. Genovese, "Medical and Insurance Costs," 146; Genovese, *Roll, Jordan, Roll*, 520; White, *Ar'n't I a Woman?*, 54, 117.

70. E. A. Davis, *Plantation Life*, 262.

71. Owens, *This Species of Property*, 47.

72. Mary Woodson to the Mayor of Alexandria (21 June 1813), Slavery Papers, Library of Congress, cited in Owens, *This Species of Property*, 48.

73. Grandy, *Narrative*, 51–52.

74. Philo Tower, *Slavery Unmasked: Being a Truthful Narrative of a Three Years' Residence and Journeying in Eleven Southern States* (Rochester: E. Darrow and Brother, 1856), 170–72.

75. Redpath, *Roving Editor*, 120.

76. Journal of Araby Plantation, Haller Nutt Papers, 205.

77. Burke, *Pleasure and Pain*, 59–60.

78. Rosengarten, *Tombee*, 456–57. See also Creel, "*A Peculiar People*", 241–42.

79. Savitt, "Use of Blacks," 343. See also Boster, "An 'Epeleptick' Bondswoman," 283–84.

80. William W. Keen, S. Weir Mitchell andGeorge R. Morehouse, "On Malingering: Especially in Regard to Simulation of Diseases of the Nervous System," *American Journal of the Medical Sciences* 48 (October 1864): 390–94; Thomas R. P. Spence, "Account of the Efficacy of Sugar of Lead, in a Case of Epilepsy," *Philadelphia Medical Museum* 2 (1806): 150; Savitt, *Medicine and Slavery*, 47.

81. Pernick, *Calculus of Suffering*, 155–56.

82. J. Marion Sims, *The Story of My Life* (New York: D. Appleton, 1898), 228–30.

83. Ibid., 230, 240 (quote on 240). See also J. Marion Sims, "On the Treatment of Vesico-Vaginal Fistula," *American Journal of the Medical Sciences* 23 (January 1852): 59.

84. See Sims, *Story of My Life*, 237–38.

85. See W. Montague Cobb, "Surgery and the Negro Physician: Some Parallels in Background," *Journal of the National Medical Association* 43 (May 1951): 148; Kiple and King, *Another Dimension*, 174; Washington, *Medical Apartheid*, 63; Byrd and Clayton, *American Health Dilemma*, 1:271; Savitt, "Use of Blacks," 343–46.

86. See Fisher, "Physicians and Slavery," 46–48; Bankole, *Slavery and Medicine*, 103.

87. "Minutes of the Society," *Transactions of the Fourth Annual Meeting of the Medical Society of the State of Georgia* IV (Savannah, April 1853): 7. See also Savitt, "Use of Blacks," 346.

88. C. W. Long, "An Account of the First Use of Sulphuric Ether by Inhalation as an Anaesthetic in Surgical Operations," *Southern Medical and Surgical Journal* 5 (December 1849): 707, 710.

89. Ibid., 711. Long mentions that, following the procedures, he procured certificates from the enslaved patient's owner and of the female patient and her husband, testifying that they was "insensible" under ether; from this evidence, it is reasonable to conclude that his female patient was free, and therefore presumably white.

90. See Robert C. Carroll, "Jackson Street Hospital Reports: Cases of Menstrual Derangement in Negro Women," *Southern Medical & Surgical Journal* 16 (May 1860): 333.

91. Fisher, "Physicians and Slavery," 45; S. M. Stowe, *Doctoring the South*, 30.

92. Savitt, "Use of Blacks," 332. See also S. M. Stowe, *Doctoring the South*, 49–50.

93. "Dr. T. Stillman's Medical Infirmary for Diseases of the Skin," *Charleston Mercury* (12 October 1838), cited in William Goodell, *The American Slave Code in Theory and Practice: Its Distinctive Features Shown by Its Statutes, Judicial Decisions, and Illustrative Facts,* 2nd ed. (New York: American & Foreign Anti-Slavery Society, 1853, repr., New York: New American Library, 1969), 87. See also Jones, *Born a Child of Freedom*, 201.

94. Savitt, "Use of Blacks," 334.

95. Fisher, "Physicians and Slavery," 46.

96. Goodell, *American Slave Code*, 86–87.

97. Senex, "On Surgical Operations," 110. See also Savitt, *Medicine and Slavery*, 288.

98. See Schwartz, *Birthing a Slave*, 218.

99. "Is the Negro Subject to Hare-Lip?" *Western Lancet* 4 (June 1845): 95; "Hare-Lip in the Negro," *Western Lancet* 4 (November 1845): 332.

100. James B. Dungan, "Double-Headed Monster," *New Orleans Medical News and Hospital Gazette* 4 (1 May 1857): 129–30.

101. Savitt, *Medicine and Slavery*, 303–4; Schwartz, *Birthing a Slave*, 212, 216–17.

102. Schwartz, *Birthing a Slave*, 212.

103. [P. Claiborne Gooch], "The Carolina Twins," *The Stethoscope, and Virginia Medical Gazette* 2 (July 1852): 394.

104. Millie-Christine [McCoy], *The History of the Carolina Twins*: *"Told in Their Own Peculiar Way" by "One of Them"* ([Buffalo]: Buffalo Courier Printing House, [1869?]), 6. In their autobiography, Millie and Christine sometimes referred to themselves as two separate individuals, and sometimes they identified themselves as a single person, Millie-Christine; I have also used both forms of identification in this chapter. See also [Gooch], "The Carolina Twins," 394–95; Schwartz, *Birthing a Slave*, 216–17.

105. [Gooch], "The Carolina Twins," 395.

106. [McCoy], *History of the Carolina Twins*, 6–8 (quote on 8). See also Joanne Martell, *Millie-Christine: Fearfully and Wonderfully Made* (Winston-Salem, NC: John F. Blair, 2000), 13–14.

107. According to one Canadian newspaper, the McCoy twins were more interesting because, unlike Chang and Eng Bunker, they could not be separated safely, but this assertion was probably not true. Martell, *Millie-Christine*, 16, 32–34.

108. [McCoy], *History of the Carolina Twins*, 21.

109. Byrd and Clayton, *American Health Dilemma*, 271.

NOTES TO CHAPTER 5

1. Q. C. Philander Doesticks [Mortimer Neal Thompson], *Great Auction Sale of Slaves, at Savannah, Georgia, March 2d and 3d, 1859* (New York: American Anti-Slavery Society, 1859), 10, accessed 7 July 2009, http://antislavery. eserver.org/travel/thompsonauction/thompsonauction.html.

2. Ibid., 1, 26.

3. Walter Johnson, "Introduction: The Future Store," in Walter Johnson, ed., *The Chattel Principle: Internal Slave Trades in the Americas* (New Haven, CT: Yale University Press, 2004), 2, 6, 7.

4. Fett, *Working Cures*, 16, 20–21; Gross, *Double Character*, 3, 8.

5. W. Johnson, *Soul by Soul*, 149.

6. Ibid., 13–14, 19–20.

7. See Tadman, *Speculators and Slaves*; Daina Ramey Berry, "'We'm Fus' Rate Bargain': Value, Labor, and Price in a Georgia Slave Community," in *The Chattel Principle: Internal Slave Trades in the Americas*, ed. Walter Johnson (New Haven, CT: Yale University Press, 2004), 55–71; Steven Deyle, *Carry Me Back: The Domestic Slave Trade in American Life* (New York: Oxford University Press, 2005).

8. Andrew Fede, "Legal Protection for Slave Buyers in the U.S. South: A Caveat Concerning Caveat Emptor," *American Journal of Legal History* 31 (October 1987): 330; Herman Freudenberger and Jonathan B. Pritchett, "The Domestic United States Slave Trade: New Evidence," *Journal of Interdisciplinary History* 21 (Winter 1991): 459–61; Berlin, *Generations of Captivity*, 170; Michael Tadman, "The Interregional Slave Trade in the History and Myth-Making of the U.S. South," in W. Johnson, *The Chattel Principle*, 128.

9. Deyle, *Carry Me Back*, 171.

10. Ibid., 118, 167–70. Michael Tadman has argued that slave traders were less likely to be involved in the sale of slaves from an estate because they were costly and did not bring much profit, but that they purchased estate slaves. Tadman, "Interregional Slave Trade," 128.

11. Franklin and Schweininger, *Runaway Slaves*, 282, 285.

12. Johnson, *Soul by Soul*, 118–19, 138–47.

13. Scale of Valuation of Slaves, Pfafftown District, Forsythe Co., NC [n.d.], Tyre Glen Papers, Box 2. See also Wahl, *Bondsman's Burden*, 37–38; Gavin

Wright, *The Political Economy of the Cotton South: Households, Markets, and Wealth in the Nineteenth Century* (New York: Norton, 1978), 143.

14. W. Johnson, "Introduction," 3.

15. Wright, *Political Economy*, 144. See also Valencius, *Health of the Country*, 64; Berry, "'We'm Fus' Rate Bargain,'" 62.

16. Tadman, *Speculators and Slaves*, 189.

17. W. Johnson, *Soul by Soul*, 138–41; Wahl, *Bondsman's Burden*, 31; Tadman, *Speculators and Slaves*, 32n22, 60, 188; Berlin, *Generations of Captivity*, 169–70.

18. W. Johnson, *Soul by Soul*, 151. For example, see Ewing v. Gist, 2 B. Mon. 465 (KY 1842), cited in Helen Tunnicliff Catterall, ed., *Judicial Cases Concerning American Slavery and the Negro*(Washington, DC: Carnegie Institution of Washington, 1926), 1:360.

19. A. J. McElveen to Z. B. Oakes, Sumterville, SC (13 July 1853), cited in Edmund L. Drago, ed. *Broke by the War: Letters of a Slave Trader* (Columbia: University of South Carolina Press, 1991), 44.

20. A. J. McElveen to Z. B. Oakes, Sumterville, SC (10 July 1853), cited in Drago, *Broke by the War*, 43–44.

21. Berry, "'We'm Fus' Rate Bargain,'" 58.

22. Bancroft, *Slave Trading*, 227; Pollard, *Complaint to the Lord*, 35.

23. See Deyle, *Carry Me Back*, 162–63.

24. Samuel Burnett to The Honorable Orphan's Court of Wilcox County [n.d.], Dick Brown (collector), Slave Records Collection, 1844–1864/n.d. See also Littlejohn v. Underhill's Executor, 2 Car. L. R. 574 (July 1816), cited in Catterall, *Judicial Cases*, , 2:29.

25. An Inventory and Appraisement . . . at the West Bank Plantation (23 July 1840), Glover Papers, Joseph Glover Estate Papers, 1840, 11-156-2, South Carolina Historical Society, Charleston; An Inventory and Appraisement . . . at the Camp Plantation (23 July 1840), Glover Papers, Joseph Glover Estate Papers, 1840, 11-156-2; An Inventory and Appraisement . . . at the Snug-It-Is Plantation (23 July 1840), Glover Papers, Joseph Glover Estate Papers, 1840, 11-156-2.

26. "Sale of Aged Slaves," n.p.

27. [List of Slaves for Sale at New Orleans by J. Beard Auctioneer, 14 March 1851], African American Miscellany File, Slavery Division: 1757–1867, n.d. See also W. Johnson, *Soul by Soul*, 55.

28. "Sale of Slaves and Stock," in Byrd and Clayton, *American Health Dilemma*, 1:263.

29. "A Prime and Orderly Gang of 25 Negroes Accustomed to the Culture of Cotton, Rice and Provisions . . ." Hutson Lee Papers, Slave Ads, 1860, 11-260-3.

30. W. Johnson, *Soul by Soul*, 152–53. For another example of a field slave who had lost an eye, see "Estate Sale! By Order of Executor . . . of the late Mr. and Mrs. Wm. Barnwell, A Prime Gang of 67 Negroes Accustomed to the Culture of Sea Island Cotton and Provisions, in Beaufort District," Hutson Lee Papers, Slave Ads, n.d., 11-260-6.

31. "Estate Sale! Hutson Lee Papers, Slave Ads, n.d., 11-260-6.

32. See Gross, *Double Character*, 215–16n3.

33. "Negro List of Southfield, Jany 17, 1860," Langdon Cheves Papers, Correspondence January 17–31, 1860 (re: estate?), 12-49-22; *List of 170 Rice Field Negroes, Belonging to the Estate of Late Hon. Langdon Cheves. To be Sold at Public Outcry at SAVANNAH, Ga., Friday, Feb. 3rd, 1860*, 43/1037, South Carolina Historical Society, Charleston. In another example from Charleston, an 1860 estate sale included a thirty-seven-year-old

woman named Kitty, who was described as "full task—prolapsus." Since buyers presumably would not expect a woman of her age to be a "breeder," her reproductive condition was listed after her qualification as a full task worker. *A Prime and Orderly Gang of Thirty-Three Negroes Accustomed to the Culture of Cotton, Rice and Provisions* . . . Hutson Lee Papers, Slave Ads, 1860, 11-260-5. See also W. Johnson, *Soul by Soul*, 143–44.

34. *For Sale by Shingler Brothers* . . . *A Remarkably Prime Gang of 235 Negroes, Belonging to the Estate of the Late General James Gadsden, November 1, 1859*, Slave Ads, 1859, Hutson Lee Papers, 11-260-2; *Prime Gang of 235 Negroes, Belonging to the Estate of the late Gen. Jas. Gadsden, . . . by Shingler Brothers, on Monday, 9th of January, 1860*, Hutson Lee Papers, Slave Ads, 1860, 11-260-3.

35. Solomon Northup, *Twelve Years a Slave: Narrative of Solomon Northup, a Citizen of New-York, Kidnapped in Washington City in 1841 and Rescued in 1853, from a Cotton Plantation near the Red River in Louisiana* (Auburn, NY: Derby and Miller; Buffalo: Derby, Orton and Mulligan; London: Sampson Low, Son, 1853), 58.

36. J. Brown, *Slave Life in Georgia*, 116–17.

37. Redpath, *Roving Editor*, 248–49; J. Brown, *Slave Life in Georgia*, 113, 117; W. Johnson, *Soul by Soul*, 130.

38. Redpath, *Roving Editor*, 247; Drago, *Broke by the War*, 48–49; W. Johnson, *Soul by Soul*, 141–42; Bancroft, *Slave Trading*, 106–7; Gross, *Double Character*, 126–28.

39. White, *Ar'n't I a Woman?*, 31–32; Redpath, *Roving Editor*, 252.

40. Charles Richard Weld, *A Vacation Tour in the United States and Canada* (London: Longman, Brown, Green, and Longmans, 1855), 299–300, 302; W. Johnson, *Soul by Soul*, 142–43.

41. A. J. McElveen to Z. B. Oakes, Montgomery (1 November 1856), cited in Drago, *Broke by the War*, 134.

42. Fett, *Working Cures*, 20; W. Johnson, *Soul by Soul*, 145; Gross, *Double Character*, 8. For a more detailed description of examination of whipping scars from an abolitionist perspective, see "A Slave Auction in Virginia," [1]–2.

43. Robert F. W. Allston Papers: Slave Papers, 1847–1853, 12-6-21.

44. Tadman, *Speculators and Slaves*, 189. See also Judith K. Schafer, "New Orleans Slavery in 1850 as Seen in Advertisements," *Journal of Southern History* 47 (February 1981): 55; Bancroft, *Slave Trading*, 106.

45. Bill of Sale for Negroes, James & Josiah [Herie?] to Saml Guy (n.d.), African American Miscellany File, Slavery Division 1757–1867/n.d. See also *Slave Bills of Sale Project* (Atlanta: African-American Family History Association, Inc., 1986); Betty Wood, *Slavery in Colonial Georgia, 1730–1775* (Athens: University of Georgia Press, 1984), 96; Wahl, *Bondsman's Burden*, 36–37; Bancroft, *Slave Trading*, 106; Tadman, *Speculators and Slaves*, 103, 189; Fett, *Working Cures*, 20–21.

46. Bill of Sale, William Guy to Samuel Guy (1 March 1811), African American Miscellany File, Slavery Division, 1757–1867/n.d; Garvins Bill of Sail [*sic*] of Susana (9 December 1813), African American Miscellany File, Slavery Division, 1757–1867/n.d.

47. [Herndon/Williams Receipt, Richmond (5 July 1849)], African American Miscellany File, Slavery Division, 1757–1867, n.d.

48. Richard Tansey, "Bernard Kendig and the New Orleans Slave Trade," *Louisiana History* 23 (Spring 1982): 170n34, 171–72.

49. Robert S. Mills to James B. Harris, Pleasant Hill (1 July 1844), Robert S. Mills Papers (Account and Letter Book), Rare Book, Manuscript, and Special Collections Library, Duke University, Durham, North Carolina.

50. Wahl, *Bondsman's Burden*, 40–41. For example, see Jordan v. Foster, 11 Ark. 139; 1850 Ark. LEXIS 21 (January 1850). LexisNexis.
51. Harriss, "What Constitutes Unsoundness?," 149.
52. H. B. Stowe, *Key to Uncle Tom's Cabin*, 254; Postell, "Mental Health," 52; Laurence J. Kotlikoff, "The Structure of Slave Prices in New Orleans, 1804 to 1862," *Economic Inquiry* 17 (October 1979): 511.
53. [Bill of Sale, Emanuel Geiger to Alexander Forsyth (6 August 1853)], African American Miscellany File, Slavery Division, 1757–1867/n.d.
54. Samuel R. Browning to A. H. Boyd Esqr. Millikins Bend, Louisiana (26 December 1848 and 2 January 1849), Archibald H. Boyd Papers, 1841–1897, Section A, Rare Book, Manuscript, and Special Collections Library, Duke University, Durham, North Carolina.
55. Henry Izard to Timothy Ford Esq., The Elms (29 January 1806), Ford-Ravenel Papers, Business & Plantation Correspondence, Negroes 1825, 11-131-3.
56. [Timothy Ford to Henry Izard (n.d.)], Ford-Ravenel Papers, Business & Plantation Correspondence, Negroes 1825, 11-131-3. In this letter, Ford implied that he would not take Willoughby as part of the gang, but her name is included in the bill of sale. Bill of Sale, State of South Carolina (1 February 1806), Ford-Ravenel Papers, Business & Plantation Correspondence, Negroes 1825, 11-131-3.
57. Timothy Ford to Sir [Henry Izard] (31 January 1806), Ford-Ravenel Papers, Business & Plantation Correspondence, Negroes 1825, 11-131-3, (emphasis in original).
58. Walter Johnson, "Review. Inconsistency, Contradiction, and Complete Confusion: The Everyday Life of the Law of Slavery," *Law & Social Inquiry* 22 (Spring 1997): 414n15.
59. McElveen to Oakes, Darlington Courthouse, SC (10 May 1854), cited in Drago, *Broke by the War*, 80.
60. J. Brown, *Slave Life in Georgia*, 115. See also Valencius, *Health of the Country*, 70.
61. *Young ads. Plumeau*, Harper 543 (S.C. 1827), cited in Catterall, *Judicial Cases*, 2:336.
62. William Wells Brown, *Narrative of William W. Brown, an American Slave* (London: Charles Gilpin, 1849), 42; J. Brown, *Slave Life in Georgia*, 112.
63. J. Brown, *Slave Life in Georgia*, 117.
64. W. W. Brown, *Clotel*, 6; W. W. Brown, *Narrative of William W. Brown*, 38–42. See also Owens, *This Species of Property*, 186, 190; Greenberg, *Honor and Slavery*, 38–39; Pollard, *Complaint to the Lord*, 35; Tadman, *Speculators and Slaves*, 98–101.
65. J. Brown, *Slave Life in Georgia*, 114–15. See also Tadman, *Speculators and Slaves*, 185; W. Johnson, *Soul by Soul*, 129; Deyle, *Carry Me Back*, 266.
66. W. Johnson, *Soul by Soul*, 138.
67. Richard Hildreth, *The White Slave: Or, Memoirs of a Fugitive* (Boston: Tappan and Whittemore, 1852), 73–74.
68. W. Johnson, *Soul by Soul*, 129.
69. Ibid., 164. See also Fett, *Working Cures*, 30–32.
70. Oral memoirs collected in the 1930s indicate strong fears of separation in the lives of slaves, and that evidence of disease or disability at market was a significant factor in preventing sales that would have destroyed families. For instance, Robert Falls, a slave born on Harry Beattie Goforth's North Carolina farm in 1840, recalled that his mother, who had been sold three separate times before Falls was born, experienced fits after Goforth "had sold her away from her baby" to speculators from North Carolina. The

men who had taken her brought her back to Goforth the next day and demanded a refund, thus reuniting Falls's family; "after that none of us was ever separated." By Falls's account, his mother continued to experience fits for the rest of her life "every change of the moon, or leastways every other moon change," yet this episode is the only one that Falls describes in any detail in his narrative. This indicates that, at least in Falls' memory, the most remarkable thing about his mother's disorder was its serendipitous ability to prevent her sale away from her family ("Tennessee Narratives XV," *Born in Slavery*). As Michael Tadman has pointed out, the desire to keep families together as much as possible was perhaps the strongest motivation to manipulate market transactions (Tadman, *Speculators and Slaves*, 9).

71. Doesticks, *Great Auction Sale of Slaves*, 11.
72. Ibid., 10–11. See also Berry, "'We'm Fus' Rate Bargain,'" 55–56.
73. Raymond A. Bauer and Alice H. Bauer, "Day to Day Resistance to Slavery," *Journal of Negro History* 27 (October 1942): 406–7. For an example of a slave whose obvious malingering compromised her sale, see Tyre Glen to Isaac Jarratt, Huntsville (24 March 1832), Jarratt-Puryear Papers, Correspondence and Papers, 1807–1849, Box 1, Folder 1830–1833, Rare Book, Manuscript, and Special Collections Library, Duke University, Durham, North Carolina.
74. Samuel G. Howe, [Interview with John Boggs], in Blassingame, *Slave Testimony*, 422.
75. Doesticks, *Great Auction Sale of Slaves*, 26. See also Berry, "'We'm Fus' Rate Bargain,'" 63–64.
76. Gross, *Double Character*, 3, 122.
77. For example, see Pleasants v. Clements, 29 Va. (2 Leigh) 474 (1831), cited in Catterall, *Judicial Cases*, 1:163.
78. Wahl, *Bondsman's Burden*, 30.
79. Tansey, "Bernard Kendig," 172–73.
80. Schafer, "'Guaranteed," 6, 34–35.
81. Schafer, "'Guaranteed,'" 308; W. Johnson, *Soul by Soul*, 183.
82. H. B. Stowe, *Key to Uncle Tom's Cabin*, 131; Gross, *Double Character*, 6, 34, 170n15; Schafer, *Slavery*, 128–30, 147–48; Wahl, *Bondsman's Burden*, 35; Thomas D. Morris, *Southern Slavery and the Law, 1619–1860* (Chapel Hill: University of North Carolina Press, 1996), 111.
83. Fett, *Working Cures*, 22; Fede, "Legal Protection," 327, 333, 338, 343; Wahl, *Bondsman's Burden*, 5.
84. Clopton v. Martin, 11 Ala. 187, 1847 Ala. LEXIS 44 (1847), LexisNexis.
85. Williams v. Ingram, 21 Tex. 300, 1858 Tex. LEXIS 82 (1858), LexisNexis.
86. Gross, "Pandora's Box," 309; Wahl, *Bondsman's Burden*, 42, 200n55.
87. Schafer, "'Guaranteed'," 310–11; Gross, *Double Character*, 54, 66.
88. Harrell v. Norvill, 50 N.C. 29, 1857 N.C. LEXIS 11, 5 Jones Law 29 (1857), LexisNexis.
89. Nelson v. Biggers, 6 Ga. 205, 1849 Ga. LEXIS 26 (1849), LexisNexis. See also Wahl, *Bondsman's Burden*, 31–32.

NOTES TO CHAPTER 6

1. Smith, *Autobiography*, 3.
2. Ibid., 21.
3. Ibid., 23–24. Smith also describes walking long distances to attend prayer meetings on Saturday evenings (26), further indicating his ability to overcome his disability to claim independence and do something important to him.

4. See Hartman, *Scenes of Subjection*, 22; Heidi M. Hackford, "Malingering: Representations of Feigned Disease in American History, 1800–1920" (PhD diss., American University, 2004), 99.
5. S. L. Grier, "The Negro and His Diseases," *New Orleans Medical & Surgical Journal* 9 (1852–53): 757; Owens, *This Species of Property*, 24; Schwartz, *Birthing a Slave*, 5, 10. See also Tadman, *Speculators and Slaves*, 179–80; Stevenson, *Life in Black and White*, 179; Rosengarten, *Tombee*, 187.
6. Cartwright, "Diseases and Physical Peculiarities," 422–24; Warner, "Idea of Southern Medical Distinctiveness, 193, 205; Pernick, *Calculus of Suffering*, 204.
7. Cartwright, "Philosophy of the Negro Constitution," 200, see also 207–8.
8. Cartwright, "Diseases and Physical Peculiarities," 424. See also Byrd and Clayton, *American Health Dilemma*, 299.
9. Fisher, "Physicians and Slavery," 172; Fett, *Working Cures*, 16, 18.
10. E. A. Davis, *Plantation Life*, 417, 419.
11. S. M. Stowe, *Doctoring the South*, 81.
12. Fisher, "Physicians and Slavery," 41; Fett, *Working Cures*, 21, 24, 29. Medical examinations were necessary for life insurance because companies could deny coverage to individuals (including slaves) suffering from chronic disease, including hernia and dropsy. Savitt, "Slave Life Insurance," 588–89.
13. Harriss, "What Constitutes Unsoundness in the Negro?," 146.
14. See Gross, *Double Character*, 8–9, 123–24, 133–34; Fett, *Working Cures*, 25.
15. [Deposition of Samuel Robinson, 6 July 1809], Butler Family Papers 1663–1950, Series 3, Box 2, Folder 6, in *Records of the Ante-Bellum Southern Plantations from the Revolution through the Civil War* (microfilm), ed. Kenneth M. Stampp, Series I, Part 5, Reel 13.
16. Thompson v. Bertrand, 23 Ark. 730; 1861 Ark. LEXIS 192 (December 1861), LexisNexis. See also Brabo v. Martin, 5 La. 275; 1833 La. LEXIS 44 (March 1833), LexisNexis.
17. A. J. McElveen to Z. B. Oakes, Sumterville, SC (27 October 1853), cited in Drago, *Broke by the War*, 59.
18. A. J. McElveen to Z. B. Oakes, Sumterville, SC (7 November 1853), cited in Drago, *Broke by the War*, 61.
19. Bankole, *Slavery and Medicine*, 165–66; Gorn, "Black Magic," 300; S. M. Stowe, *Doctoring the South*, 138; Fett, *Working Cures*, 33–34.
20. E. A. Davis, *Plantation Life*, 185. See also *Letters on Slavery* (1853), 4, Francis Cope Yarnall Papers, Diary Folder; Joyner, *Down by the Riverside*, 146; Faust, "Culture, Conflict, and Community," 89; Savitt, *Medicine and Slavery*, 149.
21. Raboteau, *Slave Religion*, 83.
22. McCaa, "Observations," 5.
23. Genovese, "Medical and Insurance Costs," 148; Morais, *History of the Negro*, 17.
24. For examples, see Henry Ravenel Day Book 1816–1834, Thomas P. Ravenel Collection, 12-313-7, South Carolina Historical Society, Charleston; Ledger 1853–1859, William L. Johnston Papers, Rare Book, Manuscript, and Special Collections Library, Duke University, Durham, North Carolina; Langdon Cheves to [Son], Columbia (12 April 1853), Langdon Cheves Papers, Correspondence January–May 1855, 12-49-1; Miss H. P. Gaillard to Edwd. Flud, Dr. 1849 [receipt], Theodore Gourdin Papers, Gaillard Family, Plantation Receipts & Accounts 1848–1850, 11-166-13, South Carolina Historical Society, Charleston. See also Genovese, "Medical and Insurance Costs," 153.
25. Richard D. Arnold to Heber Chase (13 October 1836), in Shryock, *Letters of Richard D. Arnold*, 13.

26. L. M. Lawson, "A Few Thoughts on Epilepsy," *Western Lancet* 18 (January 1857): 6, Genovese, "Medical and Insurance Costs," 148; S. M. Stowe, *Doctoring the South*, 139–40; Fett, *Working Cures*, 27.

27. J. Marion Sims, "Osteo-Sarcoma of the Lower Jaw.—Resection of the body of the bone.—Cure," *American Journal of the Medical Sciences* 11 (January 1846): 129; Fisher, "Physicians and Slavery," 47.

28. Robert F. W. Allston to Alexander W. Campbell, Matanza (2 February 1837), cited in J. H. Easterby, ed., *The South Carolina Rice Plantation as Revealed in the Papers of Robert F. W. Allston*, (Chicago: University of Chicago Press, 1945), 384. See also Jones, *Born a Child of Freedom*, 200.

29. George M. Cooke to [Drs. Carmichael] (11 December 1825), "Patients' Voices in Early 19th Century Virginia: Letters to Doct. Carmichael & Son," Dr. James Carmichael Papers, 1816–1832 and n.d., Albert and Shirley Small Special Collections Library, University of Virginia Library, Charlottesville, Virginia, http://carmichael.lib.virginia.edu.

30. Langdon Cheves to [Son], Columbia (12 April 1853), Langdon Cheves Papers, Correspondence January–May 1855, 12-49-1.

31. Kevin Lander and Jonathan Pritchett, "When to Care: The Economic Rationale of Slavery Health Care Provision," *Social Science History* 33 (Summer 2009): 170. The authors examine advertisements to purchase sick slaves as evidence that doctors sought to turn a profit, or to conduct medical experiments, but do not consider that some doctors wanted to buy slaves for clinical instruction.

32. See Savitt, *Medicine and Slavery*, 150, 171; Fett, *Working Cures*, 38, 59; Gorn, "Black Magic," 296. Some historians, like Kenneth Stampp and Marie Jenkins Schwartz, assume it was a common belief that white Southerners and slaves were too different to receive the same medical treatment, but primary evidence does not hold up this assumption. See Stampp, *Peculiar Institution*, 308–9; Schwartz, *Birthing a Slave*, 4.

33. See M. D. McLoud, "Hints on the Medical Treatment of Negroes" (M.D. thesis, Medical College of the State of South Carolina, 1850), 14, 17, Waring Historical Library, Medical University of South Carolina, Charleston.

34. See Cartwright, "Philosophy of the Negro Constitution," 204. Cartwright and others extended their self-proclaimed expertise on the specific health issues of African American slaves to make proslavery justifications. Shryock, "Medical Practice," 169. See also Baynton, "Disability and the Justification," 38; Johnson and Bond, "Investigation of Racial Differences," 336; Gross, "Pandora's Box," 290–92; Franklin and Schweininger, *Runaway Slaves*, 274–75; Bauer and Bauer, "Day to Day Resistance," 395.

35. Gross, "Pandora's Box," 294.

36. See McLoud, "Hints on Medical Treatment," 3. More specific issues of slave malingering and the role of physicians in identifying feigned illness are discussed in another chapter.

37. James O. Breeden, ed., *Advice among Masters: The Ideal in Slave Management in the Old South* (Westport, CT: Greenwood Press, 1980), 193; McLoud, "Hints on Medical Treatment," 2; Feldstein, *Once a Slave*, 182–83; S. M. Stowe, *Doctoring the South*, 162–74, 216; Hackford, "Malingering," 54. Assumptions that slave malingering was widespread were not limited to the South. For instance, in *The Opal*, a newsletter published by patients at the New York State Insane Asylum in the 1850s, a fictional conversation written between "two southern gentlemen and a negro" indicates that a thieving slave who claimed to be "crazy" might receive a lighter punishment. As the slave Bob told his owner in the story, "it is so fashionable to be crazy, master, it saves many a fellow from the State's Prison and Gallows."

"A Dialogue between Two Southern Gentlemen and a Negro, Part 1," *The Opal* (May 1852), http://www.disabilitymuseum.org/lib/docs/1258.htm.

38. McLoud, "Hints on Medical Treatment," 1. See also S. M. Stowe, *Doctoring the South*, 139–40; Hackford, "Malingering," 25, 65–68, 79–80.

39. Boster, "An 'Epeleptick' Bondswoman," 289; S. M. Stowe, "Seeing Themselves at Work," 46; S. M. Stowe, *Doctoring the South*, 172–74; Hackford, "Malingering," 23; Savitt, *Medicine and Slavery*, 162–63.

40. For example, see J. Douglass, "Surgical Cases," 300–301; Hemming, "Notes on the Surgical Pathology," 407.

41. Lander and Pritchett, "When to Care," 160–65.

42. Douglass, "Surgical Cases," 300.

43. See Harriss, "What Constitutes Unsoundness?" 15; Cartwright, "Philosophy of the Negro Constitution," 205.

44. Sims, *The Story of My Life*, 227–28.

45. William Jackson Jr. to Drs. Carmichael (18 February 1823), "Patients' Voices in Early 19th Century Virginia," Dr. James Carmichael Papers, 1816–1832 and n.d., http://carmichael.lib.virginia.edu.

46. McLoud, "Hints on Medical Treatment," 13.

47. For instance, see Hord v. Grimes, 52 Ky. 188; 1852 Ky. LEXIS 10; 13 B. Mon. 188 (June 1852), LexisNexis.

48. Owens, *This Species of Property*, 40–41. See also Shryock, "Medical Practice," 174.

49. Freemon, "Removal of Large Tumor," 401.

50. Hemming, "Notes on Surgical Pathology," 404.

51. Thomas Affleck, "On the Hygiene of Cotton Plantations and the Management of Negro Slaves," *Southern Medical Reports* 2 (1850): 429.

52. Ibid., 434.

53. [G. G. Minor to Governor James McDowell] (1 June 1843), Office of the Governor, Record Group 3, James McDowell (1843–1846), Letters Received, Box 373, Archives & Manuscripts Room, Library of Virginia, Richmond. See also Boster, "An 'Epeleptick' Bondswoman," 271–72, 284; Todd L. Savitt, "Slave Health and Southern Distinctiveness," in *Disease and Distinctiveness in the American South*, eds. Todd L. Savitt and James Harvey Young (Knoxville: University of Tennessee Press, 1988), 137–38.

54. Richard H. Shryock, "Medical Sources and the Social Historian," *American Historical Review* 41 (April 1936): 465.

55. Gross, *Double Character*, 50; Stowe, *Doctoring the South*, 51, 213; Fett, *Working Cures*, 145, 147.

56. Stowe, *Doctoring the South*, 51.

57. This was not just limited to physicians; slaveholders, speculators and others also denied the extent of injuries that slaves may have experienced from physical trauma. See Hartman, *Scenes of Subjection*, 36.

58. McLoud, "Hints on Medical Treatment," 9–10, 12. See also Savitt, *Medicine and Slavery*, 83; Fett, *Working Cures*, 190; Boster, "An 'Epeleptick' Bondswoman," 285–86.

59. White, *Ar'n't I a Woman?*, 86.

60. See Roberts, *Killing the Black Body*, 24–25.

61. Carroll, "Jackson Street Hospital Reports," 332.

62. Fisher, "Physicians and Slavery," 43–44.

63. Stevenson, *Life in Black and White*, 192–93; Wahl, *The Bondsman's Burden*, 37–38; White, *Ar'n't I a Woman*, 79–83; Fett, *Working Cures*, 191.

64. J. H. Morgan, "Essay on Causes of . . . Abortion," 117–19. See also Bauer and Bauer, "Day to Day Resistance," 406–7; Stampp, *Peculiar Institution*,

103–4; Savitt, *Medicine and Slavery*, 115–16; Fett, *Working Cures*, 179; Hackford, "Malingering," 73.

65. James B. Floyd, Adm'r v. James M. Abney and Others, 1 S.C. 114, 1869 S.C. LEXIS 12 (1869), cited Catterall, *Judicial Cases*, , 2:475; White, *Ar'n't I a Woman*, 85.

66. Journal of Araby Plantation, Parish of Madison, Louisiana [1843–1850] (195), Haller Nutt Papers, FF-3323.

67. J. H. Morgan, "Essay on Causes of . . . Abortion," 121.

68. Citizen of Mississippi, "The Negro," 420; Harriss, "What Constitutes Unsoundness?" (September 1858), 147; Savitt, *Medicine and Slavery*, 146; Rosengarten, *Tombee*, 181.

69. Bailey, "Surgical Cases," 742–43. See also Fett, *Working Cures*, 27–28.

70. Harriss, "What Constitutes Unsoundness?" (September 1858), 147. See also Owens, *This Species of Property*, 37.

71. W. Johnson, "Review," 406.

72. Smith v. McCall, 1 McCord 223–24, 12 S.C. LEXIS 91 (1821), cited in Fede, "Legal Protection," 334.

73. See Schafer, *Slavery*, 133.

74. James F. Petigru to Robert F. W. Allston, Charleston (15 April 1837), cited in Easterby, *South Carolina Rice Plantation*, 69.

75. W. Johnson, "Review," 408–9, 424 (quote on 409).

76. Fede, "Legal Protection," 322; Wahl, *Bondsman's Burden*, 1–8 (quote on 7).

77. Schafer, *Slavery*, 40.

78. Morris, *Southern Slavery*, 9–10.

79. Gross, *Double Character*, 3, 41, 44 (quote on 44). See also Gross, "Pandora's Box," 269, 310, 314.

80. Lawrence Meir Friedman, *The Legal System: A Social Science Perspective* (New York: Russell Sage Foundation, 1975), 305; Paul Finkelman, "Slaves as Fellow Servants," *American Journal of Legal History* 31 (October 1987): 271.

81. In their recent study on health-care provision for slaves, Kevin Lander and Jonathan Pritchett argue that the low number of slaves admitted to Touro Hospital in New Orleans for occupational injuries supports U. B. Phillips's argument that masters "cherished" the lives of their slaves and most did not employ them in dangerous industrial occupations. Lander and Pritchett, "When to Care," 165. However, this conclusion overlooks evidence from court cases and insurance policies, which indicates that the number of slaves in dangerous industrial occupations increased in the 1850s, and does not consider the fact that most slaves were not admitted to hospitals for medical treatment.

82. Jamie L. Bronstein, *Caught in the Machinery: Workplace Accidents and Injured Workers in Nineteenth-Century Britain* (Stanford, CA: Stanford University Press, 2007), 105–6. See also Frederick Wertheim, "Note: Slavery and the Fellow Servant Rule: An Antebellum Dilemma," *New York University Law Review* 61 (December 1986): 1112.

83. Finkelman, "Slaves as Fellow Servants," 274–79; Bronstein, *Caught in the Machinery*, 105.

84. Redding v. Hall, 1 Bibb 536 (KY 1809), cited in Catterall, *Judicial Cases*, 1:284. See also Jonathan D. Martin, *Divided Mastery: Slave Hiring in the American South* (Cambridge, MA: Harvard University Press, 2004), 139–40, 151–52.

85. Morris, *Southern Slavery*, 135–46.

86. Mullen et al. v. Ensley, 27 Tenn. 428, 1847 Tenn. LEXIS 98, 8 Hum. 428 (1847), LexisNexis. See also Morris, *Southern Slavery*, 142.

87. Louisville and Nashville Railroad Co. v. Yandell, 56 Ky. 586, 1856 Ky. LEXIS 62, 17 B. Mon. 586 (1856), cited in Catterall, *Judicial Cases*, 1:427.
88. Wahl, *Bondsman's Burden*, 10, 59.
89. Scudder v. Woodbridge, 1 Ga. 195, 1846 Ga. LEXIS 53 (1846), LexisNexis.
90. Mayor and Councils of Columbus v. Howard, 6 Ga. 213, 1849 Ga. LEXIS 28, cited in Morris, *Southern Slavery*, 142.
91. Louisville and Nashville Railroad Co. v. Yandell, 56 Ky. 586, 1856 Ky. LEXIS 62, 17 B. Mon. 586 (1856), cited in Catterall, *Judicial Cases*, 1:427–28.
92. Gross, *Double Character*, 3; Schafer, *Slavery*, 35.
93. Dabney v. Taliaferro, 25 Va. 256, 1826 Va. LEXIS 32, 4 Rand. 256 (1826), LexisNexis.
94. Jones v. Glass, 35 N.C. 305, 1852 N.C. LEXIS 43, 13 Ired. Law 305 (1852), LexisNexis.
95. Jourdan v. Patton, 5 Mart. (o.s.) 615, 1818 La. LEXIS 56 (1818), Lexis-Nexis. See also Schafer, *Slavery*, 23.
96. Goodell, *American Slave Code*, 205–6. See also T. D. Weld, *American Slavery*, 145–46; H. B. Stowe, *Key to Uncle Tom's Cabin*, 73–74.
97. George M. Stroud, *A Sketch of the Laws Relating to Slavery in the Several States of the United States of America*, 2nd ed. (Philadelphia, 1856), 235 (italics in original). See also Lydia Maria Child, *An Appeal in Favor of that Class of Americans called Africans* (Boston: Allen & Ticknor, 1833; Amherst: University of Massachusetts Press, 1996), 52; Wardens of Hyde v. Jordan Silverthorn, Ex'r, &c. 28 N.C. 356, 1846 N.C. LEXIS 62, 6 Ired. Law 356 (1846), LexisNexis; The Trustees of the Poor of Sussex County v. Hall, 3 Del. 322, 1841 Del. LEXIS 7, 3 Harr. 322 (1841), LexisNexis; Fett, *Working Cures*, 26.
98. Redford v. Peggy, 6 Randolph 316, (VA 1828), cited in Catterall, *Judicial Cases*, 1:155. See also Maddox &c. v. Allen, 58 Ky. 495, 1859 Ky. LEXIS 3, 1 Met. 495 (1859), LexisNexis.
99. Child, *Appeal in Favor*, 43.
100. Schafer, *Slavery*, 29.
101. Morris, *Southern Slavery*, 183–85. See also Wahl, *Bondsman's Burden*, 6.
102. Worley v. The State, 30 Tenn. 172, 1850 Tenn. LEXIS 84, 11 Hum. 172 (1850), LexisNexis. There is evidence that some mid-nineteenth-century physicians used castration as a surgical cure for depleting illnesses linked with masturbation, but one New Hampshire doctor who utilized the treatment admitted that it was largely unsuccessful and dangerous. Josiah Crosby, "Seminal Weakness—Castration," *Boston Medical & Surgical Journal* 29 (9 August 1843): 10.
103. Stroud, *Sketch of Laws*, 66.
104. Genovese, *Roll, Jordan, Roll*, 39–40. In *Roulhac v. White,* a North Carolina court admitted the testimony of a consumptive slave over the defendant's objections; the superior court affirmed the judgment, noting that "his Honor was correct in admitting, as evidence, the declarations of the slave as to the state of his health." This example, however, seems to be the exception that proves the rule, since Justice J. Nash also noted that the law forbidding African Americans from serving as witnesses against white persons did not apply in this case. Roulhac v. White, 9 Iredell 63 (NC 1848), cited in Catterall, *Judicial Cases*, 2:129.
105. Child, *Appeal in Favor*, 42–43.
106. Craft, *Running a Thousand Miles*, 14.
107. Schafer, *Slavery*, 30.
108. Goodell, *American Slave Code*, 194.
109. T. D. Weld, *American Slavery*, 145.
110. State v. Mann, 13 N.C. 263, 1829 N.C. LEXIS 62 (1829), LexisNexis.

111. Ibid.
112. E. A. Davis, *Plantation Life*, 43–44; Bauer and Bauer, "Day to Day Resistance," 406–7; Pollard, *Complaint to the Lord*, 41.
113. White, *Ar'n't I a Woman*, 114–15, 130; Creel, *"A Peculiar People,"* 58; Genovese, *Roll, Jordan, Roll*, 521; Jones, *Born a Child of Freedom*, 54. See also Mrs. George A. Hickox (nee Mary Catherine Brisbane), "This Paper was Read at the Monday Club Held at Washington, Connecticut, About the Year 1898," Vertical File 30-21-1 (African Americans; General), South Carolina Historical Society, Charleston, 4–5; Burke, *Pleasure and Pain*, 33.
114. Forry, "Vital Statistics," 155.
115. Clinkscales, *On the Old Plantation*, 45.
116. Bauer and Bauer, "Day to Day Resistance," 406–7.
117. Robert William Fogel and Stanley L. Engerman, *Time on the Cross: The Economics of American Negro Slavery* (Boston: Little, Brown, 1974), 119, 126. See also Gregory Brian Durling, "Female Labor, Malingering, and the Abuse of Equipment under Slavery: Evidence from the Marydale Plantation," *Southern Studies* 5 (Spring & Summer 1994): 37–38, 40, 42, 45.
118. See Gutman, *Slavery and the Numbers Game*, xii, 85–87; Stampp, *Peculiar Institution*, 103–5; Genovese, *Roll, Jordan, Roll*, 620; Savitt, *Medicine and Slavery*, 114–16, 162–65; Fett, *Working Cures*, 177.
119. Hackford, "Malingering," 5, 10, 43, 45, 47, 49, 61, 86.
120. Ibid., 44–45, 56.
121. E. A. Davis, *Plantation Life*, 329.
122. Owens, *This Species of Property*, 93–94; Stampp, *Peculiar Institution*, 128.
123. Owens, *This Species of Property*, 94.
124. See Jones, *Born a Child of Freedom*, 61.
125. Redpath, *Roving Editor*, 252–53. See also Bauer and Bauer, "Day to Day Resistance," 413.
126. [Frances] Trollope, *Domestic Manners of the Americans*, vol. 2, 4th ed. (London: Whitaker, Treacher & Co., 1832), 51. See also Owens, *This Species of Property*, 93.
127. Lewis Garrard Clarke and Milton Clarke, *Narratives of the Sufferings of Lewis and Milton Clarke, Sons of a Soldier of the Revolution, during a Captivity of More than Twenty Years among the Slaveholders of Kentucky, One of the So-Called Christian States of North America* (Boston: Bela Marsh, 1846), 125. See also Bauer and Bauer, "Day to Day Resistance," 414. Like the Virginia man Trollope described, Ennis likely attacked his hands to disable himself from the kind of field labor expected of a slave in the deep South, but he was sold anyway; one may speculate that his malingering ploy failed because Coombs wanted to punish Ennis for deliberately injuring himself, or because the master wanted to recoup some of the financial loss that Ennis generated.
128. See Bergad, *Comparative Histories of Slavery in Brazil*, 166; Jones, *Born a Child of Freedom*, 137.
129. Berlin, *Generations of Captivity*, 3.

NOTES TO CHAPTER 7

1. Louis Manigault Family Record, 1756–1887, 320, 0177.01.01.02. The name "Moses" is given in quotation marks.
2. "Negroes Brt 15 Feby 1849 for McAlpins Place adjoining Gowrie . . . Decembr 1848," Louis Manigault Papers, Box 2, Papers 1847–1849, Rare Book, Manuscript, and Special Collections Library, Duke University, Durham, North

Carolina. This may be the same Moses whom Louis Manigault acquired as "prime" field hand in 1848 or 1849.

3. Louis Manigault Family Record, 320.
4. "Statement of a Slave: Meeting in Dr. Cheever's Church," *The New York Times* (14 January 1862), cited in Blassingame, *Slave Testimony*, 171.
5. See Yetman, *Life Under the "Peculiar Institution,"* 14; [Interview with Reverend Nelson Hammock, b. 1842], *Weevils in the Wheat*, 127.
6. Downs, "The Continuation of Slavery," http://www.dsq-sds.org/article/view/112/112.
7. David W. Blight, *Race and Reunion: The Civil War in American Memory* (Cambridge, MA: Harvard University Press, Belknap, 2001), 3–4, 19, 32, 42.
8. Paper delivered by Mary M. Solari, J. Harvey Mathews chapter, United Daughters of the Confederacy, Memphis, Tennessee, *Confederate Veteran* 13 (March 1905): 123–24, cited in Blight, *Race and Reunion*, 459n57.
9. See Grace Elizabeth Hale, *Making Whiteness: The Culture of Segregation in the South, 1890–1940* (New York: Vintage Books, 1998), 52–53, 153, 205, 211; Blight, *Race and Reunion*, 395.
10. Bay, "See Your Declaration Americans!!!," 35.

Select Bibliography

MANUSCRIPT COLLECTIONS

Duke University Library, Special Collections Department. Durham, North Carolina

African American Miscellany File. Slavery Division: 1757–1867, n.d.
Archibald H. Boyd Papers, 1841–1897.
Dick Brown Slave Records Collection.
Tyre Glen Papers.
Jarratt-Puryear Papers.
William L. Johnston Papers.
Louis Manigault Papers.
Vardry McBee Letters.
Robert S. Mills Papers.
Rockingham Plantation Journal, 1828–1829.
Haller Nutt Papers.
Francis Cope Yarnall Papers.

South Carolina Historical Society. Charleston, South Carolina

African Americans: General Vertical File.
Allston Family Papers.
Robert F. W. Allston Papers.
Ball Family Papers.
Samuel G. Barker Papers.
Langdon Cheves Papers.
Ford-Ravenel Collection.
Alexander Glennie Journal (Commonplace Book).
Glover Papers.
Theodore Gourdin Papers.
Hutson Lee Papers.
Louisa Lord Papers, 1850–1862.
Thomas W. Peyre Journal, 1834–c.1850.
Thomas P. Ravenel Collection.

University of North Carolina Library, Southern Historical Collection. Chapel Hill, North Carolina

John S. Henderson Papers.
George J. Kollock Plantation Journals.
John Nevitt Record Book.

Waring Historical Library, Medical University of South Carolina, Charleston, South Carolina

Theses, Medical College of the State of South Carolina.

MICROFILM AND INTERNET ARCHIVES

Born in Slavery: Slave Narratives from the Federal Writers' Project, 1936–1938, accessed 16 March 2006 and 12 September 2008, Library of Congress, http://memory.loc.gov/ammem/snhtml/snhome.html.
Butler Family Papers, 1663-1950.
Charles Brown Papers, 1792-1888.
"Patients' Voices in Early 19th Century Virginia: Letters to Doct. Carmichael & Son." Accessed 6 July 2007. Dr. James Carmichael Papers, 1816–1832 and n.d. Albert and Shirley Small Special Collections Library, University of Virginia Library, Charlottesville, Virginia, http://carmichael.lib.virginia.edu.
Records of the Ante-Bellum Southern Plantations from the Revolution through the Civil War (microfilm), edited by Kenneth M. Stampp.
Samuel J. May Anti-Slavery Collection. Accessed 19 February 2009. Division of Rare and Manuscript Collections, Cornell University Library, http://digital.library.cornell.edu:80/m/mayantislavery.

PRIMARY SOURCES

Affleck, Thomas. "On the Hygiene of Cotton Plantations and the Management of Negro Slaves." *Southern Medical Reports* 2 (1850): 429–36.
Anti-slavery Songs: A Selection from the Best Anti-slavery Authors. Salem, OH: Trescott, 1849.
Armistead, Wilson. *A Tribute for the Negro: Being a Vindication of the Moral, Intellectual, and Religious Capabilities of the Coloured Portion of Mankind . . .* Manchester: William Irwin; New York: William Harned, Anti-Slavery Office, 1848.
Bailey, T. P. "Surgical Cases." *Charleston Medical Journal and Review* 14 (November 1859): 740–45.
Ball, Charles. *Fifty Years in Chains; or, The Life of an American Slave.* New York: H. Dayton; Indianapolis, IN: Asher & Company, 1859.
Barnum, P. T. *The Life of P. T. Barnum, Written by Himself.* London: Sampson Low, Son, 1855.
Blassingame, John W., ed. *Slave Testimony: Two Centuries of Letters, Speeches, Interviews, and Autobiographies.* Baton Rouge: Louisiana State University Press, 1977.
Breeden, James O., ed. *Advice among Masters: The Ideal in Slave Management in the Old South.* Westport, CT: Greenwood Press, 1980.
Brown, D. Tilden. "Theatrical Performances at the New York State Lunatic Asylum." *Medical Examiner* 3 (April 1847): 259–62.
Brown, John. *Slave Life in Georgia: A Narrative of the Life, Sufferings, and Escape of John Brown, a Fugitive Slave, Now in England*, edited by L. A. Chamerovzow, London: [W. M. Watts], 1855.
Brown, William Wells. *Clotel; or, The President's Daughter: A Narrative of Slave Life in the United States.* London: Partridge & Oakey, 1853.
———. *My Southern Home: or, The South and Its People.* Boston: A. G. Brown, 1880.
———. *Narrative of William W. Brown, an American Slave.* London: Charles Gilpin, 1849.

Browne, Martha Griffith. *Autobiography of a Female Slave.* New York: Redfield, 1857.

Bruce, Henry Clay. *The New Man: Twenty-Nine Years a Slave. Twenty-Nine Years a Free Man.* York, PA: P. Anstadt & Sons, 1895.

Burke, Emily. *Pleasure and Pain: Reminiscences of Georgia in the 1840's.* Savannah, GA: Beehive Press, 1991.

Campbell, Israel. *An Autobiography: Bond and Free: or, Yearnings for Freedom, from My Green Brier House: Being the Story of My Life in Bondage, and My Life in Freedom.* Philadelphia: C.E.P. Brinckloe, 1861.

Carroll, Robert C. "Jackson Street Hospital Reports: Cases of Menstrual Derangement in Negro Women." *Southern Medical & Surgical Journal* 16 (May 1860): 332–37.

Cartwright, Samuel A. "The Diseases and Physical Peculiarities of the Negro Race." *Southern Medical Reports* 2 (1850): 421–29.

———. "Dr. Cartwright on the Caucasians and the Africans." *DeBow's Review* 25 (July 1858): 45–56.

———. "Philosophy of the Negro Constitution." *New Orleans Medical & Surgical Journal* 9 (1853): 195–208.

———. "Slavery in the Light of Ethnology." *Cotton is King, and Proslavery Arguments*, edited by E. N. Elliott, 691–728. Augusta, GA: Pritchard, Abbott & Loomis, 1860.

Catterall, Helen Tunnicliff, ed. *Judicial Cases Concerning American Slavery and the Negro*, vols. 1 and 2. Washington, DC: Carnegie Institution of Washington, 1926, 1929.

Child, Lydia Maria. *An Appeal in Favor of that Class of Americans called Africans.* Boston: Allen & Ticknor, 1833; Amherst: University of Massachusetts Press, 1996.

A Citizen of Mississippi. "The Negro." *DeBow's Review* 3 (May 1847): 419–22.

Clarke, Lewis Garrard, and Milton Clarke. *Narratives of the Sufferings of Lewis and Milton Clarke, Sons of a Soldier of the Revolution, during a Captivity of More than Twenty Years among the Slaveholders of Kentucky, One of the So-Called Christian States of North America.* Boston: Bela Marsh, 1846.

Clinkscales, J. G. *On the Old Plantation: Reminiscences of His Childhood.* Spartanburg, SC: Band & White, 1916.

Craft, William. *Running a Thousand Miles for Freedom; or, The Escape of William and Ellen Craft from Slavery.* London: William Tweedie, 1860.

Crosby, Josiah. "Seminal Weakness—Castration." *Boston Medical & Surgical Journal* 29 (9 August 1843): 10.

Davis, Edwin Adams, [ed]. *Plantation Life in the Florida Parishes of Louisiana, 1836–1846, as Reflected in the Diary of Bennet H. Barrow.* New York: Columbia University Press, 1943.

DeWees, H. P. "On Paralytic and Convulsive Diseases of the Cerebro-Spinal System, Including Epilepsy, Its Physiology, Pathology, and Treatment." *The American Medical Monthly and New York Review* 15 (April 1861): 241–65, 338–63.

"A Dialogue between Two Southern Gentlemen and a Negro, part 1." *The Opal* (May 1852). http://www.disabilitymuseum.org/lib/docs/1258.htm.

Doesticks, Q. C. Philander [Mortimer Neal Thompson]. *Great Auction Sale of Slaves, at Savannah, Georgia, March 2d and 3d, 1859.* New York: American Anti-Slavery Society, 1859, accessed 7 July 2009, http://antislavery.eserver.org/travel/thompsonauction/thompsonauction.html.

Douglass, Frederick. *Life and Times of Frederick Douglass, Written By Himself . . .* rev. ed. Boston: De Wolfe & Fiske, 1892.

———. *Narrative of the Life of Frederick Douglass, an American Slave.* Boston: Anti-Slavery Office, 1845; New York: Viking Penguin, 1986.

Douglass, John. "Surgical Cases." *Charleston Medical Journal and Review* 4 (May 1849): 298–301.

Drago, Edmund L., ed. *Broke by the War: Letters of a Slave Trader*. Columbia: University of South Carolina Press, 1991.

Dungan, James B. "Double-Headed Monster." *New Orleans Medical News and Hospital Gazette* 4 (1 May 1857): 129–30.

Dunglison, R. *Human Physiology with Three Hundred and Sixty-Eight Illustrations*, 2 vols., 6th ed. Philadelphia: Lea and Blanchard, 1846.

Easterby, J. H., ed. *The South Carolina Rice Plantation as Revealed in the Papers of Robert F. W. Allston*. Columbia: University of South Carolina Press, 2004.

Fee, John G. *Autobiography of John G. Fee, Berea, Kentucky*. Chicago: National Christian Association, 1891.

Forry, Samuel. "On the Relative Proportion of Centenarians, of Deaf and Dumb, of Blind, and of Insane, in the Races of European and African Origin, as Shown by the Census of the United States." *New York Journal of Medicine and the Collateral Sciences* 2 (May 1844): 310–20.

———. "Vital Statistics Furnished by the Sixth Census of the United States, Bearing upon the Question of the Unity of the Human Race." *New York Journal of Medicine, and the Collateral Sciences* 1 (September 1843): 151–67.

Forten, [Charlotte]. "Life on the Sea Islands, Part 2." *Atlantic Monthly* 80 (June 1864): 666–76.

Freemon, J. Anton. "Removal of a Large Tumor from the Thigh of a Negro Woman, Aged 30 Years, by Professors H. L. Byrd and F. W. B. Hemming, of Oglethorpe Medical College, Assisted by Dr. W. L. Davis." *Oglethorpe Medical and Surgical Journal* 1 (March 1860): 400–404.

[Gooch, P. Claiborne]. "The Carolina Twins." *The Stethoscope, and Virginia Medical Gazette* 2 (July 1852): 394–95.

Goodell, William. *The American Slave Code in Theory and Practice: Its Distinctive Features Shown by Its Statutes, Judicial Decisions, and Illustrative Facts*, 2nd ed. New York: American & Foreign Anti-Slavery Society, 1853; New York: New American Library, 1969.

Grandy, Moses. *Narrative of the Life of Moses Grandy; Late a Slave in the United States of America*. London: C. Gilpin, 1843.

Grier, S. L. "The Negro and His Diseases." *New Orleans Medical & Surgical Journal* 9 (1852–53): 752–63.

"Hare-Lip in the Negro." *Western Lancet* 4 (November 1845): 332.

Harriss, Juriah. "What Constitutes Unsoundness in the Negro?" *Savannah Journal of Medicine* 1 (September 1858): 145–52; 1 (January 1859): 289–95; 2 (May 1859): 10–16.

Hemming, F.W B. "Notes on the Surgical Pathology and Character of the above Tumor, Removed by Drs. H. L. Byrd and F.W.B. Hemming." *Oglethorpe Medical and Surgical Journal* 1 (1860): 404–7.

Henson, Josiah. *The Life of Josiah Henson, Formerly a Slave, Now an Inhabitant of Canada, as Narrated by Himself*. Boston: Arthur D. Phelps, 1849.

Hildreth, Richard. *The White Slave: or, Memoirs of a Fugitive*. Boston: Tappan and Whittemore, 1852.

Hitchcock, President. "The Blind Slave of the Mines." *North Star*. 24 November 1848.

[Interview with Reverend Nelson Hammock, b. 1842]. *Weevils in the Wheat: Interviews with Virginia Ex-Slaves*, edited by Charles L. Perdue Jr., Thomas E. Barden, and Robert K. Phillips, 127. Bloomington: Indiana University Press, 1976.

"Is the Negro Subject to Hare-Lip?" *Western Lancet* 4 (June 1845): 95.

[Jacobs, Harriet]. *Incidents in the Life of a Slave Girl: Written by Herself*, edited by Lydia Maria Child. Boston, 1861.

Jarrot, Richard. "Amputation for Gangrene of the Foot, Successfully Performed on a Negro, at the Advanced Age of One Hundred and Two Years." *Charleston Medical Journal and Review* 4 (May 1849): 301–3.

Jefferson, Thomas. *Jefferson's Notes on the State of Virginia; with the Appendixes— Complete.* Baltimore: W. Pechin, 1800.

Keen, William, W., S. Weir Mitchell, and George R. Morehouse. "On Malingering: Especially in Regard to Simulation of Diseases of the Nervous System." *American Journal of the Medical Sciences* 48 (October 1864): 367–94.

Lawson, L. M. "A Few Thoughts on Epilepsy." *Western Lancet* 18 (January 1857): 1–7.

Life Insurance: Its Principles, Operations and Benefits, as Presented by the N.C. Mutual Life Insur. Co. Raleigh, NC: Seaton Gales, 1849.

The Life of Joice Heth, the Nurse of Gen. George Washington, (the Father of Our Country,) Now Living at the Astonishing Age of 161 Years, and Weighs Only 46 Pounds. New York, 1835.

Loguen, Jermain Wesley. *The Rev. J. W. Loguen, as a Slave and as a Freeman: A Narrative of Real Life.* Syracuse: J.G.K. Truair, 1859.

Long, C .W. "An Account of the First Use of Sulphuric Ether by Inhalation as an Anaesthetic in Surgical Operations." *Southern Medical and Surgical Journal* 5 (December 1849): 705–13.

McCaa, William L. "Observations on the Manner of Living and Diseases of the Slaves of the Wateree River." M.D. thesis, University of Pennsylvania, 1822.

[McCoy], Millie-Christine. *The History of the Carolina Twins: "Told in Their Own Peculiar Way" by "One of Them."* [Buffalo]: Buffalo Courier Printing House, [1869?].

Meaders, Daniel, ed. *Advertisements for Runaway Slaves in Virginia, 1801–1820.* New York: Garland, 1997.

Merrill, A. P. "An Essay on Some of the Distinctive Peculiarities of the Negro Race." *Memphis Medical Recorder* 4 (July 1855): 1–17, 65–77.

"Minutes of the Society." *Transactions of the Fourth Annual Meeting of the Medical Society of the State of Georgia* IV (Savannah, April 1853): 3–10.

Morgan, John H. "An Essay on the Causes of the Production of Abortion among Our Negro Population." *Nashville Journal of Medicine & Surgery* 19 (1860): 117–23.

"Negro Melodies." *The Opal* (December 1854). http://www.disabilitymuseum.org/ lib/docs/1318.htm?page = 1.

Northup, Solomon. *Twelve Years a Slave: Narrative of Solomon Northup, a Citizen of New-York, Kidnapped in Washington City in 1841 and Rescued in 1853, from a Cotton Plantation near the Red River in Louisiana.* Auburn, NY: Derby and Miller; Buffalo: Derby, Orton and Mulligan; London: Sampson Low, Son, 1853.

Nott, Josiah C. "The Mulatto a Hybrid—Probable Extermination of the Two Races if the Whites and Blacks Are Allowed to Intermarry." *American Journal of the Medical Sciences* 6 (July 1843): 252–56.

———. "Statistics of Southern Slave Population, with Especial Reference to Life Insurance." *DeBow's Review* 4 (November 1847): 275–89.

———. *Two Lectures, on the Natural History of the Caucasian and Negro Races.* Mobile, AL: Dade & Thompson, 1844.

Powell, Thomas S. "Reports of the Case Book of Thos. S. Powell, M.D., Sparta, Georgia." *Atlanta Medical & Surgical Journal* 1 (May 1856): 516–18.

A Professional Planter [Dr. Collins]. *Practical Rules for the Management and Medical Treatment of Negro Slaves, in the Sugar Colonies.* London: printed by J. Barfield for Vernor, Hood and Sharp; Hatchard, 1811. Reprinted by Freeport, NY: Books for Libraries Press, 1971.

Ramsay, H. A. "The Pulse, Cranial Dimensions, &c., of the Southern Negro Child, with some Remarks upon Infantile Therapeutics." *Boston Medical & Surgical Journal* 48 (1853): 396–402.

————. "The Southern Negro, etc." *Philadelphia Medical & Surgical Journal* 1 (1852–53): 293–97.

"Recollections of a Runaway Slave." *The Emancipator*. 11 October 1838.

Redpath, James. *The Roving Editor: Or, Talks with Slaves in the Southern States.* New York: A. B. Burdick, 1859. Reprinted New York: Negro Universities Press, 1968.

Robert, W. H. "Surgical Cases Occurring in the Practice of L. A. Dugas, M.D. Professor in the Medical College of Georgia." *Southern Medical & Surgical Journal* 3 (February 1839): 287–97.

"Sale of Aged Slaves." In *Five Hundred Thousand Strokes for Freedom*. Leeds Anti-Slavery Series, no. 17. Reprint, Miami, FL: Mnemosyne Publishing Co., 1969. Originally published London: W. & F. Cash; William Tweedie, 1853.

Senex. "On Surgical Operations." *Virginia Medical Journal* 6 (February 1856): 108–11.

"Serpent Worship among the Negroes." *DeBow's Review* 31 (July 1861): 97–99.

Shryock, Richard D., ed. *Letters of Richard D. Arnold, M.D. 1808–1876*. Durham, NC: Seeman Press, 1929.

Sims, J. Marion. "On the Treatment of Vesico-Vaginal Fistula." *American Journal of the Medical Sciences* 23 (January 1852): 59–82.

————. "Osteo-Sarcoma of the Lower Jaw.—Resection of the body of the bone.—Cure." *American Journal of the Medical Sciences* 11 (January 1846): 128–32.

————. *The Story of My Life*. New York: D. Appleton, 1898.

A Sketch in the Life of Thomas Greene Bethune (Blind Tom). Philadelphia: Ledger Book and Job Printing Establishment, 1865.

"A Slave Auction in Virginia." In *Five Hundred Thousand Strokes for Freedom*. Leeds Anti-Slavery Series, no. 49. London: W. & F. Cash; William Tweedie, 1853. Reprinted Miami, FL: Mnemosyne, 1969.

Slave Bills of Sale Project. Atlanta: African-American Family History Association, Inc., 1986.

"Slave-Branding." In *Five Hundred Thousand Strokes for Freedom*. Leeds Anti-Slavery Series, no. 23. London: W. & F. Cash; William Tweedie, 1853. Reprinted Miami, FL: Mnemosyne, 1969.

"Slavery a System of Inherent Cruelty." In *Five Hundred Thousand Strokes for Freedom*. Leeds Anti-Slavery Series, no. 7, London: W. & F. Cash; William Tweedie, 1853. Reprinted Miami, FL: Mnemosyne, 1969.

Smith, James L. *Autobiography of James L. Smith, Including, Also, Reminiscences of Slave Life, Recollections of the War, Education of Freedmen, Causes of the Exodus, Etc.* Norwich: Press of the Bulletin Company, 1881.

Spence, Thomas R. P. "Account of the Efficacy of Sugar of Lead, in a Case of Epilepsy." *Philadelphia Medical Museum* 2 (1806): 150–54.

"Statement of a Slave: Meeting in Dr. Cheever's Church." In *Slave Testimony: Two Centuries of Letters, Speeches, Interviews, and Autobiographies*, edited by John W. Blassingame, 170–72. Baton Rouge: Louisiana State University Press, 1977.

Stowe, Harriet Beecher. *A Key to Uncle Tom's Cabin: Presenting the Original Facts and Documents upon Which the Story is Founded*. London: T. Bosworth, 1853.

Stringfellow, Thornton. *Scriptural and Statistical Views in Favor of Slavery*, 4th ed. Richmond, VA: J. W. Randolph, 1856.

Stroud, George M. *A Sketch of the Laws Relating to Slavery in the Several States of the United States of America*, 2nd ed. Philadelphia, 1856.

Thompson, John. *The Life of John Thompson, a Fugitive Slave: Containing His History of 25 Years in Bondage, and His Providential Escape*. Worcester: John Thompson, 1856.

Tower, Philo. *Slavery Unmasked: Being a Truthful Narrative of a Three Years' Residence and Journeying in Eleven Southern States*. Rochester: E. Darrow and Brother, 1856.

Trollope, [Frances]. *Domestic Manners of the Americans*, vol. 2, 4th ed. London: Whitaker, Treacher & Co., 1832.

Van Evrie, John H. *White Supremacy and Negro Subordination, or Negroes a Subordinate Race*. New York: Van Evrie, Horton, 1868.

Weld, Charles Richard. *A Vacation Tour in the United States and Canada*. London: Longman, Brown, Green, and Longmans, 1855.

Weld, Theodore Dwight. *American Slavery as It Is*: *Testimony of a Thousand Witnesses*. New York: American Anti-Slavery Society, 1839.

Woods, Nancy Venture to Master [John Haywood?]. Newbern [NC], 5 February 1825, edited by Robert S. Starobin, 87. *Blacks in Bondage*: *Letters of American Slaves*. New York: New Viewpoints, 1974.

SECONDARY SOURCES

Amundson, Ron. "Disability, Ideology, and Quality of Life: A Bias in Biomedical Ethics." In *Quality of Life and Human Difference*: *Genetic Testing, Healthcare, and Disability*, edited by David Wasserman, Jerome Bickerbach, and Robert Wachbroit, 101–24. Cambridge: Cambridge University Press, 2005.

Anderson, Julie. "Review Essay: Voices in the Darkness: Representations of Disability in Historical Research." *Journal of Contemporary History* 44, no. 1 (January 2009): 107–16.

Andrews, William L. *To Tell a Free Story*: *The First Century of Afro-American Autobiography, 1760–1865*. Urbana: University of Illinois Press, 1986.

Bancroft, Frederic. *Slave Trading in the Old South*. Baltimore: J. H. Furst, 1931. Southern Classics Series, edited by John G. Sproat. Columbia: University of South Carolina Press, 1996.

Bankole, Katherine. *Slavery and Medicine*: *Enslavement and Medical Practices in Antebellum Louisiana*. New York: Garland, 1998.

Baptist, Edward E. "'Stol' and Fetched Here': Enslaved Migration, Ex-slave Narratives, and Vernacular History." In *New Studies in the History of Slavery*, edited by Edward E. Baptist and Stephanie M. H. Camp, 243–74. Athens: University of Georgia Press, 2006.

Barclay, Jenifer. "'Cripples All! Or, the Mark of Slavery': Disability and Race in Antebellum America, 1820-1860." Ph.D. Dissertation, Michigan State University, 2011.

Barrett, Lindon. "Hand-Writing: Legibility and the White Body in *Running a Thousand Miles for Freedom*." *American Literature* 69 (June 1997): 315–36.

Bauer, Raymond A., and Alice H. Bauer. "Day to Day Resistance to Slavery." *Journal of Negro History* 27 (October 1942): 388–419.

Baumgartner, Barbara. "The Body as Evidence: Resistance, Collaboration, and Appropriation in 'The History of Mary Prince.'" *Callaloo* 24 (Winter 2001): 253–75.

Bay, Mia. "See Your Declaration Americans!!! Abolitionism, Americanism, and the Revolutionary Tradition in Free Black Politics." In *Americanism*: *New Perspectives on the History of an Ideal*, edited by Michael Kazin and Joseph A. McCartin, 25–52. Chapel Hill: University of North Carolina Press, 2006.

Baynton, Douglas C. "Disability and the Justification of Inequality in American History." In *The New Disability History*: *American Perspectives* edited by Paul K. Longmore and Lauri Umansky, 33–57. New York: New York University Press, 2001.

———. "Disability in History." *Disability Studies Quarterly* 28, no. 3 (Summer 2008). http://www.dsq-sds.org/article/view/108/108.

Bergad, Laird W. *The Comparative Histories of Slavery in Brazil, Cuba, and the United States*. New York: Cambridge University Press, 2007.

Berlin, Ira. *Generations of Captivity*: *A History of African-American Slaves*. Cambridge, MA: Harvard University Press, 2003.

————. *Many Thousands Gone: The First Two Centuries of Slavery in North America.* Cambridge, MA: Harvard University Press, 1998.

Berry, Daina Ramey. "'We'm Fus' Rate Bargain': Value, Labor, and Price in a Georgia Slave Community." In *The Chattel Principle: Internal Slave Trades in the Americas,* edited by Walter Johnson, 55–71. New Haven, CT: Yale University Press, 2004.

———— and Deleso A. Alford, eds. *Enslaved Women in America: An Encyclopedia.* Westport, CT: Greenwood, 2012.

Bland, Sterling Lecater Jr. *Voices of the Fugitives: Runaway Slave Stories and Their Fictions of Self-Creation.* Westport, CT: Greenwood Press, 2000.

Blassingame, John W. "Introduction." In *Slave Testimony: Two Centuries of Letters, Speeches, Interviews, and Autobiographies,* edited by John W. Blassingame, xvii–lxv. Baton Rouge: Louisiana State University Press, 1977.

————. *The Slave Community: Plantation Life in the Antebellum South,* rev. ed. Oxford: Oxford University Press, 1979.

————. "Using the Testimony of Ex-slaves: Approaches and Problems." *Journal of Southern History* 41 (November 1975): 473–92.

Blight, David W. *Race and Reunion: The Civil War in American Memory.* Cambridge, MA: Harvard University Press, Belknap, 2001.

Bontemps, Arna. "The Slave Narrative: An American Genre." In *Great Slave Narratives,* edited by Arna Bontemps, vii–xix. Boston: Beacon Press, 1969.

Boster, Dea H. "An 'Epeleptick' Bondswoman: Fits, Slavery, and Power in the Antebellum South." *Bulletin of the History of Medicine* 83 (Summer 2009): 271–301.

————. "'Useless': Disability, Slave Labor, and Contradiction on Antebellum Southern Plantations." *Review of Disability Studies* 7 (December 2011): 26–33.

Bronstein, Jamie L. *Caught in the Machinery: Workplace Accidents and Injured Workers in Nineteenth-Century Britain.* Stanford, CA: Stanford University Press, 2007.

Brown, Vincent. "Spiritual Terror and Sacred Authority: The Power of the Supernatural in Jamaican Slave Society." In *New Studies in the History of Slavery,* edited by Edward E. Baptist and Stephanie M. H. Camp, 179–210. Athens: University of Georgia Press, 2006.

Burbick, Joan. *Healing the Republic: The Language of Health and the Culture of Nationalism in Nineteenth-Century America.* Cambridge: Cambridge University Press, 1994.

Byrd, W. Michael, and Linda A. Clayton. *An American Health Dilemma.* Vol. 1: *A Medical History of African Americans and the Problem of Race, Beginnings to 1900.* New York: Routledge, 2000.

Camp, Stephanie M. H. "The Pleasures of Resistance: Enslaved Women and Body Politics in the Plantation South, 1830–1861." In *New Studies in the History of Slavery,* edited by Edward E. Baptist and Stephanie M. H. Camp, 87–124. Athens: University of Georgia Press, 2006.

Camp, Stephanie M. H., and Edward E. Baptist. "Introduction: A History of the History of Slavery in the Americas." In *New Studies in the History of Slavery,,* edited by Edward E. Baptist and Stephanie M. H. Camp, 1–18. Athens: University of Georgia Press, 2006.

Clark, Elizabeth B. "'The Sacred Rights of the Weak': Pain, Sympathy, and the Culture of Individual Rights in Antebellum America." *Journal of American History* 82 (September 1995): 463–93.

Cobb, W. Montague. "Surgery and the Negro Physician: Some Parallels in Background." *Journal of the National Medical Association* 43 (May 1951): 145–52.

Cook, James W. *The Arts of Deception: Playing with Fraud in the Age of Barnum.* Cambridge, MA: Harvard University Press, 2001.

Creel, Margaret Washington. *"A Peculiar People": Slave Religion and Community-Culture among the Gullahs.* New York: New York University Press, 1988.

Davis, David Brion. *Inhuman Bondage: The Rise and Fall of Slavery in the New World*. New York: Oxford University Press, 2006.

Davis, Lennard J. *Enforcing Normalcy: Disability, Deafness, and the Body*. London: Verso, 1995.

DeLombard, Jeannine. "'Eye-Witness to the Cruelty': Southern Violence and Northern Testimony in Frederick Douglass' 1845 *Narrative*." *American Literature* 73 (June 2001): 245–75.

Deyle, Steven. *Carry Me Back: The Domestic Slave Trade in American Life*. New York: Oxford University Press, 2005.

Downs, Jim. "The Continuation of Slavery: The Experience of Disabled Slaves during Emancipation." *Disability Studies Quarterly* 28 no. 3 (Summer 2008). http://www.dsq-sds.org/article/view/112/112.

Durling, Gregory Brian. "Female Labor, Malingering, and the Abuse of Equipment under Slavery: Evidence from the Marydale Plantation." *Southern Studies* 5 (Spring & Summer 1994): 31–49.

Elkins, Stanley M. *Slavery: A Problem in American Institutional and Intellectual Life*. 3rd ed. rev. Chicago: University of Chicago Press, 1976.

Fabian, Ann. *The Unvarnished Truth: Personal Narratives in Nineteenth-Century America*. Berkeley: University of California Press, 2000.

Faust, Drew Gilpin. "Culture, Conflict, and Community: The Meaning of Power on an Ante-Bellum Plantation." *Journal of Social History* 14 (Autumn 1980): 83–97.

Fearnley, Andrew M. "Primitive Madness: Re-Writing the History of Mental Illness and Race." *Journal of the History of Medicine and Allied Sciences* 63 (April 2008): 245–57.

Fede, Andrew. "Legal Protection for Slave Buyers in the U.S. South: A Caveat Concerning Caveat Emptor." *American Journal of Legal History* 31 (October 1987): 322–58.

Feldstein, Stanley. *Once a Slave: The Slave's View of Slavery*. New York: W. Morrow, 1971.

Fett, Sharla M. "Consciousness and Calling: African American Midwives at Work in the Antebellum South." In *New Studies in the History of Slavery*, edited by Edward E. Baptist and Stephanie M. H. Camp, 64–86. Athens: University of Georgia Press, 2006.

———. *Working Cures: Healing, Health, and Power on Southern Slave Plantations*. Chapel Hill: University of North Carolina Press, 2002.

Fields, Barbara J. "Ideology and Race in American History." In *Region, Race, and Reconstruction: Essays in Honor of C. Vann Woodward*, edited by J. Morgan Kousser and James M. McPherson, 143–77. New York: Oxford University Press, 1982.

Finkelman, Paul. "Slaves as Fellow Servants: Ideology, Law, and Industrialization." *American Journal of Legal History* 31 (October 1987): 269–305.

Fisher, Walter. "Physicians and Slavery in the Antebellum Southern Medical Journal." *Journal of the History of Medicine and Allied Sciences* 23 (January 1968): 36–49.

Fleischner, Jennifer. *Mastering Slavery: Memory, Family, and Identity in Women's Slave Narratives*. New York: New York University Press, 1996.

Fogel, Robert William, and Stanley L. Engerman. *Time on the Cross: The Economics of American Negro Slavery*. Boston: Little, Brown, 1974.

Franklin, John Hope, and Loren Schweininger. *Runaway Slaves: Rebels on the Plantation*. New York: Oxford University Press, 1999.

Fredrickson, George M. *The Black Image in the White Mind: The Debate on Afro-American Character and Destiny, 1817–1914*. New York: Harper & Row, 1971.

Freudenberger, Herman, and Jonathan B. Pritchett. "The Domestic United States Slave Trade: New Evidence." *Journal of Interdisciplinary History* 21 (Winter 1991): 447–77.

Friedman, Lawrence Meir. *The Legal System: A Social Science Perspective.* New York: Russell Sage Foundation, 1975.

Gartner, Alan, and Tom Joe. "Introduction." *Images of the Disabled, Disabling Images.* New York: Praeger, 1987. Genovese, Eugene D. "The Medical and Insurance Costs of Slaveholding in the Cotton Belt." *Journal of Negro History* 45 (July 1960): 141–55.

———. *Roll, Jordan, Roll: The World the Slaves Made.* New York: Vintage, 1974.

Gilroy, Paul. *The Black Atlantic: Modernity and Double Consciousness.* Cambridge, MA: Harvard University Press, 1993.

Goffman, Erving. *Stigma: Notes on the Management of Spoiled Identity.* Englewood Cliffs, NJ: Prentice Hall, 1963.

Gorn, Elliott J. "Black Magic: Folk Beliefs of the Slave Community." In *Science and Medicine in the Old South*, edited by Ronald L. Numbers and Todd L. Savitt, 295–326. Baton Rouge: Louisiana State University Press, 1989.

Greenberg, Kenneth S. *Honor and Slavery: Lies, Duels, Noses, Masks, Dressing as a Woman, Gifts, Strangers, Death, Humanitarianism, Slave Rebellions, the Proslavery Argument, Baseball, Hunting and Gambling in the Old South.* Princeton, NJ: Princeton University Press, 1996.

Grob, Gerald N. *Edward Jarvis and the Medical World of Nineteenth-Century America.* Knoxville: University of Tennessee Press, 1978.

Gross, Ariela J *Double Character: Slavery and Mastery in the Antebellum Southern Courtroom.* Princeton, NJ: Princeton University Press, 2000.

———. "Pandora's Box: Slave Character on Trial in the Antebellum Deep South." *Yale Journal of Law and the Humanities* 7 (1995): 267–316.

Gunning, Sandra. "Nancy Prince and the Politics of Mobility, Home and Diasporic (Mis)identification." *American Quarterly* 53 (March 2001): 32–69.

Gutman, Herbert G. *The Black Family in Slavery and Freedom, 1750–1925.* New York: Pantheon, 1976.

———. *Slavery and the Numbers Game: A Critique of* Time on the Cross. Urbana: University of Illinois Press, 2003.

Hackford, Heidi M. "Malingering: Representations of Feigned Disease in American History, 1800–1920." PhD. dissertation, American University, 2004.

Hale, Grace Elizabeth. *Making Whiteness: The Culture of Segregation in the South, 1890–1940.* New York: Vintage Books, 1998.

Haller, John S. Jr. "The Negro and the Southern Physician: A Study of Medical and Racial Attitudes 1800–1860." *Medical History* 16 (July 1972): 238–53.

Hartman, Saidiya. *Scenes of Subjection: Terror, Slavery, and Self-Making in Nineteenth-Century America.* New York: Oxford University Press, 1997.

Herndl, Diane Price. *Invalid Women: Figuring Feminine Illness in American Fiction and Culture, 1840–1940.* Chapel Hill: University of North Carolina Press, 1993.

Hirsch, Jerrold, and Karen Hirsch. "Disability and Ex-slave Narratives." H-Civwar Post, 30 June 1994. http://www.h-net.org/~civwar/logs/archives/ log9406/0100. html.

———. "Disability in the Family? New Questions about the Southern Mill Village." *Journal of Social History* 35 (Summer 2002): 919–33.

Humphreys, Margaret. *Intensely Human: The Health of the Black Soldier in the American Civil War.* Baltimore, MD: Johns Hopkins University Press, 2008.

Iezzoni, Lisa I., and Vicki A. Freedman. "Turning the Disability Tide: The Importance of Definitions." *Journal of the American Medical Association* 299 (23 January 2008): 332–34.

Jennings, Audra. "Introduction: Disability and History." *Disability Studies Quarterly* 28 no. 3 (Summer 2008). http://www.dsq-sds.org/article/view/108/108.

Johnson, Charles S., and Horace M. Bond. "The Investigation of Racial Differences Prior to 1910." *Journal of Negro Education* 3 (July 1934): 328–39.

Johnson, Guion Griffis. *Ante-Bellum North Carolina: A Social History*. Chapel Hill: University of North Carolina Press, 1937.

Johnson, Walter. "Introduction: The Future Store." In *The Chattel Principle: Internal Slave Trades in the Americas*, edited by Walter Johnson, 1–31. New Haven, CT: Yale University Press, 2004.

———. "Review. Inconsistency, Contradiction, and Complete Confusion: The Everyday Life of the Law of Slavery." *Law & Social Inquiry* 22 (Spring 1997): 405–33.

———. *Soul by Soul: Life inside the Antebellum Slave Market*. Cambridge, MA: Harvard University Press, 1999.

Jones, Norrece T. Jr. *Born a Child of Freedom, Yet a Slave: Mechanisms of Control and Strategies of Resistance in Antebellum South Carolina*. Hanover: Wesleyan University Press; London: University Press of New England, 1990.

Joyner, Charles. *Down by the Riverside: A South Carolina Slave Community*. Urbana: University of Illinois Press, 1984.

Kiple, Kenneth F. *The Caribbean Slave: A Biological History*. Cambridge: Cambridge University Press, 1984.

Kiple, Kenneth F., and Virginia Himmelsteib King. *Another Dimension to the Black Diaspora: Diet, Disease, and Racism*. Cambridge: Cambridge University Press, 1981.

Klages, Mary. *Woeful Afflictions: Disability and Sentimentality in Victorian America*. Philadelphia: University of Pennsylvania Press, 1999.

Kotlikoff, Laurence J. "The Structure of Slave Prices in New Orleans, 1804 to 1862." *Economic Inquiry* 17 (October 1979): 496–518.

Kriegel, Leonard. "The Cripple in Literature." In *Images of the Disabled, Disabling Images*, edited by Alan Gartner and Tom Joe, 31–46. New York: Praeger, 1987.

———. "Uncle Tom and Tiny Tim: Some Reflections on the Cripple as Negro." *American Scholar* 38 (Summer 1969): 412–30.

Kudlick, Catherine J. "Disability History: Why We Need Another 'Other.'" *American Historical Review* 108 (June 2003): 763–93.

LaCom, Cindy. "'It Is More than Lame': Female Disability, Sexuality, and the Maternal in the Nineteenth-Century Novel." In *The Body and Physical Difference: Discourses of Disability*, edited by David T. Mitchell and Sharon L. Snyder, 189–201. Ann Arbor: University of Michigan Press, 1997.

Lander, Kevin, and Jonathan Pritchett. "When to Care: The Economic Rationale of Slavery Health Care Provision." *Social Science History* 33 (Summer 2009): 155–82.

Lane, Ann J. "Introduction." In *The Debate over Slavery: Stanley Elkins and His Critics,* edited by Ann J. Lane, 3–19. Urbana: University of Illinois Press, 1971.

Lapsansky, Phillip. "Graphic Discord: Abolitionist and Antiabolitionist Images." In *The Abolitionist Sisterhood: Women's Political Culture in Antebellum America*, edited by Jean Fagin Yellin and John C. Van Horne, 201–30. Ithaca, NY: Cornell University Press (in cooperation with the Library Company of Philadelphia), 1994.

Levine, Lawrence W. *Black Culture and Black Consciousness: Afro-American Folk Thought from Slavery to Freedom*. Oxford: Oxford University Press, 1977.

Lhamon, W. T. Jr. *Raising Cain: Blackface Performance from Jim Crow to Hip Hop*. Cambridge, MA: Harvard University Press, 1998.

Linton, Simi. *Claiming Disability: Knowledge and Identity*. New York: New York University Press, 1998.

Longmore, Paul K., and Lauri Umansky, "Introduction. Disability History: From the Margins to the Mainstream." In *The New Disability History: American Perspectives*, edited by Paul K. Longmore and Lauri Umansky 1–32. New York: New York University Press, 2001..

Martell, Joanne. *Millie-Christine: Fearfully and Wonderfully Made*. Winston-Salem, NC: John F. Blair, 2000.

Martin, Jonathan D. *Divided Mastery: Slave Hiring in the American South*. Cambridge, MA: Harvard University Press, 2004.

Matt, Susan J. "You Can't Go Home Again: Homesickness and Nostalgia in U.S. History." *Journal of American History* 94 (September 2007): 469–97.

McBride, David. "'Slavery as It Is': Medicine and Slaves of the Plantation South." *Magazine of History* 19 (1 September 2005): 36–39. http://www.proquest.com.

McCandless, Peter. *Moonlight, Magnolias, and Madness: Insanity in South Carolina from the Colonial Period to the Progressive Era.* Chapel Hill: University of North Carolina Press, 1996.

Mitchell, David T., and Sharon L. Snyder. "The Eugenic Atlantic: Race, Disability, and the Making of an International Eugenic Science, 1800–1945." *Disability & Society* 18 (December 2003): 843–64.

———. *Narrative Prosthesis: Disability and the Dependencies of Discourse.* Ann Arbor: University of Michigan Press, 2000.

Moore, Leroy. "Buried Alive Not Dead." *Poor Magazine Online.* 5 March 2001. http://www.poormagazine.org/index.cfm?L1 = news&story = 2.

Morais, Herbert M. *The History of the Negro in Medicine.* New York: Publisher's Co. Inc. for the Association for the Study of Negro Life and History, 1967.

Morgan, Jennifer L. "'Some Could Suckle over Their Shoulder': Male Travelers, Female Bodies, and the Gendering of Racial Ideology." In *New Studies in the History of Slavery*, edited by Edward E. Baptist and Stephanie M. H. Camp, 21–64. Athens: University of Georgia Press, 2006.

Morgan, Philip D. "The Poor: Slaves in Early America." In *Slavery in the Development of the Americas*, edited by David Eltis, Frank D. Lewis, and Kenneth L. Sokoloff, 288–323. Cambridge: Cambridge University Press, 2004.

Morris, Thomas D. *Southern Slavery and the Law, 1619–1860.* Chapel Hill: University of North Carolina Press, 1996.

Nielsen, Kim E. "Historical Thinking and Disability History." *Disability Studies Quarterly* 28 no. 3 (Summer 2008). http://www.dsq-sds.org/article/view/ 107/107.

Oakes, James. *The Ruling Race: A History of American Slaveholders.* London: Norton, 1998.

Osofsky, Gilbert. "Introduction. Puttin' on Ole Massa: The Significance of Slave Narratives." In *Puttin' on Ole Massa: The Slave Narratives of Henry Bibb, William Wells Brown, and Solomon Northup*, edited by Gilbert Osofsky, 9–44. New York: Harper & Row, 1969.

Owens, Leslie Howard. *This Species of Property: Slave Life and Culture in the Old South.* New York: Oxford University Press, 1976.

Painter, Nell Irvin. *Southern History across the Color Line.* Chapel Hill: University of North Carolina Press, 2002.

Parsons, Elsie Clews. *Folk-Lore of the Sea Islands, South Carolina.* Cambridge, MA: American Folk-Lore Society, 1923.

Pasamanick, Benjamin. "Myths Regarding Prevalence of Mental Disease in the American Negro." *Journal of the National Medical Association* 56 (January 1964): 6–17.

Pernick, Martin S. *A Calculus of Suffering: Pain, Professionalism, and Anesthesia in Nineteenth-Century America.* New York: Columbia University Press, 1985.

———. "Defining Disability: The History and Implications of Pre-ADA Controversies." Paper presented at *The Americans with Disabilities Act: Directions for Reform* symposium, sponsored by The University of Michigan Journal of Law Reform, Ann Arbor, Michigan, 4 November 2000.

Peterson, Carla L. *"Doers of the Word": African-American Women Speakers and Writers in the North (1830–1880).* New York: Oxford University Press, 1995.

Phillips, Ulrich Bonnell. *American Negro Slavery: A Survey of the Supply, Employment and Control of Negro Labor as Determined by the Plantation Régime.* New York: D. Appleton, 1918. Reprint by Gloucester, MA: Peter Smith, 1959.

Pollard, Leslie J. *Complaint to the Lord: Historical Perspectives on the African American Elderly*. Selinsgrove, PA: Susquehanna University Press; London: Associated University Presses, 1996.

Postell, William Dosite. *The Health of Slaves on Southern Plantations*. Baton Rouge: Louisiana State University Press, 1951.

———. "Mental Health among the Slave Population on Southern Plantations." *American Journal of Psychiatry* 110 (July 1953): 52–54.

Prude, Jonathan. "To Look Upon the 'Lower Sort': Runaway Ads and the Appearance of Unfree Laborers in America, 1750–1800." *Journal of American History* 78 (June 1991): 124–59.

Raboteau, Albert J. *Slave Religion: The "Invisible Institution" in the Antebellum South*. New York: Oxford University Press, 1978.

Rael, Patrick. *Black Identity and Black Protest in the Antebellum North*. Chapel Hill: University of North Carolina Press, 2002.

Reiss, Benjamin. "Letters from Asylumia: The *Opal* and the Cultural Work of the Lunatic Asylum, 1851–1860." *American Literary History* 16 no. 1 (2004): 1–28.

———. *The Showman and the Slave: Race, Death, and Memory in Barnum's America*. Cambridge, MA: Harvard University Press, 2001.

———. *Theaters of Madness: Insane Asylums and Nineteenth-Century American Culture*. Chicago: University of Chicago Press, 2008.

Roberts, Dorothy. *Killing the Black Body: Race, Reproduction, and the Meaning of Liberty*. New York: Pantheon Books, 1997.

Rosenberg, Charles E. "Framing Disease: Illness, Society, and History." In *Framing Disease: Studies in Cultural History*, edited by Charles E. Rosenberg and Janet Golden, xiii–xxvi. New Brunswick, NJ: Rutgers University Press, 1992.

Rosengarten, Theodore. *Tombee: Portrait of a Cotton Planter*. New York: William Morrow, 1986.

Samuels, Ellen. "'A Complication of Complaints': Untangling Disability, Race, and Gender in William and Ellen Craft's *Running a Thousand Miles for Freedom*." *MELUS* 31 (Fall 2006): 15–47.

Savitt, Todd L. *Medicine and Slavery: The Diseases and Health Care of Blacks in Antebellum Virginia*. Urbana: University of Illinois Press, 1978.

———. "Slave Health and Southern Distinctiveness." In *Disease and Distinctiveness in the American South*, edited by Todd L. Savitt and James Harvey Young, 120–53. Knoxville: University of Tennessee Press, 1988.

———. "Slave Life Insurance in Virginia and North Carolina." *Journal of Southern History* 43 (November 1977): 583–600.

———. "The Use of Blacks for Medical Experimentation and Demonstration in the Old South." *Journal of Southern History* 48 (August 1982): 331–48.

Scarry, Elaine. *The Body in Pain: The Making and Unmaking of the World*. New York: Oxford University Press, 1985.

Schafer, Judith K. "'Guaranteed Against the Vices and Maladies Prescribed by Law': Consumer Protection, the Law of Slave Sales, and the Supreme Court in Antebellum Louisiana." *American Journal of Legal History* 31 (October 1987): 306–21.

———. "New Orleans Slavery in 1850 as Seen in Advertisements." *Journal of Southern History* 47 (February 1981): 33–56.

———. *Slavery, the Civil Law, and the Supreme Court of Louisiana*. Baton Rouge: Louisiana State University Press, 1994.

Schwartz, Marie Jenkins. *Birthing a Slave: Motherhood and Medicine in the Antebellum South*. Cambridge, MA: Harvard University Press, 2006.

Sekora, John. "Black Message/White Envelope: Genre, Authenticity, and Authority in the Antebellum Slave Narrative." *Callaloo* 32 (Summer 1987): 482–515.

Shryock, Richard H. "Medical Practice in the Old South." *South Atlantic Quarterly* 29 (April 1930): 160–78.

———. "Medical Sources and the Social Historian." *American Historical Review* 41 (April 1936): 458–73.

Siebers, Tobin. "Disability as Masquerade." *Literature and Medicine* 23 (Spring 2004): 1–22.

Stampp, Kenneth M. *The Peculiar Institution: Slavery in the Ante-Bellum South.* New York: Knopf, 1956.

Stauffer, John. *The Black Hearts of Men: Radical Abolitionists and the Transformation of Race.* Cambridge, MA: Harvard University Press, 2002.

Steckel, Richard H. "The African American Population of the United States, 1790–1920." In *A Population History of North America,* edited by Michael R. Haines and Richard H. Steckel, 433–82. New York: Cambridge University Press, 2000.

Stevenson, Brenda E. *Life in Black and White: Family and Community in the Slave South.* New York: Oxford University Press, 1996.

Stewart, James Brewer. *Holy Warriors: The Abolitionists and American Slavery.* New York: Hill & Wang, 1976.

Stowe, Steven M. *Doctoring the South: Southern Physicians and Everyday Medicine in the Mid-Nineteenth Century.* Chapel Hill: University of North Carolina Press, 2004.

———. *Intimacy and Power in the Old South: Rituals in the Lives of the Planters.* Baltimore, MD: Johns Hopkins University Press, 1987.

———. "Seeing Themselves at Work: Physicians and the Case Narrative in the Mid-Nineteenth-Century American South." *American Historical Review* 101 (February 1996): 41–79.

Swados, Felice. "Negro Health on the Ante Bellum Plantations." *Bulletin of the History of Medicine* 10 (1941): 460–72.

Tadman, Michael. "The Interregional Slave Trade in the History and Myth-Making of the U.S. South." In *The Chattel Principle: Internal Slave Trades in the Americas,* edited by Walter Johnson, 117–42. New Haven, CT: Yale University Press, 2004.

———.*Speculators and Slaves: Masters, Traders, and Slaves in the Old South.* Madison: University of Wisconsin Press, 1989.

Tansey, Richard. "Bernard Kendig and the New Orleans Slave Trade." *Louisiana History* 23 (Spring 1982): 159–78.

Thielman, Samuel B. "Southern Madness: The Shape of Mental Health Care in the Old South." In *Science and Medicine in the Old South,* edited by Ronald L. Numbers and Todd L. Savitt, 256–75. Baton Rouge: Louisiana State University Press, 1989.

Thomson, Rosemarie Garland. *Extraordinary Bodies: Figuring Physical Disability in American Culture and Literature.* New York: Columbia University Press, 1997.

Valencius, Conevery Bolton. *The Health of the Country: How American Settlers Understood Themselves and Their Land.* New York: Basic Books, 2002.

Wahl, Jenny Bourne. *The Bondsman's Burden: An Economic Analysis of the Common Law of Southern Slavery.* Cambridge: Cambridge University Press, 1998.

Warner, John Harley. "The Idea of Southern Medical Distinctiveness: Medical Knowledge and Practice in the Old South." In *Science and Medicine in the Old South,* edited by Ronald L. Numbers and Todd L. Savitt, 179–205. Baton Rouge: Louisiana State University Press, 1989.

Washington, Harriet A. *Medical Apartheid: The Dark History of Medical Experimentation on Black Americans from Colonial Times to the Present.* New York: Doubleday, 2006.

Wertheim, Frederick. "Note: Slavery and the Fellow Servant Rule: An Antebellum Dilemma," *New York University Law Review* 61 (December 1986): 1112.

White, Deborah Gray. *Ar'n't I a Woman? Female Slaves in the Plantation South,* rev. ed. New York: Norton, 1999.

Whiteneck, Gale. "Conceptual Models of Disability: Past, Present, and Future." In *Workshop on Disability in America: A New Look*, edited by Marilyn J. Field, Alan M. Jette, and Linda Martin, 50–66, Appendix B. Washington, DC: National Academies Press, 2006.

Wickberg, Daniel. "Heterosexual White Male: Some Recent Inversions in American Cultural History." *Journal of American History* 92 (June 2005), http://www.historycooperative.org.proxy.lib.umich.edu/journals/jah/92.1/wickberg.html.

Wood, Betty. *Slavery in Colonial Georgia, 1730–1775*. Athens: University of Georgia Press, 1984.

Wright, Gavin. *The Political Economy of the Cotton South: Households, Markets, and Wealth in the Nineteenth Century*. New York: Norton, 1978.

Wu, Cynthia. "'The Mystery of their Union': Cross-Cultural Legacies of the Original Siamese Twins." PhD diss., University of Michigan, 2004.

Yetman, Norman. *Life under the "Peculiar Institution": Selections from the Slave Narrative Collection*. New York: Hold, Rinehart and Winston, 1970.

Index